LOVE
in the
FILM

LOVE
in the
FILM

WILLIAM K. EVERSON

Citadel Press   •   Secaucus, N.J.

First edition
Copyright © 1979 by William K. Everson
All rights reserved
Published by Citadel Press
A division of Lyle Stuart Inc.
120 Enterprise Ave., Secaucus, N. J. 07094
In Canada: General Publishing Co. Limited
Don Mills, Ontario
Manufactured in the United States of America by
Halliday Lithograph, West Hanover, Mass.
Designed by William R. Meinhardt

Library of Congress Cataloging in Publication Data

Everson, William K
  Love in the film.

  1.   Love in motion pictures.   I.   Title.
PN1995.9.L6E9   791.43′0909′354   79-19087
ISBN 0-8065-0644-X

Dedicated to
JANETTE SCOTT
the lovely young star of *Now and Forever*
whose vibrant and touching performance in
that fifties film is the epitome of what
love and romance on the screen *used* to be.

Acknowledgements

As usual, I should like to thank Jacques Ledoux of
the Royal Film Archive, Belgium, for his good will
and help, The British Film Institute, The Museum of
Modern Art, Gene Stavis of the American Cinema-
theque, and Bill Kenly of Paramount Pictures, for
help with certain key stills. Special thanks are also
due to Eddie and Peta Smith for their cooperation
and skill in making the high-quality frame blow-ups
from often quite worn 16mm prints.

But most especially I should like to acknowl-
edge a debt that we *all* owe to Alex Gordon, formerly of 20th Century-Fox, for his successful cru-
sade to find and save many of their silent and early
sound classics. Were it not for him, films like *Pilgri-
mage, Six Hours to Live* and *Zoo in Budapest* would
not exist to be discussed in this book, or to be seen.

Credits

The credits for the films under review are consistent
in that leading players, directors, writers and cameramen—*basic* credits—are always listed. Supplementary credits, for art direction, music, editing,
etc., are indicated only where those crafts have particular bearing on the films under review, or where
they are interesting in themselves because of the
subsequent career of the person involved.

Contents

Introduction

The two plot elements most common to all film are love and crime. Love is an emotion; crime a physical act. Between them, singly and more often jointly, they provide the motivation—and the linking narrative thrust—of most films, whether they be comedy, horror, science-fiction, or from any other genre. Even when history is put on the screen, its facts are often reemphasized (or totally rewritten, as in *Suez*) so that love is frequently the force which changes the destiny of nations. And political decisions, in actuality formed by expediency, economics or patriotism, are frequently diverted and debased, becoming the criminal acts of greedy individuals. There *are* films which contain neither love nor crime, but they are rare and if one were to make up a list of such films, one would probably find it heavily weighted in favor of the documentary—the only genre that might totally avoid both ingredients, although one might argue that the documentary is frequently utilized to protest "social crime," and that that kind of injustice is as dramatic as straightforward lawbreaking.

The musical? Certainly it is a genre unto itself, not notable for the utilization of strong emotional love stories. Yet boy's pursuit of girl, or his need to "prove" himself to the girl by staging that big show, is invariably the linking narrative thread on which the music is hung, while certain musicals—like *Hallelujah I'm a Bum* and *One Touch of Venus*—do deal very specifically with idealized love. If one takes the plotless compendium ballet film such as *Tales of Hoffmann*, love is very much a part of the motivation of the ballets themselves. Even if one is backed into a corner with the all-male war film (such as *Journey's End*) the element of love can still be very prominent. Love for the girl—or wife—back home can often be far more strongly expressed through yearning than through physical presence. Moreover, love need not necessarily be for a *person*; the war film (and again, *Journey's End* is a good example) allows for the expression of love of cause, love of honor, love of country.

If the word "love" is ambiguous, then the phrase "love story" as related to film (or play or novel) is more ambiguous still, and frequently overlaps into what one can only term the territory of the "romantic" film (or play or novel). A great love story is usually made "great" by the power of its theme or the passion of its playing; a great "romantic" film, however, depends far more on a *welding* of those elements with others—particularly the elegant stylistics of writing, directing and photography. As an easily identified example, I would consider the 1937 *The Prisoner of Zenda* one of the really great romantic films of all time. By definition, the film is actually a swashbuckler, yet it has comparatively little of the action normally considered an essential of that genre. It contains only two real love scenes, one of them short and almost casual. Yet its romanticism is so strong that I would find it unthinkable *not* to include it among the highlight films in this survey of love on the screen. Conversely, I have *not* included *Camille* (of a year earlier) despite its having all the earmarks and requirements of the great love story. It is a magnificent showcase for the beauty and artistry of Greta Garbo, and the directorial skill of George Cukor, and is a handsome, elegant film to watch. Yet somehow it lacks passion: we admire and we enjoy, but we are not moved. And one thing the love story *does* demand of its audience is that it *care*—that it delight in a happy ending, or sorrow at a sad one.

Quite incidentally, the words "love" and "romance" are among the most frequently used in the whole lexicon of film titles, and to Hollywood they were interchangeable, without differences in gradation. *Love* and *Romance* were both titles for equally heavy Garbo vehicles. *Love on the Run* was used for a generally light-hearted Gable/Crawford movie, while *Romance on the Run* was Republic's comeback for a Donald Woods/Grace Bradley frolic. The only distinction that Hollywood made is that it used the word "love" far more. And while "romance" was generally used in a simple context (*The Romance of Happy Valley*), "love" was occasionally used in an implied sordid sense (*The Love Racket, The Love Trap*).

Perhaps all I am trying to do in this introduction is to stress the enormity of the involvement of love in film ever since films began, the ambiguity of the word itself, and most important of all, that love —or the interpretation of it—being a very personal thing, choices of films to illustrate that emotion will be very personal and often very arbitrary as well.

Not only is love a personal emotion, but it is also a very changeable one. There were times when love was expressed openly, honestly and with a great deal of sentiment; other times when the emotions, though no less deep or honest, were concealed. Changing attitudes towards women (in life, and therefore in film too) can render behavioral patterns of another day hopelessly out of date to a later audience. The gallant, gentlemanly demeanor of a lover or husband as protector, and his beloved as a serflike recipient of his largesse, was not only acceptable but expected in an earlier period. Today it would be considered insulting—and in fact some of the tenderest lines of dialogue in love stories of the thirties and forties are often greeted with hisses by movie audiences of the 70s.

All of us tend to be most excited by that period of films in which we first discover them, and it makes objective criticism of film both difficult and unreliable. To a person growing up in the 1970s, the element of realism in 70s films must make the escapism and the romanticism of the 30s akin to fantasy, and to him a director like Paul Mazursky (*An Unmarried Woman*) probably seems a far greater director that an earlier romantic like Frank Borzage. Thanks to archives, television, film study programs at schools and universities, and revival theatres, the *past* of film is far more readily available today than ever before, and can be seen side by side with the present. Older filmgoers can view these revivals by casting their minds back to the conditions (personal, historic and otherwise) under which the films were originally made and shown, and they may have little sympathy either for the current films—or the conditions which spawned them. On the other hand, young contemporary moviegoers are bombarded by the mass media with news, information, opinions, editorializing and propaganda. They *fully* understand the contemporary scene, and the films that are a product of it, whereas they have little or no insight into parallel conditions twenty, forty or sixty years ago. Older filmgoers are doubtless appalled (as I must confess I was) by the language and moral tone of a contemporary film like *Saturday Night Fever* and (if such a choice were possible) would want no part of a world like that. Yet a contemporary, city-dwelling 70s youth would probably find nothing wrong or dishonest with its attitudes.

With such ambiguity, there obviously can be no *definitive* critical history of love on the screen, nor, due to the enormous size of the subject, a fully comprehensive historical survey. What follows therefore is a decidedly personal choice. In some cases titles have been selected largely because of the sincerity of the films, or because of the points they make, or merely because they are lovely films that deserve to be far better known. I offer no defense for including an obscure little British film such as *Return to Yesterday* and overlooking *Gone With the Wind.* The latter has had whole books devoted to it, and needs no further nod of approval here. Hopefully, the individual essays will not only explain why those films are included, but will also prompt readers to seek them out if they are unfamiliar, and urge local television stations or revival houses to play them, if they are available.

But if the films are very much personal choices, they are also films very typical of the eras in which they were made, and the introductory chapters to each significant era should help to clarify their position within that era. And not only clarification, but supplementary information, is essential to an understanding of the filmic treatment of the love story, and the changing times in which they were made. For example, there have been many films about implied or actual lesbian love which have been alternately erotic or tender, but overall *sympathetic.* The male homosexual on the screen, however, was used initially as the butt of jokes (sometimes genuinely funny and performed without malice, but too often coarse and offensive) and in more recent years for dramatic or shock values. But the orthodox commercial cinema still does not take kindly to the *sympathetic* treatment of homosexual relationships. If attitudes change, that may well offer a major breakthrough, providing a screen outlet for hitherto untapped theatrical and literary works, and biographical studies. With that possibility in mind, this whole book may seem quaintly out of date in a few years. But by that time, perhaps we'll have made contact with other planets, established working relationships with outer-space archives, and we'll all be busily delving into other galaxy genres and investigating the careers of Saturn's equivalents of D. W. Griffith and Clara Bow. In any event, I suspect that the further evolution of love in film will be increasingly more clinical and correspondingly less romantic, and I shall be happy to leave the updating of this volume to other less sentimental hands.

11

The Teens

Fairbanksian romance was lighthearted and gallant rather than torrid, but his efforts to woo and win his girl provided the basis for many of his early acrobatic comedy-thrillers. One of the best was 1919's HIS MAJESTY THE AMERICAN, in which Marjorie Daw was Doug's leading lady.

Robert Harron and Mae Marsh made a popular romantic team for D.W. Griffith in early Biograph shorts as well as later features. Here they play prehistoric cavedweller lovers in 1912's MAN'S GENESIS.

For there to be a mere two titles to represent the love story from 1900 to 1920—and one of those two films merely a short—may seem somewhat drastic, and quite certainly it's an evaluation open to serious argument.

But it took ten of those years for movies to evolve from the novelty stage and to tell well-structured stories, still limited for the most part to a single reel, or fifteen minutes, of running time. Although players were beginning to establish a rapport with audiences by 1910, the star system was still in the future—and a popular, or an idealized, star image was always one of the basic requisites for an effective love story. Considering that techniques were still evolving, and that the whole art of direction—and of manipulating audience emotions —was still new, it's surprising how effective some of these early story films could be on a purely emotional level. 1912's *A Mender of Nets*, a poetic little one-reeler directed by D. W. Griffith, is almost an embryonic *An American Tragedy*. It's a surprisingly sophisticated little film, both in its writing and underplayed acting, and even in its photographic treatment. Mary Pickford, almost at the peak of her youthful beauty, is posed against lyrical seascapes and photographed in stunning closeups by the great Billy Bitzer. She becomes a symbol of almost-within-reach yet ultimately unattainable beauty and happiness, just as was Elizabeth Taylor in the much later *A Place in the Sun*. Mabel Normand on the other hand—likewise anticipating the photographic treatment of Shelley Winters in the parallel role in that later film—is photographed in shadows, away from the sea, and in slovenly clothes and makeup. Unusual and even remarkable though it was however, *A Mender of Nets* could do no more than scratch at the surface and indicate *some* of the potential power of the movies in telling a great love story.

Two factors continued to work against the de-

Dustin Farnum and the Indian actress Red Wing in the oft-filmed THE SQUAW MAN (1913), forerunner of many films about the "impossibility" of interracial love.

velopment of the genre at least until 1920. One of course was the Victorian sense of romance and melodrama that still pervaded the movies—and the phrase "Victorian" is meant not in a critical sense, but in a purely descriptive one, for the Victorian age had literally passed into history only a few years earlier. The movies, and the stories and novels on which they were frequently based, were still concerned with simple and well-defined virtues and vices. The virtuous heroine was juxtaposed with the dynamic and aggressive vamp; between them, they could offer pure love—or impure sex. But there was no shading, no mingling of the two extremes. This did not preclude the making of good movies, but it did rather shift the emphasis into the areas of romance, or straight drama. Mary Pick-

ford's *Stella Maris* (1918) is both a very good and an incredible film—the latter because it chose to fly in the face of Pickford's popularity, and present a decidedly grim story. It's about wasted love and thwarted love rather than fulfilled love.

At the other end of the spectrum one finds a film like *A Cumberland Romance* (1920) starring Pickford's leading rival, Mary Miles Minter. It's appealing because of its very simplicity and "prettiness"—lovely outdoor locations, superb photography, and a magnificent use of tinted and toned stock.

Between these two extremes, there were the Cinderella romances of Lillian Gish and Mae Marsh, the heavier romantic dramas of Norma Talmadge, and the frothy romantic comedies of her

16

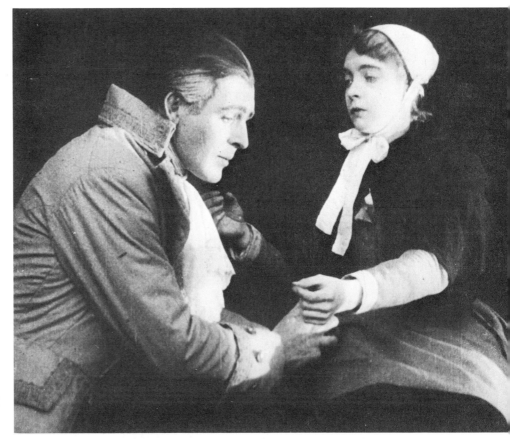

ENOCH ARDEN (1915) with Wallace Reid and Lillian Gish.

sister Constance. There was nothing wrong with these films. They were escapist and they were entertaining; they more than met the demands of fans and exhibitors; and because the industry was not yet geared to aggressive competition (it had no need to be, since it was *the* entertainment medium, with radio still in the future, and television but a science-fiction dream) the films deliberately cultivated a "sit-back-and-be-entertained" manner, and rarely came to grips with life in the way necessary to produce a really moving love story.

Then there was a second factor to be taken into consideration. The enormous success of D. W. Griffith's *The Birth of a Nation* in 1915 eased, and even encouraged, the segue into much longer films. But it also, unwittingly, dictated their shape too. Producers, impressed by the money it had made, and directors, in awe of Griffith's filmmaking genius, used it as a pattern, and at least until 1920, the majority of films were made in its image. There were subplots to cut away from—and to; interwoven characters; flashbacks; spectacular climaxes that were built mathematically. This made for some extremely lively films, but it didn't help the cause of good acting—or the creating of sustained charac-

ters, so essential in a love story. One of the reasons that Mary Pickford was such a reigning star in the teen years was that she was one of the few female stars big enough to control her own image and the construction of her own films. With all their variety (comedies, dramas, westerns, costume pieces, tragedy), she remained the point of focus throughout. She was able to build and sustain a characterization that was not fragmented by the demands of a narrative where editing and cross-cutting were the paramount concerns. True, the fast pacing of films in this period did not prevent great performances. Mae Marsh's acting as the young wife and mother in *Intolerance* (1916) is both brilliant and moving; but it is even more so in the source film, *The Mother and the Law* (1914), which Griffith cut and reshaped and used as the centerpiece for *Intolerance*, surrounding it with French, Biblical and Babylonian stories. Griffith's later *Hearts of the World* (1918) had all the potential for being a really tender love story as well as a war spectacle, in its depiction of a young love torn asunder by the war, during the course of which the young bride is driven to temporary insanity. Lillian Gish's performance was her subtlest and most mature to that point, but all too

17

Mae Marsh's performance as the young wife and mother in Griffith's INTOLERANCE (1916) represented the finest screen acting to that date.

often, having reached peaks of emotion or hysterical intensity, the film just drops her, reverts to action and melodrama, and by the time it picks her up again, the momentum is lost.

The movies' pre-1920 years are by no means barren ones. The films of those years have youth, innocence, vitality and optimism—both in their plot content, and in their own style, for they are made by directors possessed of those same qualities, and excited by what they are discovering about film. But basically, the films of those years appeal to the senses rather than to the emotions. While the selection of only two films to illustrate this period is obviously arbitrary, it is perhaps significant that both are the result of the collaboration between two of the foremost artists of the period—D. W. Griffith and Lillian Gish.

Lillian Gish, as the young wife and mother, spies on her philandering husband.

The Mothering Heart

American Biograph, 1913.

Directed by D. W. Griffith. Camera: G. W. Bitzer.

With: Lillian Gish, Walter Miller, Viola Barry, Charlie Murray, Kate Bruce.

It is not at all unusual to find exceptionally strong dramatic stories in the one- and two-reel pre-feature films of 1910 to 1913. The sheer number of them, and the need to maintain as much variety as possible, meant that some pretty offbeat material was offered, accepted and produced, merely because of the need to keep up a steady stream of production. Too, the star system was not really established as yet, so that audiences would not be disappointed or dismayed if a favored player turned up in an unsympathetic role, or in a tragic one. Finally, the mass audience for movies was still an essentially working-class one, bolstered by the still very large waves of immigrants. While one might have assumed that this kind of audience was the one for which escapist entertainment would have been most in demand, at the same time the more progressive directors—and certainly D. W. Griffith headed the list—also felt that the audience would respond emotionally to problems and situations it knew and understood.

On its own merits, *The Mothering Heart*—a film that runs for only about sixteen minutes—is hardly a permanent classic. But in a *comparative* sense it is; for 1913 it is daring both in its content and in its faith in the ability of an audience to recognize all its subtleties.

Griffith's short films for Biograph between 1907

Following the death of her child, she wanders disconsolately into her garden . . .

and 1913 can very roughly be divided into two groups: the chase films, melodramas, Civil War stories and Westerns which he made primarily to develop and polish new methods of editing and the staging of action, and those other films—ranging from Tolstoy's *Resurrection* to Norris's *A Corner in Wheat*—where theme was more important than technique. A number of the latter group had included quite strong little emotional stories, usually involving redemption in one form or another (particularly the reformation of the alcoholic), but there were relatively few bona fide love stories. One exception was the the already mentioned 1912 *The Mender of Nets*, in which the hero (Charles West) loves the beautiful fisherman's daughter (Mary Pickford) but in an earlier liaison has made another girl pregnant—this latter role played surprisingly well by Mabel Normand, her normal vivacity covered by nondescript clothing and makeup which makes her look plump and relatively plain. (The parallel with Elizabeth Taylor and Shelley Winters

in *A Place in the Sun* is quite striking.) The wronged girl's father tries to kill the erring lover, but is prevented from doing so by Pickford, who, sacrificing her own happiness, persuades the boy that his duty is to marry the other girl. The film concludes with a lovely closeup of Mary Pickford, sitting outside her hut atop a cliff, helping her father with his fishing nets and, with a sigh of wistful resignation, remarking that "*Somebody* has to mend other people's broken nets."

With its maximum use of rugged outdoor land- and seascapes, striking closeup images and dramatic editing, *A Mender of Nets* was one of Griffith's most sophisticated films to 1912. It is a measure of the incredibly rapid strides he was making at that time that *The Mothering Heart*, made only the following year, seems infinitely more mature. It starred Lillian Gish and Walter Miller, a romantic duo that Griffith used in a number of films of the period (*The Musketeers of Pig Alley* and *An Unseen Enemy* were others). As in his later romantic teaming of Mae Marsh and Robert Harron, the feminine role was the stronger and more dramatic one. The male's role was to be weak, passive, sometimes even unsympathetic.

In *The Mothering Heart*, Lillian Gish and Walter Miller are a young, happily married couple. On a visit to a nightclub, however, the husband attracts the attention of a flirtatious woman at a nearby table, and is infatuated with her. In the ensuing weeks, he deceives his wife and carries on an affair with the woman, totally under her spell, though to her he is merely a passing adventure. He is away from home so much that he is unaware that their young baby is ailing. The baby in fact dies, and in a most remarkable scene, Lillian Gish, as the distraught mother, wanders almost somnambulistically into their garden and then, in a frenzied paroxysm of destruction, seizes a hoe and hits out at all the plants and young trees, seeking to kill them. Then, returning to her trancelike state, she returns to the house where the husband—chastened by the discovery of the death of his child, thrown over by the other woman who has gone on to another affair—is waiting for her. At first the wife is hard and unforgiving; then, unwittingly, she finds the dead child's pacifier in the crib. There is a full screen closeup of her hand fondling the head of the pacifier—the borders of the screen blacked out to emphasize the action, which must be one of the first examples of explicit sexual symbolism on the screen. Then she almost thrusts the pacifier at her husband. The climax is thus not so much one of a happy reunion, but almost one of desperation, the wife suggesting that only via another child does their love, and their marriage, stand a chance of survival.

As if fully understanding the psychological depth and importance of his story, Griffith gives *The Mothering Heart* quite surprisingly elaborate production values. The nightclub is exceptionally spacious, yet in keeping with the kind of enlarged roadhouse that it would have been in its suburban California setting. The details of decor and clothing (particularly in respect to the contrasting hats and dresses of the two women) are carefully thought out, and the bit players well chosen. The tall, handsome, muscular uniformed doorman of the nightclub seems to have been cast just for the effect of one scene towards the end. Initially, since he always opens the door for the straying husband and his new paramour, he seems to symbolize the glamour of the new lifestyle he has assumed. But when the husband is finally tossed aside by his temporary mistress, the action takes place outside the club doors. The husband's shame is compounded by the

contempt of the doorman, who smiles superciliously at this expected turn of events. Because he is a tall, striking figure—much taller than the husband —it is possible for that all-important smile of scorn to register with*out* Griffith going into a closeup to underline it.

Subtle, underplayed acting was a trademark of the better Griffith Biographs; Blanche Sweet, Henry B. Walthall, Mae Marsh and others had all, by this time, given performances which even today, hold up by virtue of their sensitivity and restraint and need no apologies or explanations. Even so, the three lead performances in *The Mothering Heart* are quite exceptional. Although only in her mid-teens, Lillian Gish is utterly convincing as the more mature mother—as convincing as she was as the naive teenager in *True Heart Susie*, which she was to make for Griffith some six years later. Moreover, she manages to downplay her own beauty, to make the mother serious, even a little dowdy, so that the husband's straying to the exciting other woman becomes understandable. Walter Miller, as the husband, is likewise restrained and sincere, and suggests that he might well have become a major actor had not his striking good looks and virility sidetracked him into a career as a serial hero, where he developed a series of poses and mannerisms that stayed with him until the end of his career in the early 1940s.

But perhaps the most exciting performance of all is that of Viola Barry as the adventuress. She wasn't the first screen vamp—Helen Gardner had beaten her to the punch—nor was she the most famous since, from 1914 on, Theda Bara assumed that role. But in 1913, she was certainly the *best*, and her interpretation so modern and subtle that it works even today. Facially, she had the finely-chiseled features of Mary Astor—but coupled to the voluptuous body of that twenties vamp, Nita Naldi. Her low cleavaged gown was worn with tremendous style, as though she was totally unaware of the effect it was having on her victims. Moreover, there was nothing obvious or "sinful" about her vamping approach. She was able to snare Walter Miller's attention (and ours) with a glance. Her attraction was enhanced by the fact that Griffith did not see fit either to condemn her as an "evil woman" or to punish her. She merely goes on to another adventure at the end of the film; it is Miller, the husband, who has "sinned" and is punished.

In the rather clear-cut separation between "good" woman and "bad" that characterized American movies of the teen years, Viola Barry would have had rather tough sledding. She was too

. and, in a frenzy, destroys the rosebushes.

healthily sexy to fit into the fashionable niche for screen heroines, yet too attractive to play vamps, who had to come off second-best to the virginal heroines. Fortunately, she was married to up-and-coming director Jack Conway, and a career was not uppermost in her mind—though her beauty, casual elegance and real acting style in this film suggest that her lack of ambition was a major loss to the silent screen.

In any event, whether one classifies *The Mothering Heart* as a love story, a romance, or an emotional drama, it is an almost Freudian film, and very probably the first American film that can make that claim.

22

True Heart Susie

Paramount-Artcraft, 1919.

Directed by D. W. Griffith.
Scenario: Marian Fremont.
Camera: G. Bitzer.

With: Lillian Gish, Robert Harron, Loyola O'-Connor, Walter Higby, George Fawcett, Clarine Seymour, Kate Bruce, Carol Dempster, Robert Cannon.

One of a group of films loosely referred to as "rural romances," *True Heart Susie* came, in one sense, midway in Griffith's career. The initial spectacles, *The Birth of a Nation, Intolerance* and *Hearts of the World,* were behind him; the big spectacles of the 20s (*America, Orphans of the Storm*) lay ahead. At this particular time, Griffith was trying to retrench financially—his entrapment by bank loans and other debts had already begun—and also to put the war behind him, and deal with the people and the landscapes of his childhood in Kentucky in a series of less ambitious but often lyrical little films.

True Heart Susie is one of the best of these, and certainly the most romantic, but one sees it today under a disadvantage. No original negative or prints appear to have survived, and all circulating copies in this country and elsewhere seem to derive from a copy held by the British Film Institute in London—itself far from a really good print. The interiors of the film now seem black and shadowy, and the exteriors lack the radiance of the sunshine. Fortunately, a similar if lesser Griffith film, 1920's *The Greatest Question,* does survive in the form of one or two good prints made from the original negative, and by studying that, with its superb lighting and dramatic use of landscape, one can at least mentally project *True Heart Susie* with all the pictorial beauty it once had. It is quite a tribute to the film, and the sensitivity of the performances by Lillian Gish and Robert Harron, that it plays as well as it does despite the handicap of dark and lackluster prints several generations away from the original.

Griffith, ever the showman (though he often pretended not to be), was aware that after his earlier spectacles audiences expected something "Big" from him, constantly tried to add stature to these smaller films by portentous opening titles. *True Heart Susie* opens with a title claiming that every incident in it is taken from life, and goes on to dedicate itself to all the women of the world who wait for the great love that never comes. Actually, 1919 audiences might have been equally impressed had Griffith just leveled with them and admitted that

True Heart Susie was an amalgamation of themes from Charles Dickens, the author whose influence (both structurally and thematically) was to dominate Griffith's work. Most specifically, *True Heart Susie* derives from *Great Expectations* and the latter portions of *David Copperfield*.

Its underlying theme is quite simple. Susie, very much in love with William—who only halfheartedly reciprocates—scrimps and saves to put him through college. He is unaware of her sacrifices, thinking his benefactor to be a stranger from the city who once passed through their rural community and promised to help. When he returns from college, ready to take a position as minister, Susie assumes that they'll marry, and misinterprets several of his remarks as a confirmation of that. However, his attention goes to the gaudy Bettina—all paint, powder and silk stockings—and it is she that he marries. Bettina however, only wants the security of the marriage, and after the wedding is a poor wife, who looks slovenly about the house, won't cook hot meals, and complains of boredom. Both Susie and William think wistfully of what might have been, but never confide their thoughts to each other—and when Susie realizes that Bettina is deceiving William, she keeps quiet about it. On one occasion, Bettina sneaks away to a wild party with her friends, on the way collecting a book that her husband needed. The party breaks up late, and Bettina is drenched in a torrential downpour. She contracts pneumonia, and William feels responsible, knowing nothing of the party and thinking that it was all brought about by her thoughtful act in collecting the book for him. On her deathbed, Bettina is about to confess, but William prevents her and, to quote a rather lovely Griffith subtitle, "She dies as she lived—a little unfaithful." Despite the previous emptiness of his marriage, William is so moved that he vows never to love or marry again, and Susie is too loyal to him to tell him the truth. Inadvertently however, the truth does come out, and, belatedly, William and Susie are married.

It is a simple story, simply told, with no need for the subplots or intercutting of Griffith's more ambitious works. (Actually, Griffith's cutting in the post-*Intolerance* period tended to remain innovative in conception, but to get increasingly slipshod in execution—and *True Heart Susie* offers early evidence of Griffith's carelessness in this direction, although the nonmatching cuts are not as serious or as obvious as they would be in the following year's *Way Down East*.)

The film really wins one over by its sincerity and by the strength of its performers. Its beginning is not too promising. Lillian Gish's Susie seems so much the innocent trusting child that marriage to her would seem to offer very little. (Comedian Harry Langdon seems to have based many of his expressions and pantomimic gestures on Lillian Gish's performance in this film, and occasionally—through no fault of hers—one has the uncanny feeling of watching Langdon rather than Gish, which also tends to downplay the romantic involvement.) Robert Harron is first seen as a rather gawky youth, and his metamorphosis into a far more mature man (aided by a moustache to which he calls attention by constantly preening it) shows again what a remarkably subtle actor Harron could be. But his slighting of Susie gains him little audience sympathy; one can hardly blame him for choosing the more exciting Bettina, and yet at the same time one feels that in a way they deserve each other.

It is at this point that the film shifts gears, and stops telling its story only in terms of incident. From here on in there are far more closeups of both Gish and Harron in which their sadness and isolation is conveyed by the subtlety of facial expression and Bitzer's lighting. Perhaps too, in this latter portion of the film, there is more drawing upon the original plot construction of Dickens, who, quite unknowingly of course, manipulated people and details in a decidedly cinematic manner. Whatever the reasons, the film becomes both touching and moving in its final third, and many of the apparent loose ends of the opening suddenly fall into place. Earlier it had been established that Susie and William never quite managed to kiss—even when he was going away to college. Both tried, sincerely but clumsily, and both withdrew before the kiss could be accomplished. This awkwardness is maintained until the penultimate scene, when William approaches Susie to admit his love and propose marriage. Even here, Griffith keeps them apart: Susie is seen at the window of her cottage, leaning out to water flowers; William is shown only as a hesitant shadow.

The final scene is a repeat of one of their years-earlier walks down a country lane, and a closing title *hopes* that they'll be happy, and asks the audience to imagine their rekindling the love of their earlier, innocent years. There's no doubt that it's a happy ending—yet the sense of possible separation, and the shadow of the unhappy marriage to Bettina, is retained. It's a subtle and mature ending to a minor Griffith classic which offers a great deal more sophistication and emotional depth than,might at first seem apparent.

The Twenties

Clara Kimball Young was fond of flamboyant romances that pitted her against a number of widely assorted partners—and problems—before the ultimate happy ending. Typical was 1922's THE HANDS OF NARA, with John Orloff.

In some ways, the twenties represented a peak for the purely escapist romantic film. Perhaps because women had just acquired the vote and thus a nominal equality, more films in the twenties (than in any other period) seemed to be about women—and women who dominated.

Many of the top female stars—Colleen Moore, Mary Pickford, Gloria Swanson, Nazimova—at one time or another guided their careers as their own producers. Other major stars—Clara Bow, Greta Garbo, Norma Talmadge, Constance Talmadge, Lillian Gish, Dolores Costello, Vilma Banky, Alice Terry, Pola Negri—were put into essentially romantic vehicles that were showcases for their beauty and vivacity first, and in many cases for their acting talent second. Art direction, set design and the sheer beauty of glistening camerawork likewise

reached new heights in the twenties, and all of this pictorial beauty tended to put the love story into a somewhat unreal category.

This is not for a moment to suggest that the 20s romantic film was all artifice and escapism. Some works of remarkable honesty were made in this period. The love story—courtship, marriage, disintegration, reunion—in King Vidor's *The Crowd* (1928) was superbly handled, and magnificently acted by Eleanor Boardman (in particular) and James Murray. A similar pattern (except that marriage did not come until the end of the film) was followed in D. W. Griffith's poetic yet grim *Isn't Life Wonderful?* (1924), beautifully acted by Carol Dempster in what was unquestionably her finest screen performance. In some instances, a great performance transformed what was otherwise fairly

In their only co-starring film, Douglas Fairbanks and Mary Pickford took on Shakespeare in THE TAMING OF THE SHREW (1929), a vigorous romantic comedy that captured the robust sense of fun that had probably been present when it first played in Elizabethan theatres.

27

VARIETY (1925), with Emil Jannings and Lya de Putti a strong psychological drama of love, lust and murder. Eventually both stars, together with the producer, the director and the cameraman, came to Hollywood.

THE DARK ANGEL (1925): Ronald Colman and Vilma Banky.

THE TEMPTRESS (1926): Greta Garbo's second American movie, an exotic romance opposite Antonio Moreno.

Mimi's death scene in King Vidor's LA BOHEME (1926); John Gilbert and Lillian Gish.

LOVE 'EM AND LEAVE 'EM (1926): Louise Brooks as the temptress who has temporarily won Lawrence Gray away from her sister (Evelyn Brent).

A handsome pair of lovers in an incredibly handsome film: TEMPEST (1927), with John Barrymore and Camilla Horn.

LOVERS (1927): Ramon Novarro and Alice Terry.

Stories of mother love were extremely popular in the twenties, and in fact two boxoffice blockbusters ushered the twenties in and out. At left, OVER THE HILL with Mary Carr and Johnnie Walker; right, Margaret Mann waits at Ellis Island in John Ford's FOUR SONS (1928).

trite material into something rather special, as was the case with another Griffith film, *The White Rose* (1923) and a lovely performance from Mae Marsh.

But for the most part, elegance and glamour dominated. It is interesting that while the 20s represented a new high point in fan interest in the movies, the publicity machine still tried to maintain a wide gulf between fan and star. The star was still royalty—even, in some cases, a kind of deity. In the 20s, only a handful of movies like *The Extra Girl* or *Ella Cinders* dealt with the possibility of an "ordinary" person going to Hollywood and becoming a star. In fact, in both of those films (and in others) the girl doesn't make it, and is happy to return to a humdrum small-town life and a happy marriage. (In the Depression years of the 30s, the *A Star Is Born* genre of film really proliferated—and the incidence of failure was virtually nil!)

The films chosen to represent the 20s in this book are essentially those that still work, on their own terms, today—whether it be a realistic film like *Smouldering Fires*, or a grand-scale extravaganza like *Don Juan*. *Not* included is a film like *La Bohème* (1926), which one can certainly admire for its

directorial finesse (King Vidor), its superb camerawork (Sartov), and above all for its magnificent Lillian Gish portrayal. But one is touched by Gish's frailty and overawed by her acting technique, not moved by Mimi's plight. It's a cold film—something a love story just cannot be.

Aviation movies enjoyed a big boom at the end of the twenties; one more popular for its romance than its thrills was 1928's LILAC TIME with Colleen Moore and Gary Cooper.

An early talkie, and a good one, was Frank Capra's FLIGHT (1929), first sound aerial epic, with a Miles Standish-inspired love triangle between Jack Holt and Lila Lee, shown here, and Ralph Graves.

William K. Howard, though best known as a director of high-powered thrillers, made some quite touching romantic stories too. Here he directs Janet Gaynor in CHRISTINA (1929).

The 20s love story had advantages that talkies did not. Dialogue, emotions and motivations were not spelled out. Skilled directors often injected a note of ambiguity, leaving it to the audience, in a sense, to add the final directorial touch. An emotional person could turn a restrained film into a florid one; a cold person could tone down a film to his own emotional level. Audience involvement in the silent film was a major factor in its success: it called for both imagination and participation on the part of the beholder, and in return offered a kind of universality.

Unfortunately, the silent film *needs* that participation, as well as offering it as a kind of bonus. There's an art to "reading" the silent film which is largely unknown by contemporary audiences reared on television. Television, basically, is illustrated radio. The housewife can leave her set switched on, wander about the house doing her chores, and still have the relevant information relayed to her aur-

This scene from Howard Hawks' THE AIR CIRCUS (1928) indicates the kind of charming artificiality that marked love scenes of the period. However, with the right lighting and blue-toned stock, this backdrop of sky and moon would look much more effective. Atop the veranda Arthur Lake watches Sue Carol and David Rollins.

ally. Television spells everything out, leaving nothing to nuance or the imagination. Moreover, it invites *casual* enjoyment. A family will sit around watching, discussing, talking, breaking the continuity frequently for forays to the icebox—while television itself has a deliberately fragmented construction to accommodate commercials. The results of all this can be seen in any contemporary movie theatre, where audiences alas talk as casually as they do at home, frequently about matters not even related to the film on the screen, and make frequent sidetrips to the concession stands. A silent film (or at least, the good ones) just cannot live and breathe without the participation and concentration of its audience. In some cases, the crux of a whole film may be in a scene of only a few seconds. If one misses that scene, through turning aside to talk, or

Garbo's last silent was an ultra-stylish melodrama, THE KISS (1929), in which she was romantically teamed with Conrad Nagel.

walking to the Coke machine, the whole impact of the film can be minimized. (Imagine missing the few seconds in Keaton's *The General* where the fleeting expression on an officer's face is the *climax* to a prolonged and spectacular action scene, or the minute inside the church in *Sunrise*!

One can hardly condemn contemporary audiences for succumbing to the blandishments of television, but it does load an unfair burden onto the movie love stories of the 20s. Their pictorialism, their exoticism and above all their honest sentiment, are qualities virtually alien to current audiences. The people best able to "read" silent films are those who have lived with them for years, or better still, lived through their heyday.

Charles Farrell and Janet Gaynor continued their romantic alliance under Frank Borzage's direction in LUCKY STAR, a novelettish film with outstanding art direction. In the scene at right interferring mother Hedwig Reicher tries to convince Janet Gaynor that she'd be better off with a husband other than Farrell.

32

One of the best films of the late twenties was F.W. Murnau's CITY GIRL (1929), another one in the then-popular group of city-girl-versus-the-elements-finds-true-love sagas, a theme that had fascinated William K. Howard, Victor Sjostrom and other top directors of the period. Mary Duncan, Edith Yorke, Charles Farrell and Dawn O'Day (Anne Shirley).

The thirties offer an entirely different situation, affected not only by sound, but also by censorship restrictions. Films of the 30s too, offer subtleties and sophistication that TV does not. But the sound film is not a different language, and doesn't require a special ability to "read" it. Current audiences might look at an early 30s love story like *Only Yesterday* and conceivably find it old-fashioned—but at least they would understand *why* they felt that way. The 30s were never able to create a timeless, universal classic like *Sunrise* (though they achieved it in other areas, such as the musical, via *Love Me Tonight,* or the horror film, via *King Kong* and *Freaks*). Its love stories were resolutely locked in to the period in which they were made, but within those boundaries there are more that survive well then can be found within the rather different boundaries of the silent film.

This of course is no reflection on the films of

COQUETTE (1929): With John Mack Brown as her leading man, Mary Pickford won an Academy Award. The film's dated quality isn't helped today by the fact that this is the play that Ben Hecht—and John Barrymore—lampoon so mercilessly in *20th Century*.

the 20s; rather it is a reflection on audiences, and on changing tastes. One would like to hope that in years to come mass audience tastes *will* change again, that entertainment won't be a matter of sitting passively and accepting rather than injecting a part of oneself. (After all, in sports the greater exhilaration comes from participating, not from spectating, and the parallel can certainly be extended to any of the arts.) If that day ever comes to pass, then the great repertoire of 20s romantic films (and despite many sad losses, much does still survive) may well come into its own again. In the meantime, films like *Sunrise* and *Smouldering Fires* are ready and waiting to reward those who take the trouble to see —and read—them properly.

A minor but fascinating romantic drama from 1929, a talkie remake of a Norma Talmadge silent, was THE LOCKED DOOR in which, as in so many early talkie love stories, romantic problems were thrashed out in very clearly enunciated tones. Although it had its primitive moments, it was better than many of the ilk. Wife Barbara Stanwyck (in her first major role) watches sister Betty Bronson (the enchanting Peter Pan of five years earlier, somewhat out of place in a modern drama) and husband William Boyd.

33

Conrad In Quest of His Youth

Paramount, 1920.

Directed by William De Mille. Screenplay by Olga Printzlau from the novel by Leonard Merrick. Camera: Guy Wilky. Art Director: Wilfred Buckland.

With: Thomas Meighan, Kathlyn Williams, Mabel van Buren, Mayme Kelso, Bertram Johns, Charles Ogle, Ruth Renick, Margaret Loomis, Sylvia Ashton, Eddie Sutherland.

For a company that had Cecil B. De Mille, Rudolph Valentino and Clara Bow under contract at various times during the 20s, Paramount also offered a curious undertow of extremely quiet, gentle little films, many of them simple romances that derived from plays or books—and in many cases must have been more satisfying in their original form. In transforming them faithfully to the screen, at times they were *so* faithful that they were also uncinematic, and thus somewhat pointless. Typical was *Doomsday* (1928), from a Warwick Deeping novel, a quiet little triangle romance set on an English farm, and starring Florence Vidor and Gary Cooper. Nothing happened that wasn't entirely predictable, and while it was a pleasing film, it seemed to offer nothing that wasn't done better in the novel.

Nevertheless, if nothing else, this substantial—if forgotten—group of films from Paramount offers an interesting reflection of theatrical and literary tastes of the day, and *many* of the films, seemingly at odds with the commercial requirements of the period, have a great deal of taste and dignity. Paramount had a virtual monopoly on the James Barrie material, and at least two of their mid-20s Barrie adaptations, *Peter Pan* and *A Kiss for Cinderella*, are superlative films. (Both are covered in some detail in an earlier Citadel book, *Classics of the Silent Screen.*)

Conrad in Quest of His Youth is a film in this tradition: a gentle story about a wealthy retired army officer who feels that life—and love—have passed him by, and goes back to seek his past, with the same kind of bittersweet results that one finds in the film's unofficial French and female parallel, *Un Carnet de Bal.*

Although not placed on a level with *Way Down East* or *The Devil's Passkey, Conrad in Quest of His Youth* was nevertheless considered one of the better films of 1920. It was liked, however, more as an individual film than as an adaptation of the then very popular novel by Leonard Merrick. Critics were quick to point out that the adaptation popular-

34

Thomas Meighan, a major star of the silent period, now somewhat forgotten.

ized it, changed wit to broader humor, and removed potentially controversial elements. Having said that, they were happy with the film as an entity. William De Mille, Cecil's brother, and always a specialist in gentle, civilized, often stage-derived material in which emotional depth and romantic power crept up on one almost unawares, was obviously an ideal director for it at the time—though a few years later, Herbert Brenon, director of the two Barrie films mentioned earlier, would have been even better. One can see why Barrie endorsed the original novel so much, since even in the simpler form in which it reached the screen, it has a Barrie-like quality to it.

One of the reasons for the slightly awry screen treatment *may* be that it was a mistake to entrust a highly personal and sentimental *male* viewpoint to a highly sophisticated *female* scenarist. However,

this may be an unfair judgment, since De Mille certainly would have had enough power to make his own changes. The following year, incidentally, Printzlau did the screen treatment for Barrie's *What Every Woman Knows*. Another reason that the film doesn't *quite* come off is that Thomas Meighan, if not a dashing type, certainly looked too virile and too young to be in a position of despair over lost youth and unfulfilled dreams. Perhaps Lewis Stone might have pulled it off better. Nevertheless, in its own quiet way, *Conrad In Quest of His Youth* is rather a moving film, and we rejoice when he does finally find the woman he loves. It's hardly an overpowering love story—much of the narrative is deliberately light, almost making fun of the futility of trying to go back—yet it lingers persuasively in the mind rather longer than many of the bigger, more obvious love stories of the 20s.

In a scene deleted from the American version, Lars Hanson, as Gosta Berling, the defrocked priest, taunts his friends by pretending to invoke the spirit of the Devil.

The Saga of Gosta Berling

Svenska-Biograf Film, Sweden, 1923/24.

Directed by Mauritz Stiller: scenario by Ragnor Hylten-Cavallius, from the novel by Selma Lagerlof. Camera: Julius Jaenzon.

With: Lars Hanson, Greta Garbo, Jenny Hasselquist, Mona Martenson, Ellen Cederstrom, Karin Swanstrom, Gerde Lundequist, Torsten Kammeren, Svend Tornback, Otto Elg Lundberg, Sixten Malmerfelt.

Although hardly a Greta Garbo *vehicle* (she was still known as Greta Gustafson when she made it, and it was her first dramatic role, following some advertising shorts and a knockabout comedy) it is interesting that *The Saga of Gosta Berling* is one of her most successful and pleasing films when considered in terms of its success as a romance.

Silent Scandinavian cinema is sparsely represented in U.S. archives, and but rarely shown. (And when it *is* shown, it is unfortunately greeted with apathetic attendance, which tends to discourage further attempts to restore interest in this stimulating national cinema.) It is particularly fortunate therefore that *The Saga of Gosta Berling* survives

and is even reasonably accessible, since it is in many ways both an ideal introduction to silent Swedish cinema, and a summing up of its best and most characteristic qualities. It is as though one had to choose *one* film to represent all American cinema of the 30s, and selected *Gone With the Wind*. *Gone With the Wind* was certainly not the best or most important Hollywood film of the 30s (though it was the most popular), but it was thoroughly American in theme, and with its star roster and production values was illustrative of the kind of film that Hollywood did best. In many ways, *The Saga of Gosta Berling* can fit into a like classification, though it also transcends it: apart from being both a popular and a typical Swedish film, it was also an exceptionally good one. In a sense too, although made in the early half of the twenties, it was the climax of the Swedish film's Golden Age. Director Mauritz Stiller and stars Lars Hanson and Greta Garbo (along with another great Swedish actor/director, Victor Sjøstrom) were promptly signed up by Hollywood—and with the cream of their small industry gone, Sweden had to content itself with using its remaining talent to produce films for local consumption only.

Greta Garbo, at extreme left, plays the Italian countess transplanted to Sweden, where marriage into an old aristocratic family makes her mistress of the house.

That *The Saga of Gosta Berling* is as moving as it is on a personal level is something of a tribute to its stars, for in a story sense, it is a "big" picture, full of epic passions and larger-than-life motivations. It is based on an enormously popular novel by Sweden's most prolific and successful author, Selma Lagerlof, and is the kind of narrative that nobody writes any more, and that only the oldsters (more's the pity) take the trouble to read. Most of the flaws of the film, such as they are, derive from the original material—and a respect for it which prevented simplification.

The film's greatest drawback is a multiplicity of characters, and the sketchy motivation given to many of them. This is partially due to the fact that the original novel was so well known in Sweden that for native audiences little exposition was needed, and due also to the film's having been substantially shortened for release outside of Sweden. Cut virtually in half, the U.S. version yet managed to retain all but one really key scene; the shortening was accomplished mainly by trimming within scenes (which tended to be somewhat protracted) and thus quickening the pace of the film considerably. In both versions, the film takes its first half to establish its characters and lay the framework for the various themes that interweave with one another; the second half is devoted to almost nonstop, sweepingly colorful incident, with a dramatic (and exceedingly

well staged) fire, and a flight from wolves across a frozen lake, as highlights.

Early German and early Swedish silents shared many traits, but in certain key ways they were almost totally opposed. German film was noted for a brooding intensity and an introspection, the latter especially noticeable in the acting. Swedish drama, and of course Swedish national characteristics, have equally recognizable traits. A typical Emil Jannings performance, contrasted with the flamboyant and stylized acting of Lars Hanson in this film, provides an instant clue to some of the differences. Far from being introspective, Swedish dramatists and actors are very demonstrative in their neurotic torturings and self-doubts. There are never any *minor* problems in the Swedish drama, and solutions are never reached by discussion but always by self-cleansing acts of violence—duels, suicides, plagues, holocausts of fire. Regardless of the source material—and *The Saga of Gosta Berling* overlaps into *Jane Eyre* almost as much as it does into *Gone With the Wind*—some echo of Strindberg is never very far away. Swedish writing, and Swedish film, are marked by an intense affinity with the soil—a love of both land and property. Landscape is often used symbolically in *The Saga of Gosta Berling* in the way that it had earlier been used by Griffith. Quite incidentally, very few films are better examples of the way Griffith's influence extended to Eu-

In a shot that gives hints of the Hollywood-groomed beauty to come, Garbo comforts Jenny Hasselquist, who is hopelessly in love with Gosta.

rope: in structure as well as in individual scenes and compositions, it is a virtual copy of Griffith, though never in a lazy sense.

So much happens in *The Saga of Gosta Berling* that it is sometimes difficult to pin it down to being a love story. In a very loose sense, Gosta Berling—a rebellious defrocked priest—is the film's Rhett Butler. But he is a self-sacrificing idealist, torn between destroying himself and redeeming himself by helping others. There is little of the reckless, aggressive cavalier in the character itself, but Lars Hanson's striking features, and the way he sits a horse or wears a black cloak, somehow transform him into a much more romantic figure than was probably intended. The subplots include the story of a group of army pensioners who turn on their feudal "master"; a matriarch who is turned out of her house by a vengeful husband and who in turn seeks redemption by serving the now ailing mother who had once put a curse on her; and a somewhat complicated story of yet another woman turned out of her house (by angry parents) who is rescued from the snow by Gosta Berling. She loves *him* desperately—and is ultimately struck down by a plague. With so much going on, there is hardly time for the basic love story—especially since Garbo plays a woman apparently married to a local aristocrat. It is

not until the closing reels that it is discovered that the marriage is invalid, thus freeing her to marry Gosta. Throughout the film, the Hanson-Garbo relationship is one of gradually developing love, and then desperation with the realization that it is hopeless. Yet despite the incident-packed narrative, it is the love story of these two that commands the greatest attention. Garbo was a lovely, serene creature even then—but a little plump, lacking in experience as an actress, and accordingly a trifle lacking in grace. There aren't even very many closeups of that incredible face. Yet somehow the magic was already there, and despite the complicated activity of the rest of the film, we miss her when she isn't on screen. Without her, *The Saga of Gosta Berling* might well have been that—a saga of atonement. *With* her, it becomes a romance and a love story.

The great love that develops between Gosta and the countess seems doomed, until her marriage is revealed to be legally invalid.

Pauline Frederick

Smouldering Fires

Universal, 1924.

Produced and Directed by Clarence Brown. Story by Sada Cowan, Howard Higgin and Melville Brown. Camera: Jackson Rose.

With: Pauline Frederick, Laura LaPlante, Malcolm MacGregor, Tully Marshall, Wanda Hawley, George Cooper, Helen Lynch and, as extras, Arthur Lake, Bert Roach and George Lewis.

"Whether we win it to hold it; or win it to lose it; or never win it at all, the greatest thing in all the world is—LOVE!"

From this little piece of prose, a catchline in Universal's original ads, it is apparent that *Smouldering Fires* is what is loosely termed "a woman's picture"—and it's a good one. The Pauline Frederick vehicles of the 20s were the counterparts of the vehicles for Kay Francis and Ruth Chatterton in the early 30s, and to a degree, to some of the Bette Davis vehicles of the late 30s and early 40s.

Its plot is basically familiar and predictable. Pauline Frederick plays a highly successful businesswoman who has never had time for love or even romantic dalliances on the side. She falls in love suddenly and desperately with one of her young factory employees (Malcolm MacGregor)— one of the few underlings who is not a "yes" man. His initial interest in her is a mixture of admiration and as a means of introducing his own progressive new ideas into the company. However, despite opposition and a realization of their age difference, he too falls in love with her, and they set a marriage date. In the meantime, she dreams of a romantic honeymoon and tries to restore as much of her youth as possible by arduous beauty treatments. At this stage, enter her young sister (Laura LaPlante) who is at first delighted by the marriage news, but assumes it is to be with a much older man. When she meets the bridegroom-to-be she is shocked, and is sure that he is only after her sister's money. Ulti-

Jane Vale (Pauline Frederick) is trying to find out the name of the man whom her sister Dorothy (Laura LaPlante) loves so hopelessly. Catching sight of her husband (Malcolm MacGregor) in the garden, she calls his name—and notices her sister's startled reaction in a reflection in the window. A complicated chunk of narrative information is thus conveyed in a single shot.

When business executive Jane Vale falls in love for the first time, she hides her long-standing creed and motto in a drawer.

mately however she is convinced of his sincerity, but by this time the two youngsters, constantly thrown together, are falling in love themselves. They are about to confront the older woman with the truth and call the marriage off when they suddenly realize how desolate she would be from the shock. The marriage goes off on schedule and is apparently a happy one. Only gradually, and quite accidentally, does the older woman realize that her young sister's unhappiness is due to an apparently hopeless love. Despite her own great happiness, she pretends that the marriage was a mistake and that she wants to return to a concentration on her business alone. She'll arrange a divorce, knowing that the two youngsters will get together.

With due respect to the intelligent acting—and its importance in a film like this—director Clarence Brown is its real star, and his contributions of taste and imagination are important ones. For years Brown was taken for granted as a highly competent but perhaps not particularly innovative director. This was an understandable reaction, since not only did he deliberately avoid showy technique, but also virtually all of his films in the late 20s and on through to the mid-50s were glossy MGM showcases for their biggest stars—Garbo, Gable, Crawford, Harlow, Loy. With so much elegance, such production values and dominating personalities it was often hard to see what the director's contribution was. That's one of the reasons why a film like *Smouldering Fires* is so valuable today; a relatively unambitious film, its plot—and treatment—are of at least equal importance to the stars, and there's very little window-dressing between what Brown as a director is doing, and what the audience sees on screen. Even the script of this film survives, and one can see that Brown *deleted* rather than expanded, taking out flowery subtitles and elaborate bits of business and expressing the same ideas visually.

Director Clarence Brown

40

Brown conveys much of his information by carefully arranged three-shots. In the final one—the last shot of the film—the facial expressions of themselves explain the film's ultimate solution.

Aware that triangle dramas have a limited range of plot ramifications, Brown rejects most of the expected mechanics of plotting. There are none of those endless complications and misunderstandings that usually plague this kind of fare. Moreover, Brown doesn't make it easy for the audience by suddenly turning the older woman into the nominal villain, or a shrew, as so often happens. All three are likable, decent people, and despite the ultimate tidiness of the ending, all are hurt in one way or another. If only by the avoidance of cliché the film offers real surprises and more important, maintains a kind of honesty. For his extremely effective fadeout, Brown uses only a simple three-shot, itself a variation on similar compositions that he had employed earlier at similar critical moments (and incidentally, a pictorial method—and trademark—that he used throughout his career). The result is that without backup subtitles, and in one single shot (the characters' positions within the frame, and their expressions making any written information unnecessary) Brown wraps up the film very neatly, both distilling the *current* dilemma *and* indicating its future solution. Moreover, the shot involves the audience even more than usual, since they are almost *forced* to think for themselves rather than having it all spelled out for them.

Visually the film is handsome without ever being showy. The photography is tasteful and inventive, the camera moving quite frequently, but always for a purpose. The few exteriors (notably some Yosemite locations) are particularly well shot, and the sets elegant and lavish. (It's a particular pleasure to see *height* in movie sets now, when the current trend, echoing the CinemaScope age, is to emphasize width and horizontal design.) The sets are cunningly convincing too; despite a comparative lack of detail, the factory *looks* like a factory.

Smouldering Fires came out late in 1924, when too much was going on for it to attract the attention it deserved; theatre screens were full of big prestige films like *Peter Pan* and *Isn't Life Wonderful?*, huge popular hits (*Romola, The Thief of Bagdad*), controversial critical "successes" (*Greed*) and plain 1920s vintage bread-and-butter pictures like *Silk Stocking Sal.* Nevertheless, trade press reviews were uniformly good, all singling out Brown's direction, while Universal thought so highly of the film that it was the spearhead picture of their current 21-feature release schedule. Universal also reprinted in the trade papers a letter of praise from an exhibition group, and while one can never put too much stock in this kind of letter—too often neither spontaneous nor genuine—at the same time this one is worth reprinting in part. It seems particularly topical in the late 70s and so applicable to contemporary production patterns when, unfortunately, there are few directors around with the taste and integrity of Clarence Brown, and the need for films of his type has to be filled rather mechanically (and not very efficiently) from Disney and certain independent producers. Addressed, of course, to Carl Laemmle, president of Universal, the letter said:

"I want to thank you for giving to the industry a picture of modern life without cigarette-smoking women, cocktail-drinking flappers, hip-flasks, rolled hose and other props so noticeable in current attractions . . . this picture, in addition to being a wonderful drama, is certainly a relief . . . from a standpoint of drama and entertainment, one of the most entertaining pictures in many moons. . . . Director Brown had plenty of opportunity to resort to questionable scenes, but he availed himself of none of them—he kept the picture clean and wholesome; in lieu of wild parties and indecent exposure, he gave us scenes to make the most confirmed grouch laugh. I believe it my duty to lend my moral support to the class of film you have produced here. The industry needs more of this kind, less of the other kind, if we are to survive." (Signed by S. N. Chambers of the Consolidated Amusement Company, Wichita).

It may well have been support like this, and the frequent use of the words "clean" and "wholesome" in describing the film, that caused Universal to delete from the American version one of the more mature touches. In this scene (still extant in one rare European print) the wife wakes early in the morning, and slips out of bed quietly so as not to wake her husband. In the bathroom she removes her curlers and face cream, prettifies herself, and slips back into bed—so that she'll look as young and attractive as possible when her husband awakens. Even though this scene is gone, however, many equally poignant ones remain, including at least two where the wife is made aware of her age by the totally unwitting cruelty of younger people at a party.

Smouldering Fires is not a picture of sweeping passions or powerful love scenes, but it is as subtle as its title—and one of the most moving, and most honest, films about love from Hollywood in the 20s.

Son of the Sheik

United Artists, 1926.

Directed by George Fitzmaurice. Produced by John Considine, Jr. scenario by Frances Marion and Fred de Gresac from the novel *The Sons of the Sheik* by Edith M. Hull. Camera: George Barnes. Art Direction: William Cameron Menzies.

With: Rudolph Valentino, Vilma Banky, George Fawcett, Montague Love, Karl Dane, Bull Montana, Agnes Ayres, Charles Requa, Erwin Connelly, William Donovan, Bynanski Hyman.

Valentino and Garbo were unquestionably the divinities (as opposed to mere royalty) of the romantic stars of the 20s, and it is unfortunate indeed that they never had the opportunity to co-star—an opportunity that would almost certainly have presented itself had Valentino elected to stay with Metro in 1921 instead of moving over to Paramount.

Garbo was certainly the better served of the two. Unlike economy-conscious Paramount, MGM had no qualms about spending small fortunes on their films, cultivating their stars' images in every way possible, and reshooting and polishing as much as they felt necessary. Whatever their other merits or shortcomings, MGM's Garbo films were almost swamped in decor, sumptuous sets and costuming, and stunning photography. Nor did they forget that they were star *vehicles*; topping all of this elegance was Garbo herself. Her own magnetism plus the gloss of the visuals sometimes made one forget how shallow and clichéd her plots often were. Moreover, in films like *Flesh and the Devil* and *Love*, she was costarred with John Gilbert, whom she expected to marry. Their love scenes were tastefully handled, yet their passion could not help but show through, resulting in a smoldering on-screen eroticism.

Valentino wasn't so fortunate. With the excep-

When Ahmad (Rudolph Valentino) and Yasmin (Vilma Banky) keep a romantic tryst at a desert oasis, Ahmad is captured and beaten by bandits, and believes Yasmin to have led him into a trap.

tion of one encounter with Gloria Swanson, he was never co-starred with anyone of equal magnitude, so that the opportunities for sexual and romantic give-and-take never presented themselves. (Had Paramount teamed him with Pola Negri, they might have had their own tempestuous love duo to match Garbo and Gilbert.) Too many of his Paramount films were disappointing in different ways: *Moran of the Lady Letty* was a rugged and surprisingly enjoyable melodrama, but hardly a film to enhance his romantic reputation. *Monsieur Beaucaire* was handsomely mounted, but slow and stodgy; when the story itself held no excitement, and little sense of pace, there was nothing he could do to liven it up. Although a success at the time, *Blood and Sand* seems naive and dated, and is hampered by Valentino's considerate (but not always helpful) trait of pitching his acting level to that of his leading lady. In *Blood and Sand,* he had two. Nita Naldi's vamp was wild and rather marvelous—sheer ham, but played with an elan and an animal quality that made it work. But in trying to match his emotional peaks to hers, Valentino overacted badly, resorting to nostril-quivering and other facial contortions which suggested that he was in pain rather than ecstasy. On the other hand, his love scenes (few, and sub-

dued) with his screen-wife, Lila Lee, were naturalistic, restrained and rather dull. And in the one really exotic movie in which he had played—1920's *Camille,* before he left Metro—star Nazimova made sure that audiences *knew* she was the star. Valentino had few opportunities and fewer close-ups. Limited already to a role that called for little more than passive reactions to Nazimova's tempestuous theatrics, he was further pushed into the background by the dynamic and bizarre semi-surreal sets designed by his wife-to-be, Natacha Rambova.

It is both fortunate and sad that in 1926 *Son of the Sheik* should prove to be such a successful vehicle for him. Fortunate because it makes up for all the mistakes and disappointments of earlier films, and provides us with a record in which he lives up to his legend. Sad because it was his last film—he died, suddenly, at the age of thirty-one, just as the film was going into release—and because with this film, he finally seemed to have found *exactly* the right approach. Had he lived, and continued to make films in the same style, he might have chalked up an unbroken string of successes—at least until the end of the silent era.

His previous film, *The Eagle* (1925), seemed to

be almost an introduction to *Son of the Sheik*. It had, not at all coincidentally, the same producer, the same cameraman, the same art director, and the same leading lady—Vilma Banky—whose cool, classic beauty made her an ideal visual mate for Valentino, while her subdued acting style (perhaps partially occasioned by her limited knowledge of English, for she was newly arrived from Hungary) meant that he too, could adopt a similarly relaxed manner of acting. Clarence Brown, who directed *The Eagle*, was certainly the finest director with whom Valentino had worked since his earlier association with Rex Ingram. Brown handled the film almost in a Lubitsch vein, and brought out Valentino's sense of comedy. Without being tongue in cheek, *The Eagle* managed to suggest that it wasn't meant to be taken too seriously, and yet at the same time allowed its romantic and dramatic moments to be played entirely straight.

But *Son of the Sheik* worked even better, and established *exactly* the right note for Valentino. While its director, George Fitzmaurice, wasn't as talented or as creative as Clarence Brown, he was ideally suited to this particular film. Although he'd made serious films, and good ones, his forte was always the larger-than-life romp, the film that for all its size and elegance, was meant to be first and foremost *fun*. Even his *Mata Hari* with Garbo, despite its tragic ending, is remembered not as a sad film but as an exhilarating piece of romantic espionage melodrama.

In *Son of the Sheik* everything seemed perfectly scaled to support, but not threaten, Valentino's own dimensions. William Cameron Menzies' sets—the desert oasis, the Sheik's encampment, the small desert city with its white walls and palm trees—provided a background that was both appropriate and romantic, but never overpowering. The old-fashioned tale made the most of its melodrama: the villain's henchmen were not just scoundrels or outlaws, but were referred to as "a band of mountebanks," while of the Number One Heavy, Ghabar the Moor, we were told (via subtitle) that his crimes outnumbered the sands of the desert. In the hands of Montague Love, this seemed entirely feasible. But this richness of melodrama never once descended to self-lampoon, and never before had Valentino had so many excellent opportunities to display his virility and athletic prowess. There was grace as well as vigor in his many riding and fighting scenes, and the script cunningly allowed for the display of his torso on several occasions, even throwing in a few bondage and torture scenes for the kinkier fans! And then of course there were the love

Later Ahmad kidnaps Yasmin, and shows her the scars from his beating prior to taking his own revenge on her.

scenes—ranging from the first casual flirtation to a passionate moonlight encounter in the ruins of an old fort and on to an almost obligatory rape scene. The latter occurs when Valentino mistakenly believes that he has been betrayed by his Yasmin and lured into a trap; actually the scene is there as a kind of throwback to the original *The Sheik*, although that much overrated earlier film actually pulled its punches at that crucial moment, and allowed the hero's conscience to change his mind. The love scenes are played with a sense of erotic power that is quite remarkable even today, and certainly neither dated nor laughable. Valentino, his passion building as he kisses his Yasmin's arm, working his way up to a full embrace, creates a romantic image that has just never been topped—with all the explicit "action" and nudity allowed in contemporary films. (In fact, nude love scenes in the biographical film by Ken Russell, *Valentino*, were dull, tableaux-like, and quite laughable in the way they were so uncomfortably posed in order to be both erotic and respectable at the same time!)

With its glistening photography and fast-moving narrative—despite its melodramatic action and boy-meets-loses-gets-girl complications, and with Valentino in a dual role as his own father thrown in for good measure, the film still only runs for a brisk 70 minutes—*Son of the Sheik* not only confirms that Valentino *was* a good actor, but also manages to be the best and definitive Valentino vehicle. It's good to know that it'll still be around a few hundred years hence to illustrate what all the shouting was about back in the twenties—and, on its own terms, doubtless more effective than ever, if the coarseness so prevalent in 70s love stories continues downhill at its present rate of descent!

Ultimately realizing that Yasmin is innocent, Ahmad rescues her from the clutches of the villainous Ghabah, played by Montagu Love.

Don Juan

Warner Bros., 1926.

Directed by Alan Crosland. Screenplay by Bess Meredyth, suggested by the poem by George Gordon Byron. Camera: Byron Haskin. Art Direction: Ben Carre.

With: John Barrymore, Mary Astor, Warner Oland, Montague Love, Estelle Taylor, Willard Louis, Myrna Loy, Jane Winton, John Roche, June Marlow, Yvonne Day, Philippe de Lacy, John George, Helene D'Algy, Phyllis Haver, Josef Swickard, Gustav von Seyffertitz, Nigel de Brulier, Hedda Hopper, Helen Lee Worthing, Emily Fitzroy, Sheldon Lewis, Gibson Gowland, Dick Sutherland.

Technology played a mean trick on John Barrymore by delaying the arrival of the talkie until he was just past his prime as a romantic idol. And the economics of the industry were such that, in those early Depression years, the opulent romantic swashbuckler was considered both out of date and an expensive luxury. By the time swashbucklers were restored to favor in the mid-1930s, those few extra years added to Barrymore's age made all the difference, both in his appearance, and in his abilities. His magnificent voice allowed him to play the mature lover in such fine talkies, many of them of stage origin, as *Reunion in Vienna* and *Grand Hotel*. And he was such a superb pantomimist, with such control over his body and nuance of facial expression, that the *absence* of voice in his many silent romances was hardly a handicap. But it would have been marvelous to have had a filmic record of Bar-

47

Don Juan tilts with the infamous Lucrezia Borgia, played by
Estelle Taylor.

rymore the romantic idol at his peak, roaring out defiance—or whispering endearments—with that combination of theatrical bravura *and* subtle underplaying (almost a forerunner of The Method at times) that was so uniquely his.

All of Barrymore's silent romances are larger than life, and each has its own particular assets. In *Tempest* it is the beauty of the camerawork: in *When a Man Loves* it is the grotesquerie of a "mad" scene, and the sheer gall with which the *Manon Lescaut* story, which it purports to be, is tossed aside for a typical Hollywood happy ending. *The Beloved Rogue* impresses most of all with its stunning sets and Gothic design, and one or two Barrymore set pieces where he demonstrates how little he really needs his voice to plumb the depths of drama and emotion. Only *Eternal Love*, thrown together in a hurry to help offset some of the losses on the two Barrymore vehicles that preceded it, and made while Barrymore was suffering from a painful eye infection, could be considered an out-and-out failure, a mistake for both Barrymore and director Ernst Lubitsch. Fortunately it came at the very end of the silent period, and its exhibition life was brief.

Quite apart from its subject matter, *Don Juan* is almost the perfect showcase for Barrymore as The Great Lover. It affords him every opportunity to run the emotional gamut. In the film's prologue he is the betrayed and vengeful husband, walling up his wife's lover, instructing his son that women are to be used but never *loved*, and ultimately, aging and tired, struck down by a jealous mistress to repeat his philosophy of love with his dying breath. In the film proper, Barrymore, as the grown-up son, is the cape-swirling cavalier who makes a practice of seducing every available (pretty) wife in town, in one memorable sequence juggling (and satisfying) three women at one time, while an irate husband pounds on the door. Then ultimately comes true love and genuine passion—and reformation.

Although a swashbuckler, most of the physical action of this long film is reserved for the final two reels, with its magnificent duel sequence, jailbreak and climactic chase. But until that point, the film moves effortlessly from farce to romance to straight drama, for the most part played straight by a distinguished cast of character actors, but played with a definite tongue in cheek, and a Comedie Française lightness of touch, by Barrymore himself. The constant change of venue, that many sets, the regular introducing of new characters, and the pace within the scenes themselves, make it seem a very modern, sprightly film despite the fact that it is virtually all byplay until those closing reels. While it would

In the prologue, John Barrymore as Don José, Don Juan's father, taunts his faithless wife (Jane Winton).

have been a joy to hear Barrymore lending his voice to many of the elegant comedy highlights and beautifully played love scenes with Mary Astor, at the same time dialogue would have introduced a note of reality that might have been harmful. Certain scenes have a fantasylike quality that just wouldn't have worked had dialogue been present. One of the most sophisticated and jauntily played sequences has Don Juan turning first to one woman, and then to another, assuring each in whispered tones that he loves her alone. In subtitle form, his declarations of love—identical for each woman—are both amusing and believable. However, had Barrymore *spoken* the lines—loudly enough for the audience to hear—the whole illusion would have been shattered. Backing up Barrymore's own elegance in these scenes is the beautifully arranged score played by the New York Philharmonic, in which every element of Barrymore's gait and every changing nuance of mood is matched by the music.

Mary Astor and Barrymore had been desperately in love when they made *Beau Brummel* together two years earlier. In her autobiography, Mary Astor rather poignantly recalls how she looked forward to this reteaming with Barrymore. As much in love with him as ever, she hoped—now that they were both free to marry—that working on *Don Juan* together would perhaps result in their marriage. But Barrymore in the meantime had met and fallen in love with Dolores Costello, and it was she that he would marry. Although there are rela-

tively few love scenes in *Don Juan* (the plot contrives to have Barrymore disillusioned in his new-found love after an early meeting, and to regain his faith only near the end of the film), the ones that are there are played with both passion and poetry. It must have been painful for both of them, Astor especially, but none of their offscreen feelings project into those moving onscreen scenes.

While Barrymore is at the very core of the film's success, he is backed up magnificently by director Alan Crosland, a particularly felicitous teammate who seemed to share Barrymore's taste, his love of good theatre, and also his lack of pretension. There is nothing pompous or pedestrian about *Don Juan* and it *moves* constantly. Too, a tremendous amount of credit must go to veteran art director Ben Carre and his associates. While obviously an expensive production, *Don Juan* was still made with all eyes open for possible economies. The set design makes particularly cunning use of space and lighting. One has an impression of a never-ending array of spectacular sets (until the final horseback chase, every foot of the film is staged within the studio) and sumptuous decor. And of course, so much is happening within that space that one's attention never has to wander to examine the sets in detail. And that of course is what good art direction is all about—to establishing a convincing and evocative frame against which the action can play. *Don Juan* is a showcase for superb art direction almost as much as it is a showcase for John Barrymore.

Barrymore with his leading lady, Mary Astor, about to shoot a scene that apparently was subsequently eliminated, since he wears no makeup like this in the final (and still very long) version.

Seventh Heaven

Fox, 1927.

Directed by Frank Borzage Scenario by Benjamin Glazer, from an original story by Austin Strong. Camera: Ernest Palmer. Sets: Harry Oliver. Assistant Director: Lew Borzage.

With: Janet Gaynor, Charles Farrell, David Butler, Ben Bard, Marie Mosquini, Albert Gran, George E. Stone, Gladys Brockwell, Emile Chautard, Brandon Hurst, Jessie Haslett, Lillian West, Henry Armetta.

Seventh Heaven has always been regarded as perhaps the "definitive" love story of the silent screen, and in many ways it is, although it achieves that status almost in spite of itself. Director Frank Borzage's genius has always been in his uncanny ability to wring pathos and emotion from the most commonplace of situations, or to sidestep a cliche and make it seem fresh and human. There's a moment near the end of *Flirtation Walk* (a mid-30s musical romance) in which the professional soldier (Pat O'Brien) watches proudly as the men he has trained graduate. Instead of concentrating on O'Brien, Borzage cuts away to a little girl who tugs at her father's coattails and, pointing to O'Brien, remarks, "Look Daddy, that man's crying." Or similarly in the follow-up *Shipmates Forever*, there's a potentially lugubrious situation in which a young cadet, about to be washed out of the Annapolis class, is saying goodbye to his comrades in the locker room. The scene gets increasingly sentimental, and the young cadet is just about to break down and cry; moments before he does so, the locker door swings open, obscuring his face—and the extent of his emotion is hidden, leaving it to the audience to supply the level of pathos according to their own individual standards. Even if these scenes had been written into the original scripts—which seems unlikely—they would probably have read as maudlin and heavy-handed. Somehow Borzage was able to turn these scenes, and a dozen others like them, into deeply emotional moments, without one ever knowing quite how he pulled it off. In this respect, perhaps his most incredible achievement was in the 1934 *No Greater Glory*. The tragic ending is predictable from the beginning; we see it creeping up inexorably as the film progresses; yet when it arrives, it has the shock and poignancy of a total surprise.

In many ways, the best Borzage films are the "little" ones (comparatively speaking) like *No Greater Glory* and *Man's Castle*, where he is able to conjure beauty and sadness out of the reality of life. But *Seventh Heaven* is far from a "little" film, and at times its sheer size seems in danger of swamping that delicate Borzage magic. It's an extremely handsome film, and the sets, ranging from Paris sewers and streets to rooftops, all beautifully lit and photographed, are so attention-getting in themselves that they occasionally threaten to divert the spotlight from the love story itself. Even Borzage is occasionally seduced by the beauty of his sets. When Chico takes Diane to his top floor apartment in a rambling old Parisian lodging house, the set is split so that the camera can move upwards to keep pace with them as they progress from floor to floor. Around the fourth floor, the single camera movement is interrupted for a cutaway to Chico pausing, thus permitting the same high set, redecorated, to be used again for the remaining four flights! Later on, a similar camera movement traces a downward path, and at the very end of the film, Chico's return is accomplished by a dizzy shot looking down the stairway, with Chico's face, small at first, growing larger and more recognizable as he climbs those stairs to rejoin his Diane.

The Paris of the first two-thirds of the film is entirely studio created; with the coming of World

Diane (Janet Gaynor) shows off the dress in which she will be married to Chico.

War I, the camera ventures into the genuine outdoors for the first time, to create the sense of reality that can destroy Diane and Chico's sheltered private world. But since their love story is essentially a modern fairy-tale, even the war scenes—for all their spectacle—cannot be consistently realistic. Glass shots and other camera tricks stylize the genuine exteriors, and the many miniatures—particularly in the scenes of the taxicab army rushing to the front—likewise lend an aura of deliberate unreality to these scenes.

Chico (Charles Farrell) works as a cleaner in the sewers, and looks forward to the day when he can work in the sunshine.

The film, though never boring, is also far too long. The only print available for study today is of the full, original, twelve-reel road-show version. When put into general release, it was shorn of some 35 minutes—a rather drastic reduction from such a smoothly flowing film. It is difficult to tell how efficiently this cutting was done, but it may have reduced the Diane-Chico love story to less epic proportions. In the full version, there is a tendency for the lovers to become symbols, modern counterparts of Romeo and Juliet. With the film's often quite poetical subtitles, and its elements of mysticism, it is all too easy to read allegory into what was originally an unpretentious romance.

Yet with all the pitfalls of the film's size, and the additional one of a somewhat unsubtle musical score, less effective by far than the music in the same year's *Sunrise,* and prone to turn drama into melodrama and melodrama into Grand Guignol, the film still works. It is both human and touching. Much of the credit of course goes to Borzage, but in this particular case the major credit perhaps goes to the two stars—Charles Farrell and Janet Gaynor—whose sincerity and sheer likability always come to the rescue when the plotting gets out of hand.

On its own level, the plot—divorced from its too sumptuous production values—is appropriately slender and serviceable enough. Diane is a street waif, constantly whipped and browbeaten by her vicious sister—marvelously portrayed by Gladys Brockwell. When Diane deliberately throws away a chance for the two of them to go and live with stuffy relatives (she feels that they have sunk too low to live with "decent" people), she is whipped mercilessly by her sister, and only saved by the intervention of Chico, a romantic sewer worker who dreams of the stars and working in the fresh air. In a later altercation with the police, Chico saves the situation by claiming that Diane is his wife. To avoid complications, Diane moves in with him—on a purely platonic level—to back up his story when it is investigated. She falls deeply in love with him; Chico, on the other hand, pleasant and thoughtful but extremely self-centered, is unaware of her feelings. Finally however, he does respond, and proposes marriage. The war intervenes before the ceremony can be performed, and Chico and Diane solemnly marry themselves to each other, calling on God to witness the validity of their union. Immedi-

The convoy of taxicabs, rushing men to the front for the defense of Paris, is a spectacular highlight of SEVENTH HEAVEN.

53

ately thereafter, Chico leaves for the front, first promising Diane to come to her every day at eleven, when they will talk to each other, mentally, across the miles that separate them. For both, this daily telepathy sustains them through years of war. During a major battle however, Chico is seriously wounded. Diane is told by the village priest, who had been at the front with the regiment, that Chico died in his arms. For the first time, Diane's faith is shaken. But as the armistice sounds, Chico returns, blinded, to his Diane—still a romanticist and an optimist, assuring Diane that he will not stay blind for long.

On a purely realistic level, the story is full of absurdities, and they are not always helped by the grandiose scale of production. When Nana, Diane's sister, turns on her, the whipping is a prolonged assault through the streets, the mobile camera tracking along with them through the impressive sets. Diane collapses by one of the raised grilles to the sewers—from which Chico pops at a superbly timed moment to stay Nana's hand. When war is declared, in true movie tradition the regiment has to leave for the front "within the hour" even though, up to that point, there has been no reference to anyone's serving in a regiment, undergoing training, or being issued uniforms. The troops marching back to Paris en masse just *as* the Armistice is sounded certainly seems a case of foolhardy anticipation on somebody's part, and the ability of the weakened and blinded Chico to find his way back for such a propitiously timed moment likewise seems a little dubious.

On the other hand, this isn't *The Big Parade;* it is really Cinderella transferred to World War I, and the charm of its two stars makes it work. And the sentiment inherent in warime partings and reunions is something that Borzage was always able to manipulate superbly well, as witness, films as diverse as *Farewell to Arms* and *Stage Door Canteen.* Perhaps the scenes that work best are those that are not particularly "real" and appeal primarily to the emotions—such as the scenes (underplayed, as Borzage's most effective emotional scenes always were) of Diane and Chico at their daily eleven o'clock "meetings." This bit of business worked so well that Fox repeated it verbatim a decade later in *The Little Princess,* though as between father and daughter (Ian Hunter and Shirley Temple) rather than lovers.

Just how successful *Seventh Heaven* is one can judge more easily by looking at the many follow-ups that sought to recapture its magic. In 1928, Fox literally tried the impossible. They wanted to repeat the *prestige* success of Murnau's *Sunrise* and couple it with the *commercial* success of *Seventh Heaven.* The result was the reuniting of the Borzage-Gaynor-Farrell team for *Street Angel.* To give credit to Fox's ideas of computerized box-office formulas, the film *was* a huge popular success, but it couldn't match either of the films that inspired it. Its opening reel and a half was magnificent, stylized stuff—Borzage had obviously studied Murnau's work, and that of other German masters—and the film started off like the apotheosis of all German UFA films, with borrowings not only from Murnau but Lang as well. Magnificent sets, superb composition and lighting, a mobile camera, symbolic and geometric groupings of masses of people: ten years of the best of German technique seemed distilled into fifteen minutes. It wasn't possible to maintain this pitch of virtuosity and the film didn't try, though it did return to that style for its closing reel. In between, however, was a story more farfetched and rambling than that of *Seventh Heaven,* and worse, it asked to be taken seriously as a work of art. Again, and fortunately, it was saved by the fresh and enthusiastic work of its stars, and it was always good to look at. But it was too pretentious for its own good, and the Borzage magic had too few chances to work.

Or again, one can look to the sound remake of *Seventh Heaven,* produced exactly ten years after the original. With all of its defects (including too typical typecasting from Fox's stock company, and the elimination of the taxicab "big parade" to the fighting front), its major defect is that it *talks*—and James Stewart (resolutely non-French) and Simone Simon (undeniably French, but certainly no waif) are forced to put into lame dialogue the emotions that were expressed visually in the old version, and appropriately so since one of the points of the story was the reticence of the couple in expressing, or being *able* to express, deep feelings. Poor Henry King, an admirable director, seemed fated to be associated with inferior remakes of silent classics. Apart from *Seventh Heaven,* he was also given D. W. Griffith's *Way Down East* to remake, and his own silent classics, *Tol'able David, Stella Dallas* and *The White Sister,* as well as his early talkie *State Fair,* were all remade (by others) as far less inspired sound films.

Seventh Heaven is certainly (along with *Sunrise*) the perfect illustration of the advantages of the silent film within the genre of the love story. Somehow its flaws seem insignificant and the beauty, the poetry and the romance take over. In the sound film, those qualities are too often stifled—as they are in life itself—by logic and reality. The timeless, universal qualities of the fable and the fairy-tale no longer apply.

Two of the many Gaynor/Farrell follow-ups: the dramatic and very Germanic late silent STREET ANGEL (1928), and the delightful early musical SUNNY SIDE UP (1929).

The woman from the city (Margaret Livingston) tempts the farmer (George O'Brien) and urges him to murder his wife.

Sunrise

Fox, 1927.

Directed by F. W. Murnau. Screnario by Carl Mayer from the story "The Trip to Tilsit" by Hermann Sudermann. Camera: Charles Rosher, Karl Struss. Production Design: Rochus Gliese. Asst. Art Director: Edgar Ulmer. Assistant Director: Herman Bing. Musical score arranged by Hugo Riesenfeld.

With: George O'Brien, Janet Gaynor, Margaret Livingston, J. Farrell MacDonald, Bodil Rosing, Ralph Sipperly, Jane Winton, Arthur Housman, Eddie Arnold, Gino Corrado, Sally Eilers, Barry Norton, Robert Kortman.

Sunrise may well be the finest achievement of the silent American cinema; quite certainly it is a film that demonstrates to the full just what the silent film was capabe of. Made as sound was already making its first inroads, it is both the peak and the climax of silent film. Titles are few, and information is conveyed by nuances of acting and by visual means. The elaborate color toning and tinting is dispensed with in favor of superb black-and-white photography in which subtleties of lighting and composition achieve the same emotional results that the use of color would a few years earlier. Even the silence is a distinct advantage. Without dialogue to lock it into a period or a geographic locale, the film takes on the quality of a fable—a film of no particular time, valid and moving in *all* times.

Writing about *Sunrise* (for me at least) presents certain problems. Having written about it on many occasions, there is the danger of repetition, of seeming casual about a film that provokes both enthusiasm and strong emotional reaction. There is also a purely legal problem, since publishers have a habit of not liking their material reused in the way that filmmakers often do, taking whole blocks of stock footage to use again in a remake of the same film. However, *Sunrise* is one film that really needs to be *seen* rather than just read about, and fortunately it *can* be seen—even in a limited theatrical revival, though exhibitors unfortunately seem a little reluctant to give it a chance. Stills of the film, as

In the city, the contrite husband protects his wife from the traffic and tries to win back her confidence.

The visit to the restaurant, with both of them too upset to eat.

can be seen, certainly testify to the beauty of its design and camerawork. Its story, like most of Murnau's themes, is simple in outline if more complex in its ramifications. A farmer is tempted by his newly acquired mistress to murder his wife. He plans to do so, but being an innately decent man, cannot. Their gradual, painful reconciliation during the ensuing day in the nearby city, as the wife overcomes her fear and regains faith and love, is intensely moving and almost guaranteed to bring tears to the eyes. Certain moments, such as the hus-

band's remorse and desperate reaffirmation of his own love as he and his still frightened wife watch a wedding ceremony, are so poignant that they can hardly fail to touch audiences. Other aspects are more personal, and are likely to move one more or less depending on one's own experiences of life. Just as those who have been harmed or bereaved by war, or have spent time in prisoner-of-war camps, must inevitably absorb more emotionally from Renoir's *La Grande Illusion* than those who have not been touched by war at all, so *Sunrise* must be a

F.W. Murnau, sitting behind cameraman Charles Rosher, shoots the sequence in which the farmer will attempt to drown his wife.

Reunited, the happy pair visit a photographer's salon for a posed portrait—but the photographer catches them in a happy unposed embrace.

At a huge fairground, the now thoroughly reconciled pair perform an exhilarating peasant dance.

tremendously moving experience for married couples who have drifted apart, and even more so for those who have reunited.

Murnau has sometimes been accused, because he was a homosexual, of being "incapable" of depicting love on the screen. This is nonsense. There is no finer or more sensitive celebration of love in film anywhere than his *Sunrise*. It is one of the very few serious films where one doesn't feel offended when audiences hiss the mistress at the end, as she makes her defeated return to the city. Audiences are so involved in the film that it becomes a neces-

sary release of their own collective emotion, and it is invariably followed by applause (not the polite recognition of a great film, but genuine delight in and approval of the happy ending) for the film's stunning final moments—as the husband and wife kiss, the embrace turns into a sunburst which wipes all detail from the screen, save its own shimmering image, an image that cuts to the very final scene, a long shot shot of the farmhouse, from behind which the sun rises. It is, as critic Griel Marcus commented, like the face of God bursting through the screen.

The Thirties

Few decades have seen as much filmic change as the 30s. It started with technological change—the coming of sound and the increase in the use of color. Within a few years, the industry's concern-over possible Governmental intervention in the area of censorship brought about its own self-imposed censorship in the form of the Production Code, a rigid set of rules which occasioned endless frustrations and limitations for directors, and literally re-shaped the majority of Hollywood product into "wholesome" family fare. By the end of the 30s, with audiences tiring of this never-never-Land, and showing it by falling attendance at the box office, and with Hollywood aware too of the probably impending loss of their European markets due to the threats of World War II, there was yet another change—back to the subject matter of the free-wheeling pre-Code days, but with careful adherence to the basics of the Code. Love and sex were matters given particular attention by the Code and the differences in the pre-Code and post-Code love stories are quite striking.

The movies were still relatively young in 1930, and so were most of its major stars. Youth and beauty were salable commodities, and while Hollywood didn't exactly try to destroy stars, or trade them in, like automobiles, for newer models, nevertheless its own films conveyed the idea that age was something of a sin. In an early musical, *Show Girl in Hollywood*, Blanche Sweet plays an "aging" movie star of thirty (!) who admits to being a has-been and acknowledges retirement as the only answer. In one of the early Garbo talkies, *Romance*, Lewis Stone plays Garbo's lover and steps aside because, in his own words, spoken in a tone of resignation, "I'm *fifty*—I've *lived* my life!" Still later in the 30s, a very virile Edward Arnold proposes marriage to Frances Farmer who laughs hysterically at his absurd suggestion and calls him an old man. These value judgments seem ludicrous today, but they were thoroughly in keeping with Hollywood's idea of love and romance being for the young. If it had been suggested then that Gloria Swanson and Joan Crawford could later stage

Hollywood's best romantic movies in the first few years of the sound era. There's an honesty and a lack of pretension to many of these films which have enabled them to remain surprisingly durable. For one thing, the coming of sound and the Depression coincided. Both for economy reasons, and for reasons that seemed artistically valid at the time, Hollywood concentrated on contemporary themes, and even relatively unimportant films like William Wellman's *Other Men's Women* had a ring of casual truth to them—in their details of day-to-day living, if not in their basic plots. Many of the Warner films of this period, dealing more than any other studio with themes taken from contemporary life, had quite surprisingly mature relations as their foundation: Edward G. Robinson and Genevieve Tobin as his loving but snobbish and ambitious wife in *Dark Hazard*, or Warren William, Ginger Rogers and Mary Astor in Warners' own forerunner to *Brief Encounter, Upperworld*.

With the whole art of screenwriting suddenly new and back to square-one following the transition to sound, Hollywood took many a shortcut in those early talkie years by relying on plays (even unproduced plays) and novels, where the structure and dialogue was prewritten. Recent hits were brought to the screen, and theatrical vaults scoured for old

A DEVIL WITH WOMEN (1930) is a routine film, but of historical interest in that it introduced Humphrey Bogart as the romantic lead (seen here with Mona Maris). His performance was good enough to make one wonder why nobody spotted his potential that early.

comebacks playing older women, or that Cary Grant, John Wayne and James Stewart would go on playing romantic leads into their sixties, nobody would have given the idea any credence whatsoever. Just as Blanche Sweet, *in* her thirties playing a woman of thirty was considered an anachronism, so Gloria Swanson—in her early fifties playing a woman of fifty in *Sunset Boulevard*—was considered something of a freak, although the passage of twenty years and the staying power of many established stars had extended the age barrier somewhat.

There's a remarkable concentration of some of

THE DEVIL TO PAY (1930): Though only a trifle, this was a remarkably sophisticated early sound film, and is still undated. Myrna Loy was the third side of the triangle represented here by Ronald Colman and Loretta Young.

OVER THE HILL (1931) was a remake of the silent classic with Mary Carr, the definitive "mother love" film. With James Dunn and Mae Marsh.

SVENGALI (1931), one of the great Gothic movies, a romantic as well as a melodramatic classic, starred John Barrymore as the mesmerist who hypnotizes Trilby, played by Marian Marsh, into loving him.

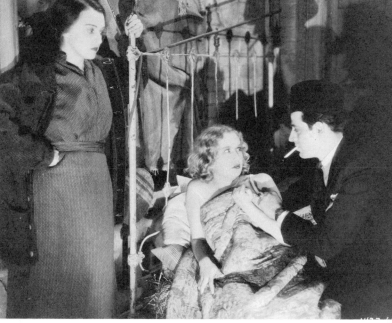

Lust often ran parallel with love in early thirties movies. In GRAND HOTEL (1932) financier Wallace Beery makes his intentions abundantly clear to stenographer Joan Crawford, while THE STORY OF TEMPLE DRAKE (1933), based on William Faulkner's Sanctuary, has the distinction of having almost singlehandedly brought about the crackdown by the Production Code. Florence Eldridge watches with mild concern as Jack LaRue makes his wishes known to captive heiress Miriam Hopkins.

63

BACK STREET (1932): the first of the three versions of Fannie Hurst's classic tearjerker starred Irene Dunne and John Boles.

RED DUST (1932): almost the definitive Gable-Harlow vehicle; torrid, unsubtle, yet with a delightful sense of humor.

A striking contrast to the gutsy and very physical love of *Red Dust* was the spiritual love of De Mille's THE SIGN OF THE CROSS (1932), in which Roman libertine Fredric March finally goes to his death in the arena for the love of virginal Christian Elissa Landi

The most elegant of all Ernst Lubitsch's romantic comedies, TROUBLE IN PARADISE (1932). Herbert Marshall and Kay Francis inspect the bed once used by Kay's former secretary. "She must have been very happy in this bed," remarks Marshall. "*Too* happy; that's why I fired her," is the reply.

The same year Norma Shearer played opposite Leslie Howard again, and also opposite Fredric March, in SMILIN' THROUGH.

In A FREE SOUL (1932) Norma Shearer is loved by Leslie Howard, but becomes the mistress of gangster Clark Gable. Lionel Barrymore, above, with Shearer, played her alcoholic father and won an Academy Award for his performance.

TAXI (1932), with James Cagney and Loretta Young in a casual and abrasive romance typical of the Depression years.

Despite its background of melodrama, Josef von Sternberg's SHANGHAI EXPRESS (1932) was essentially a love story, and an unforgettable meeting of the classic features of Clive Brook and Marlene Dietrich.

MGM's first two Tarzan movies, TARZAN THE APE MAN (1932) and TARZAN AND HIS MATE (1934) were surprisingly sensual and erotic in their romantic scenes, and indeed the second film had to be somewhat trimmed to conform to censorship rulings on its later reissue. In these two scenes from the second film, Jane (Maureen O'Sullivan), visited by friends from the outside world, tries on a new gown that they have brought, but soon reverts to her traditional jungle garb.

ones. The romantic cinema of those days offered such a wide divergence of material as *Reunion in Vienna* (Robert Sherwood's stage vehicle for the Lunts, tastefully transferred to the screen for John Barrymore and Diana Wynyard under Sidney Franklin's sensitive direction), *Tonight Is Ours*, a minor early Noel Coward play dusted off and turned into a lush and sometimes sensual romantic tour de force of Claudette Colbert and Fredric March, who were both so stunningly handsome then, and so richly costumed and photographed, that thanks to their sheer presence this little piece of trivia seemed almost important.

The talkies had turned Ronald Colman into a major star almost overnight, and his assured and relaxed playing, and flawless diction, turned almost every Colman vehicle into a romantic event. Best of all was *The Devil to Pay*, 1930's most sophisticated film, and still totally undated. From a Frederick Lonsdale play, it had charm, wit and maturity, a perfect example of a pre-Code film that could be freewheeling in its morals (Colman had Myrna Loy as his mistress before settling down to woo and win Loretta Young as his wife) and still remain in the very best of taste at all times.

On an equally unpretentious level, one of several adaptations of the Arnold Bennett novel and play *Buried Alive*, 1933s *His Double Life*, was a charming espousal of the virtues of love and marriage. Lillian Gish and Roland Young made an ut-

terly engaging married couple, whose love was British, restrained, diplomatic and apparently lacking in passion, but certainly made marriage look like a comfortable, cozy and highly satisfying institution.

Another major hit (from 1933) was the screen version of Noel Coward's play *Cavalcade*, a classic love story dealing not only with the love of two people (Clive Brook and Diana Wynyard) but also with the love of family, of tradition and of country. *Cavalcade* rarely plays nowadays, and when it does it is not greeted with enthusiasm. Attitudes have changed so much that it now seems like a visitor from another planet, more's the pity, and audiences find it stuffy.

Molnar's *The Guardsman*, brought to the screen as the only co-starring movie vehicle for the Lunts, is perhaps too much of a comedy of manners to be discussed on the purely romantic level, but the sophistication of its battle of the sexes owed much to the freedom of the pre-Code screen. (Just how much can be gleaned by looking at MGM's later musical remake, *The Chocolate Soldier*, a Nelson Eddy vehicle with all the innuendo and ambiguity watered down). *The Guardsman*, dealing as it does with a husband-and-wife acting team, each talented, temperamental and jealous of the other, was naturally a perfect vehicle for the Lunts. Apart from their skill and impeccable timing, their natural rapport throughout was evident.

The pre-Code era was also responsible for such

Very touching and in many ways superior to its later glossy Hollywood remake was the 1933 British version of THE CONSTANT NYMPH with Victoria Hopper and Brian Aherne.

Although almost forgotten today and eclipsed by David Lean's later version, the 1933 GREAT EXPECTATIONS had considerable merit, and a great deal of charm in the romantic teaming of Jane Wyatt as Estrella and Phillips Holmes as Pip.

Another 1933 film of real charm was HIS DOUBLE LIFE. Set in England, but filmed entirely in the Astoria, Long Island, Studio, it featured the offbeat but entirely felicitous teaming of Roland Young and Lillian Gish, brought together by a matrimonial bureau.

ONLY YESTERDAY (1933): John Boles, Universal's likeable cad-in-residence, goes over some of his old *Back Street* ground in a role that actually foreshadows that of Louis Jourdan in a later Universal film *Letter from an Unknown Woman*. Margaret Sullavan was particularly touching as the woman he seduces and forgets.

THE POWER AND THE GLORY (1933): Colleen Moore and Spencer Tracy as the married couple who are finally torn asunder by his own ambition and his love for a younger woman; a remarkable film that is considered a stylistic forerunner of *Citizen Kane*.

Playwright and screenwriter Preston Sturges in 1933, the year he wrote *The Power and the Glory*. He had the unique ability of being able to handle love stories with extreme tenderness, as in *Remember the Night* and *Christmas in July* (discussed later) or to satirize them with cynical barbed wit (as in *The Lady Eve* and *The Palm Beach Story*).

REUNION IN VIENNA (1933): Witty, dramatic and poignant, a superb screen translation of the Sherwood play. John Barrymore and Diana Wynyard were both at their elegant best, quite able to divert attention from MGM's art-deco sets, which in this scene even included a fireplace replica of the Empire State Building.

delightfully amoral romantic escapades as the rough-and-ready Gable-Harlow vehicle *Red Dust*, Lubitsch's most elegant film *Trouble in Paradise*, and the rough-hewn crime melodrama *I Cover the Waterfront*, in which the Ben Lyon–Claudette Colbert romance is both piquant and touching. It's consummated well before wedding bells ring, and no bones are made about the fact that Claudette's old reprobate of a father—played by Ernest Torrence—makes an occasional visit to a bordello!

Just as many a director, such as rough-housing Raoul Walsh, found his style severely handicapped by the Code, so quite a few stars had a more dynamic screen persona in those pre-Code years. Gable was such a romantic phenomenon, and so carefully groomed to peak romantic stardom in the mid-to-late thirties, that it would obviously be untrue to claim that either his popularity or his virile image were impaired by hewing to Hollywood's moral tone. Still, some of the most endearing moments of his career come from his pre-Code films, such as his audaciously offhand farewell remark to Jean Harlow—"So long, it's been nice having you!"—at the midway point of *Red Dust*.

On the distaff side, Norma Shearer too— though probably neither she nor MGM would agree —exuded a sexuality in the early 30s that was re-

Certainly the most famous romantic film of 1934 and one of the most famous of all time—though it is referred to as a comedy as often as it is as a love story—Frank Capra's IT HAPPENED ONE NIGHT with Clark Gable and Claudette Colbert.

THE WORST WOMAN IN PARIS? (1934) was a delightful and mature romantic comedy, much in the Lubitsch manner, and directed by Monta Bell, in the twenties one of Lubitsch's major rivals. Both sophisticated and sentimental, it is never shown today but deserves to be. Adolphe Menjou and Benita Hume co-starred.

fined out of existence in such later films as *Romeo and Juliet* and particularly *The Women*, where her character (in the original stage version) needed to manipulate sex in order to win back a straying husband, but in the film was made to be such a paragon of virtue as to be unaware of such tactics. One of the reasons for her popularity in her early 30s movies was admittedly one that does no credit to her male audience, namely that she projected an image of a high-quality call-girl. There was no question about Miss Shearer's offscreen integrity or her place among the Hollywood aristocracy; indeed, it was that very position, and her roles in films like *Riptide* and *A Free Soul* (where she becomes the mistress of gangster Gable, who uses her and slaps her around), that gave her screen image such a voyeuristic appeal: the unattainable ideal that is suddenly "available" for a price. (It was this kind of juxtaposition that helped to catapult Marilyn Chambers to the top of the heap of porno stars from a "pure" beginning as the Ivory Snow Girl!) MGM was wise not to overplay its hand, and Miss Shearer was still given the not infrequent prestige plum—such as Noel Coward's *Private Lives*—but still, the sensual pre-Code Shearer was an attractive and provocative figure.

MGM had a positive genius for taking the life

THE SCARLET EMPRESS may not have been 1934's greatest love story, but it was certainly the most bizarre and told against the most spectacular and baroque settings of old Russia that even Josef von Sternberg had ever used! Marlene Dietrich was Catherine of Russia, and John Lodge (later the Governor of Connecticut) was Count Orloff, most colorful of her many lovers.

Most of the George Arliss vehicles had subsidiary love stories since he was by then too mature a player (in his sixties) to play romantic leads. In THE HOUSE OF ROTHSCHILD (1934) the strong romantic subplot was carried by Robert Young and Loretta Young.

DEATH TAKES A HOLIDAY (1934) was a disappointing film, too much of its dramatic value swamped by its lush decor, but its romantic element was made memorable by the luminous performance of Evelyn Venable, a much-wasted actress, shown here with co-star Fredric March.

DARK HAZARD (1934): An unusual little Warner film, in which Edward G. Robinson plays a compulsive gambler, deeply in love with his wife (Genevieve Tobin). His compulsive gambling loses him her love, and in a surprise last-reel switch, he *doesn't* win her back. He settles down to a new life with a new love—a greyhound!

Though associated with the *Thin Man* movies and later wacky comedies, and typecast as the perfect married couple, Myrna Loy and William Powell were romantically teamed in far more dramatic love stories as well. This pose is from EVELYN PRENTICE (1934), and earlier they had made *Manhattan Melodrama*.

70

UPPERWORLD (1934): An offbeat film from a Ben Hecht story, something of an unofficial variant on *An American Tragedy*. Warren William is the successful businessman who becomes involved in an affair with showgirl Ginger Rogers.

BOLERO (1934): Basing this film on fact, even if somewhat loosely, entailed a tragic ending. A pity, since it was otherwise such an enjoyable example of hokey Hollywood romantic schmaltz, done with flair and style, that adherence to the truth seemed a liability in this case. In any case, it was a very handsome showcase for George Raft and Carol Lombard.

"B" Westerns were not usually strong on love stories. An exception was 1935's WHEN A MAN'S A MAN, based very loosely on a Harold Bell Wright novel. Excellent playing by George O'Brien and Dorothy Wilson (here escaping from a mine cave-in) was enhanced by genuinely lyrical photography from Frank B. Good.

One of the classic French studies in obsessive love was Jean Renoir's adaptation of Zola's LA BETE HUMAINE (1938), with Simone Simon and Jean Gabin.

Simple, rural romances, reminiscent of the silent Charles Ray films, became, in the thirties, the province of the small independent companies, who did not own their own theatres, couldn't bank on large metropolitan exposure, and thus aimed their product more at the small towns. The novels of Gene Stratton Porter provided especially useful material for these low-key romances. Here are scenes from two Monogram versions. In 1934 Eddie Nugent and Marian Marsh starred; in 1938 it was Eric Linden and Jean Parker.

out of its stars and putting them on pedestals in the post-Code years. Jeanette MacDonald, in her Lubitsch years at Paramount, was a saucy, lively, vivacious—and certainly sexy—young lady, with an excellent sense of comedic timing. In her operettas MGM managed to turn her into a sexless and matronly figure, who still managed to exert a certain amount of appeal only because she was cast opposite the wooden and stolid Nelson Eddy.

Shearer's *A Free Soul*, more of a sex drama than a love story, holds up extremely well today, especially so in that it is the kind of seedy underworld story that director Clarence Brown had little sympathy for and usually tried to avoid. Apart from the dynamic Shearer presence, it is also interesting in that its romantic male leads—played by Clark Gable and Leslie Howard—blueprint to a remarkable degree the roles those two actors would later play in *Gone With the Wind*.

The coming of the Code at the end of 1933 coincided with the beginning of the extended production of "B" movies and the tapering off of the higher-level "programmer" pictures which, as their classification indicates, found their own level. Programmers usually had sufficient length (around 70 minutes) and star value to play top of the bill, solo, double-bill, or bottom of the bill, depending on the theater and its location. They were brisk, never overblown, often surprisingly personal films into which directors or writers could inject real style. Among the programmers discussed in upcoming

pages are such films as *Six Hours to Live, Hot Saturday* and *One Way Passage*.

While a certain number of these films continued to be made, in the main Hollywood preferred to separate its big and little product rather more obviously, by putting all the money and the stars into the "A" product, and using the "B"'s as clearly defined supporting fare. The decision was a major loss in terms of lovely little films like *One Way Passage* which would soon be spoiled by overlength and overproduction. One of William Dieterle's finest films was the literate and ornate *Madame Du Barry* of 1934, a triumph of sophisticated writing and ensemble playing. None of his later, artificially expanded Paul Muni biographical "prestige" features could hold a candle to it, and one of them, *Juarez*, was literally twice as long.

One of the key functions of the Code seemed to be to "legitimize" love, and to take as much passion out of it as possible. Marriage was mentioned as early—and as often—as possible. Even on wedding-night scenes, double beds were much in evidence. Seductions, when unavoidable, usually took place offscreen, sometimes so ambiguously that one could never be quite sure that they did. And when the proof came a reel or two later in the form of a baby, the expectant mothers-to-be were wheeled into the delivery room with nary an ounce of extra flesh to give the game away. Pregnancies were remarkably chic and flattering to slimly-tailored suits in the 30s. Dialogue was frequently—and

The much-filmed Pierre Louys novel *The Woman and the Puppet*, dealing with obsessive love and a woman who systematically wrecks the lives of men who fall under her spell, became a peculiarly personal film for Josef von Sternberg in THE DEVIL IS A WOMAN (1935). It has been suggested that von Sternberg was trying to make a fairly obvious statement by having Lionel Atwill, a Sternberg look-alike, play the lead in this, the last of the von Sternberg–Marlene Dietrich collaborations.

DAVID COPPERFIELD (1935), one of the best of Hollywood's forays into Charles Dickens, had a particularly pleasing romantic team in Frank Lawton and Madge Evans.

Perhaps intended as an imitation Nick and Nora Charles, Robert Young and Constance Cummings nevertheless made an original and very likeable much-in-love sleuthing marital duo in REMEMBER LAST NIGHT? (1935).

Definitely not included as a joke, James Whale's 1935 THE BRIDE OF FRANKENSTEIN included one or two very touching moments as the Monster (Boris Karloff) dreams of love and happiness. Had he not been rejected by a mate (Elsa Lanchester) who had no reason to be quite so particular, domestic bliss might well have taken over at this point—and prevented a steady downhill spiral of sequels.

WALPURGISNACHT (1935) was one of the few Swedish Ingrid Bergman films to get a U.S. release—under the less sinister-sounding title of *First Love*. Most of her Swedish films were love stories, and rather tormented ones at that. Sharing this scene with her is one of Sweden's finest pioneer actor-directors, Victor Seastrom, who abandoned directing (except for one British film) in the sound period to concentrate on acting.

For contrast, a typical early portrait of the Hollywood Bergman. For once the glamour treatment did not destroy the star's natural grace and charm.

Island-reared Dorothy Lamour enjoyed romance—and her first kiss—with Ray Milland in JUNGLE PRINCESS (1936) and the follow-up HER JUNGLE LOVE. In both films chaste romance was made even more innocent by the comic interpolations of Lynne Overman and a chimp. Thereafter Ray Milland left the field to Jon Hall and Robert Preston, but Overman and the chimp made periodic returns.

obviously—inserted into films to stress that no hanky-panky was going on. When, in *Camille*, the two lovers enjoy a holiday in the country, Garbo is given a line to emphasize that she and Robert Taylor are staying at separate hotels. Imported foreign films frequently had marriages grafted into them, either by subtitled references or by the interpolation of often nonmatching stock footage, while the added newspaper headline became a convenient way of ensuring climactic retribution. (European films often had the temerity to let killers get away with crimes, or at least not to stress their capture. Hollywood always tidied up after them, even though it sometimes meant a very lame and obviously doctored climax, as in the British *A Window in London* where a *crime passionel* among vaudeville artists is honored by a front-page headline in the New York *Daily News*!)

However, the language of the Production Code was quickly assimilated by the sophisticated filmgoers, who could read between the lines, or nimbly side-stepped by directors like Lubitsch. His *Bluebeard's Eighth Wife* of 1938 is quite surprisingly risque in its sexual implications—but it is sanctified by the fact that the protagonists (Cooper and Colbert) are married.

The language of the Code can most graphically be studied by looking at a pre-Code film and its post-Code equivalent or, in some cases, remake. James Whale made the highly sophisticated *A Kiss Before the Mirror* in 1933, and remade it just five years later at the height of the Code. Apart from shifting its locale from Europe to America, virtually

Somewhat more mature than Lamour's jungle high jinks was another 1936 movie DODSWORTH, an adult love story despite the Production Code. In this scene: Walter Huston and Mary Astor.

At one time considered Hollywood's most happily married couple, Robert Taylor and Barbara Stanwyck carried their romance over into movies as well—best of all perhaps in a rousing mid-thirties melodrama, THIS IS MY AFFAIR.

every moral stand was reversed. The hero (Frank Morgan in the original, Warren William in the remake) was a defense attorney pre-Code, and a prosecuting attorney post-Code; a clear-cut case of marital infidelity in the original became a case of suspected (and disproven) infidelity in the later version. Critics were surprisingly blasé and apparently unknowing about the changes that had been wrought, however. In 1936, Hollywood bought the 1935 play *Sweet Aloes* that had served as a successful vehicle for Evelyn Laye and Diana Wynyard. Warners turned it into an equally successful screen vehicle for Kay Francis, soon disposing of that troublesome title and renaming it *Give Me Your Heart*. Critics were generally quite enthusiastic, commenting on the "maturity" and "sophistication" of the film. The adjectives are not entirely misplaced, but so inured had critics become to the restrictions of the Production Code that none seemed to feel it necessary to comment on the excessively genteel quality of the film. Never, surely, has an illegitimate child (or a legitimate one for that matter) been conceived, carried and delivered in such a state of concealment and decorum that one only gets hints of it until it is a fait accompli. But *then*—the sufferings, the accusations, the guilt, all to make sure that the audience is well aware that sin never goes unpunished, and that even those innocently involved must pay along with the guilty. Today of course this stance quite removes the film from the realm of reality, and the pleasing art direction, with its cottages, castles and spacious interiors, further stresses the artificiality. We can enjoy it without condescension, but also without involvement.

Perhaps that most sums up the romantic film of

A memorable love story despite its pretentions to being an epic: COME AND GET IT (1936), with Walter Brennan, Edward Arnold and, in a truly memorable performance, the tragic Frances Farmer.

the later thirties. Just as the vicious, honest early gangster films had shifted to becoming big action shows—metropolitan Westerns—so had the romantic film become a "show" largely separated from, and certainly larger than, life. The most memorable love stories of the later thirties—*The Prisoner of Zenda, Algiers*, certainly the much overrated *Wuthering Heights*—all share this quality. Because of this inflated cinematic love, one was often surprised

75

To the dismay of many youngsters, romance very much outweighed action in the 1936 UNDER TWO FLAGS, until the rousing final reel. In a classic romantic triangle, spitfire Claudette Colbert loves Ronald Colman, finally laying down her life for him and paving the way for him to marry aristocratic but much less interesting Rosalind Russell.

THE GARDEN OF ALLAH (1936): Its absurd story-line worked against its being taken too seriously, but the magnificent early Technicolor camerawork and the flawless playing of Charles Boyer, Marlene Dietrich and Basil Rathbone helped to make it enjoyable and even memorable in its own way.

to come upon the genuine article in the most unlikely place—a humble "B" western like George O'Brien's *When a Man's a Man* (1935) for example. An above-average Western by any standards, with a logical and sensible storyline and no action merely for its own sake, it also features a surprisingly moving triangle love story involving George O'Brien, the graceful and almost forgotten actress Dorothy Wilson, and Paul Kelly. With poetic black-and-white photography (by Frank Good) that would have done credit to a John Ford film, it's a most unusual little film—and Dorothy Wilson's simple, agonized statement "Oh, I love him so!" (speaking about George O'Brien) carries more sincerity and genuine emotion than ALL of the pictorially interesting but otherwise very cold *Wuthering Heights*.

One of the thirties' last big romantic hits, *When Tomorrow Comes*, skillfully confected to be a pre-

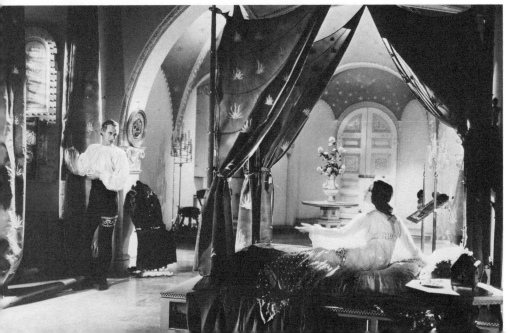

ROMEO AND JULIET (1936): Leslie Howard and Norma Shearer, earlier screen lovers in *Smilin' Through* and *A Free Soul*, were somewhat mature to play Shakespeare's teen-aged lovers, but the decor alone (this set is but one of many really stunningly designed sets) captured a truly romantic flavor.

Throughout the thirties and forties, Fred MacMurray and Claudette Colbert made an almost inspired romantic teaming in a contemporary and preferably comic millieu. Their one attempt at a serious period love story—1936's MAID OF SALEM—was a gallant misfire.

In many ways one of the most romantic films of the late thirties was Disney's first full-length animated fairy tale, SNOW WHITE AND THE SEVEN DWARFS (1937)—although the Prince's role was virtually eliminated from the final release version, except for beginning and end appearances. The ecstatic expression on Snow White's face somewhat belies her alleged innocence, and one is entitled to a raised eyebrow or two concerning the decidedly phallic appearance of the Prince's sword!

sold Charles Boyer–Irene Dunne follow-up to their successful *Love Affair,* while a slick and certainly enjoyable film on its own level, does rather sum up the artifice of the Hollywood love story of the period. Another early foray into *Brief Encounter* territory, it plays its story out against glossily romantic and melodramatic backgrounds. The main bone of contention is Charles Boyer's invalid wife, whom he cannot honorably divorce. The film comes to its climax with this problem unresolved, the love affair clearly chaste and unconsummated, and Irene Dunne promising to wait as long as necessary. But earlier it has been quite clearly established that Boyer's wife is given to drink, and to being careless with lit cigarettes and matches. The finale does spare us the expected scene of a telegram arriving with news of the wife's charred remains, but the unmistakable impression is left that Irene Dunne won't have too long to wait!

ANGEL (1937): One of the most handsome romantic couples of the thirties, Marlene Dietrich and Herbert Marshall.

The operatic trimmings made the Jeanette MacDonald–Nelson Eddy musicals almost aggressively romantic. Best, and most tasteful, was the 1937 MAYTIME.

A YANK AT OXFORD (1938): A variation on the *Camille* scene that Lionel Barrymore had played with Garbo two years earlier. Here he pleads with Vivien Leigh to extricate his son (again Robert Taylor, as in *Camille*) from a romantic entanglement so that he can *(a)* graduate from Oxford and *(b)* marry Maureen O'Sullivan.

Big-scale Westerns were a rarity in the thirties, except at Paramount. Randolph Scott and Joan Bennett were the pleasing lovers in THE TEXANS (1938).

Tyrone Power was not only Fox's No. 1 romantic idol, but he was also their stock hero for disaster movies, taking on a desert sirocco *(Suez)*, flood and earthquake *(The Rains Came)* and the Chicago fire in IN OLD CHICAGO (1938). Here Alice Faye finds that he has just tricked her into marriage for political reasons—but he is reformed, and reunited with her, after a three-reel reconstruction of the fire.

THE CITADEL (1938): King Vidor's version of the Cronin novel was both an important (if softened) social indictment and a solid love story. Robert Donat and Rosalind Russell starred, with Rex Harrison and Ralph Richardson heading a strong supporting cast.

Contrived perhaps, but one of the most effective tear-jerkers of the thirties: DARK VICTORY (1939), with Bette Davis and George Brent.

VESSEL OF WRATH (THE BEACHCOMBER) (1938): One of the more offbeat yet most appealing ''romantic'' castings was that of husband-and-wife team Charles Laughton and Elsa Lanchester in an adaptation of the Somerset Maugham story.

Quite certainly the most famous romantic film of all time, and one which epitomized the glossy expertise of Hollywood of the late thirties, GONE WITH THE WIND was released in 1939. At left, Clark Gable and Vivien Leigh; right, Leslie Howard and Vivien Leigh.

GRAND HOTEL (1932) with John Barrymore

AS YOU DESIRE ME (1932) with Melvyn Douglas

MATA HARI (1932) with Ramon Novarro

The Greta Garbo vehicles of the 30's represent a romantic trend almost in themselves, with the decade's most beautiful face on view in a series of elaborate love stories taken from classic literature, popular fiction and history. These are just a few of the highlights.

ANNA KARENINA (1935) with Fredric March

CONQUEST (1937) with Charles Boyer

CAMILLE (1936) with Robert Taylor

THE PAINTED VEIL (1934) with Herbert Marshall

Daddy Long Legs

Fox, 1931.

Directed by Alfred Santell. Screenplay by Sonya Levien and S. N. Behrman from the novel by Jean Webster. Camera: Lucien Andriot.

With: Janet Gaynor, Warner Baxter, Una Merkel, Claude Gillingwater, John Arledge, Edwin Maxwell, Effie Ellsler, Kendall MacCormak, Kathleen Williams, Louise Closer Hale, Sheila Mannors, Elizabeth Patterson.

Daddy Long Legs was filmed earlier, in 1919, as a Mary Pickford silent, and would be done again in 1955 as a glossy Technicolor vehicle for Fred Astaire and Leslie Caron. (Shirley Temple's 1935 *Curly Top* was also a remarkably faithful remake, save for turning one orphan into two so that the romantic element could be salvaged—and, outrageously, the film carried no writing credit acknowledging its source)

From 1927 through the early thirties, Janet Gaynor had unofficially assumed Mary Pickford's "America Sweetheart" throne, and this *Daddy Long Legs* is one of the most enjoyable, typical, and least pretentious films from that relatively brief but highly profitable reign. It's based of course on one of the most popular books of Jean Webster. Unlike the books of Lloyd Douglas, an author who enjoyed particular acclaim, popularity and movie attention in the thirties, the books of Jean Webster do not date.

Popular novelists in the teen years still had their roots in a Victorian age, and sentiment and simplicity were key elements. The popularity of some of these writers is, today, extremely hard to fathom. Harold Bell Wright, for example, was both a clumsy and a dull writer. Hollywood took note of his popularity, bought his novels, but usually used little more than his titles—and often enhanced his *own* reputation by making of their rewritten versions something far better and more substantial. But Jean Webster's books *did* have merit. It is unlikely that anybody coming across them for the first

Warner Baxter is the millionaire/philanthropist who adopts her, delights in getting her letters, but refuses to identify himself or get emotionally involved.

It's a story of the longing for love, rather than love itself. The heroine is a maturing orphan, who is overworked and exploited at the orphanage, though beloved by all the smaller children whom she protects and befriends. A visiting millionaire, one of the trustees, takes pity on her and arranges to adopt her and give her a thorough schooling, as long as his identity remains unknown. All she sees of him is his distorted, long-legged shadow as he leaves the orphanage—hence the nickname of the title. He is a kindly man, but a busy one. He wants to be kept informed of his ward's progress, and takes great joy in the long letters she writes him, but wishes to remain emotionally uninvolved. However, circumstances do bring them together—without of course the orphan knowing that this is her benefactor. Ultimately she falls in love with him, and goes to her guardian to get his permission to marry, feeling somewhat disloyal with her affections apparently split between two men—only to find that her rather mature beau and her Daddy Long Legs are one and the same.

As can be seen, nothing really *happens* in *Daddy Long Legs*. There is no market for a book like that today, and no market for a film based on it. It is literally a visitor from a lost world, and therein is one of the key ingredients of its charm. Stories like this need above all else genuine honesty in their sentiment—enough discipline not to exploit and vulgarize the sentiment, and yet at the same time no sense of being embarrassed by that open sentiment. It also needs brevity in the telling, so that the basically uneventful story never drags, that one doesn't have to wait for the predictable moments to catch up with the anticipation, and so that clichés, if they

time in the 70s would be wildly excited by them, but those who read them when they were fresh, usually find that on rereading today, they retain all their charm. Likewise, *Daddy Long Legs* was a film that was tremendously popular in its day, and was remembered with affection. It's not easily seen today —in fact only one or two prints are known to exist —but it is no letdown to those who saw it then, and are lucky enough to make its acquaintance again.

Janet Gaynor plays the oldest girl in the orphanage, champion of all the younger children.

All pretenses and deceptions dropped, the couple admit their love for each other at the fadeout.

Only a few years later the film was remade as CURLY TOP, the Gaynor role being split between Shirley Temple and Rochelle Hudson, with John Boles, Warner Baxter's alter-ego at Fox, taking over the Baxter role.

develop, are never tiresome. At a tight 73 minutes, *Daddy Long Legs* fills these easier-said-than-done strictures rather nicely, and it is certainly helped along by the grace and charm of Janet Gaynor. Warner Baxter must have been the most overworked actor in all of Hollywood during the 30s, appearing at his home lot, Fox, in picture after picture, often as a kind of resident Ronald Colman, Clark Gable or Errol Flynn, when the scripts called for personalities like that but the budgets didn't, and on frequent loanouts to Columbia, Warners and MGM. Yet, despite the number of films he made, and the correspondingly large percentage of *bad*

ones, he always gave of his best—and seemed particularly suited to his role here as the tired, world-weary millionaire, not quite as old as his cares make him appear, and able to be rejuvenated by the love of a younger woman.

At the time, the mildly "jazzed-up" 30s background of collegiate parties might have seemed an undue deviation from Jean Webster's original milieu, but today the 30s seem almost as unsophisticated as the pre-20s—even to some casual racial slurs—and the passage of time has enabled the film to create its own period flavor.

Although it came early in her career, WATERLOO BRIDGE offered Mae Clarke her best role—and she gave her finest performance in it.

Waterloo Bridge

Universal, 1931.

Directed by James Whale. Scenario by Tom Reed and Benn Levy. From the play by Robert L. Sherwood. Camera: Arthur Edeson. Art Director: Charles D. Hall.

With: Mae Clarke, Kent Douglas*, Doris Lloyd, Ethel Griffies, Enid Bennett, Frederic Kerr, Bette Davis, Rita Carlisle, Billy Bevan.

After having been missing and presumed lost for forty years, *Waterloo Bridge* suddenly emerged from hiding (in the MGM vaults) in the late summer of 1977. It was of particular interest to film scholars, since it was not only the *one* film missing from the twenty-odd films directed by James Whale in a brief (eleven-year) film career, but as his first in a long association with Universal, it was a particularly key film.

*Kent Douglas was later known as Douglas Montgomery.

Few films hold up to expectations after so long an absence; *Waterloo Bridge* does, although it must be admitted that it did not have (as so many lost films do) a legendary reputation to live up to. In all honesty, too, its quite remarkable qualities are more striking if one is more familiar with the generally static quality of Hollywood stage adaptations in 1931, and especially if one is familiar with the extraordinary strides that the former stage director was making in film at that time. *Waterloo Bridge* is a considerable step forward from Whale's previous film, *Journey's End* (1929), another war play, just as *Frankenstein*, released only three months after *Waterloo Bridge*, exhibited further spectacular progress. *Waterloo Bridge* too is an invaluable early piece of the jigsaw illustrating Whale's entirely unique method of creating filmed theatre. But even allowing for these perhaps academic reasons for admiring *Waterloo Bridge* today, it needs neither apology nor explanation, but can stand on its own as a love story that is still touching and moving.

Thanks to two subsequent remakes (both of them more elaborate, but less honest and realistic) the basic story must be quite familiar by now. A young soldier on leave in World War I meets and falls in love with a young dancer in a London show. He wants to marry her, and takes her to meet his aristocratic parents. There she admits the truth, that she is really a prostitute. The young man's mother, though sympathetic and admiring the girl's honesty, convinces her that such a marriage could never work. The girl runs away, but her soldier finds her just before he has to report back. In a final meeting on Waterloo Bridge, where they first met, he tells her that her background doesn't matter, and extracts her promise to marry him on his return. She agrees, and, secure in his love for her, he goes confidently back to the war. As soon as he has gone, however, she deliberately walks into the open in a bombing raid and is killed.

Comparison with the 1940 remake is perhaps the best way to stress the straight-line simplicity of the original. The new version, made as a big, glossy, MGM spectacular, a fitting vehicle for Vivien Leigh's follow-up to *Gone With the Wind*, was, in its own way, a richly romantic and extremely entertaining vehicle. Beautifully photographed and mounted, it did contain some memorable sequences and images—especially the lovers' candlelight dance before their final parting—and Mervyn LeRoy directed it, if not with delicacy, then at least with confidence and taste. But overall were the signs that this was a big MGM film first, and an adaptation of the Sherwood play second, with both eyes on the Production Code and the need to present their new star with a flattering image. First of all, the whole story was placed in a flashback framework to give it an up-to-date relevance to World War II: right away this removed the immediacy, and turned tragedy into nostalgia. Secondly, the characters were upgraded to the glossy women's magazine level. Robert Taylor was no longer a plain enlisted man, but an officer, and the aristocracy of his parents was aggrandized to the point where they were now a duke (C. Aubrey Smith of course!) and his duchess. The mediocre chorus hoofer of the original now became a promising young ballet dancer with a major career before her if (like the dancer

The ordeal of meeting a high-society family that knows nothing of her background; left to right, Enid Bennett, Douglass Montgomery, Mae Clarke, Bette Davis, Frederick Kerr.

in *The Red Shoes*) she can keep romance out of her life and concentrate on her art. Morally she is above reproach, and takes to prostitution only when she believes her beloved is dead. (Her new profession is suggested only briefly and very discreetly!) It must be admitted that the skill and beauty of Vivien Leigh compensated to a large degree for the artificiality of the writing, and that Robert Taylor was also surprisingly good as the officer. On its own level, it was an engrossing, efficient, and highly entertaining movie.

The original *Waterloo Bridge* is perhaps *less* efficient at the business of tearjerking since it is not concerned with being a great love story. Myra, as played by Mae Clarke, is hard-bitten from the beginning, constantly trying to head off the romance which she knows can only end in disaster. Emotional scenes develop, but no big love scenes. Douglas Montgomery has an extremely difficult role to handle, since most of it consists of silent reactions, and he has to convey the sense of hurt rebuff and overwhelming love via, in many cases, nonvocal facial expressions. Mae Clarke's performance is quite outstanding, and makes one wish all the more that she had become a major star and been given better roles by Hollywood. (Whale used her twice more, in *Frankenstein* where she was understandably overshadowed, and in *The Impatient Maiden* where her performance was again first-rate.)

There is one particularly touching scene where Myra has returned to her streetwalking profession, picked up a rather agreeable officer (Billy Bevan) and then, suddenly conscience-stricken, turns on him and sends him away. Moments later she relents, not only because she needs the money, but more because she genuinely regrets her rudeness to a man who seemed a decent sort. But it is too late: his taxi carries him away, while her cry—"I'm sorry mister, I didn't mean it!"—echoes in the street. Many of her big emotional scenes have the camera tracking in to a full closeup, to duplicate the effect of an actress spotlighted on stage, and she carries these difficult moments off with extreme skill. Underplaying is clearly not called for at such moments, but, probably under Whale's direction, she manages to hide most of her face with her arms, so that the scenes are not overwrought and the audience still has a chance to bring its imagination to bear. Mae Clarke's remarkable performance has a great deal to do with the film's surviving emotional validity.

The supporting cast, including a number of Whale regulars, is extremely good. Ethel Griffies as the harridan of a landlady provides both comic punctuation and dramatic emphasis, and the scene in which she gets her comeuppance from Douglas Montgomery is as much an audience-pleaser on film as it must have been on stage. Enid Bennett is just right as the mother—this actress had a sensitivity in mature roles that she lacked as a younger actress (the Maid Marian of Fairbanks's *Robin Hood* for example)—and Frederic Kerr, in what is virtually a dry-run for his Baron Frankenstein, is a delight as the slightly deaf old duffer who never seems to come to grips with reality, but is a sensitive soul despite his crustiness and detached patter. Even Bette Davis, in a very small role, is charming and effective, indicating that she might have been both a star and an actress much earlier had she worked for more directors like Whale and fewer like Hobart Henley!

Pictorially the film is extremely handsome, with a good deal of camera mobility and some extremely effective overhead shots. As was Whale's style—still only formulating, and to be developed and refined over the next few films—the details are *realistic*, yet the composition and the art direction somehow suggest the artifice of the stage. This is particularly true of the scenes on Waterloo Bridge, where the backgrounds—of a searchlight-bedecked London—are accurate and realistic enough for conviction, but where the perspective of depth is off ever so slightly and where the position of the camera likewise manages to implant the idea of theatre rather than actuality.

Whale's use of offstage sound is likewise theatrical, and for 1931 quite experimental. The transition from London to the countryside in the sequence where the soldier takes his girl for a ride in a car is partially accomplished by the offscreen sound effects, the hooters of London traffic giving way to the sounds of roosters crowing. This seems an obvious enough device today, but it was not so obvious then; indeed, as late as 1934 Frank Capra was taking credit for introducing such new uses of sound into his *It Happened One Night*. However, on at least one occasion Whale's use of sound effects is sardonic as well as functional; the moo of a cow is heard just as the soldier settles down in his car seat, his wide eyes and happy countenance an exact parallel to cowlike contentment!

Waterloo Bridge more than confirmed Whale's importance as a major new director in 1931, and was well liked by the public and well reviewed by the critics. Oddly enough, the only two criticisms made by *The New York Times* today seem particularly unjustified. Their critic complained that Whale had too little material to work with; today, while that material is admittedly direct and uncomplicated, the one criticism is that, at 81 minutes, the

Robert Taylor and Vivien Leigh in the glossier remake.

film seems too short to allow Whale to develop its emotional content to the fullest, and the climax, when it comes, is just a shade premature. Secondly, and harder to understand, the *Times* complained that the war scenes were "exaggerated." In actuality, there are very few war scenes and they are not overdone. What the *Times* probably meant was that they were stylized rather than totally realistic, and since this was so early in Whale's attempts to reshape theatre into film, the failure to recognize his subtlety of design is understandable. There is, however, one unfortunate weakness in the climactic bombing raid in that the editing appears to have Mae Clarke look up, see the falling bombs, and walk into their path to be obliterated by a direct hit from one of them! The scene, as it exists, is far too abrupt and frankly illogical; one suspects that originally it may have been a longer scene and that Uni-

versal, even though this was well before the Production Code stricture forbidding "suicide as a plot solution," may have recut the scene to give it a more ambiguous flavor. It's a pity: the scene has the value of sudden theatrical shock, but it lacks the filmic rhythm and dramatic logic that the rest of the film preserves so well.

Quite incidentally, the locale of the old Waterloo Bridge (the bridge that now stands at the same location is a wider, more streamlined affair) is used far better in this film than in the two remakes (the second was *Gaby* with Leslie Caron) where it seemed merely an arbitrary landmark chosen at random. Here it is explained early in the proceedings that it is a logical thoroughfare for streetwalkers, who wait there for the troops coming home on leave and walking across the bridge from Waterloo Station.

One Way Passage

Warner Bros., 1932.

Directed by Tay Garnett. Screenplay by Wilson Mizner and Joseph Jackson from a story by Robert Lord. Camera: Robert Kurrle.

With: William Powell, Kay Francis, Aline McMahon, Warren Hymer, Frank McHugh, Frederick Burton, Douglas Gerrard, Herbert Mundin, Ruth Hall, Allan Lane, Willie Fung, Roscoe Karns, Dewey Robinson, Stanley Fields.

One Way Passage was one of those near-fluke successes that came out of the assembly-line programmers that Warners churned out with such efficiency in the early 30s. Almost all of them were good audience pictures, short, snappy, well acted, and directed, photographed and edited with the usual Warner team spirit. Directors and writers had a surprising amount of freedom on these lesser pictures, and every so often one would come along that was imbued with an unusual sense of directorial style, or a particularly neat script, or perhaps an especially felicitous star-teaming.

One Way Passage certainly had the last two elements in spades, and this is in no way intended to denigrate the third factor, Tay Garnett's direction. Garnett started out in the late twenties with thick-ear melodramas, and continued right through until the sixties, with films like the Dietrich–Wayne *Seven Sinners* coming off best. He had a particular penchant for sea stories, all of which bore some

Dan (William Powell) takes Joan (Kay Francis) ashore with the admonition of the doctor (Frederick Burton) to avoid any excitement.

Joan collapses, however, and Dan sacrifices his own chance to escape by taking her back to the ship.

kind of personal stamp since although they were made for different companies at different periods and often in a totally different mood, there were overlapping elements common to all. There's very little to link a rousing adventure tale like *Slave Ship*, made five years after the romantic *One Way Passage*, yet both films get under way with the same trio of barroom singers engaged in the same kind of mood-establishing comedy. *China Seas* and *Trade Winds* are further examples of Garnett's seagoing dramas.

One Way Passage is often referred to as Garnett's best picture, as well it may be, but one suspects that critics single it out because it stands alone, like an oasis of repose in a sea of Garnett melodrama—just as Henry Hathaway's *Peter Ibbetson* is so often isolated from his rousing melodramas and westerns and feted as *his* best picture. One often wonders why these directors didn't return to the genres that had brought them such acclaim. The sneaking suspicion persists that perhaps they were smart enough not to press their luck, knowing instinctively that it was the writing or the acting that made those particular films work so well.

Kay Francis and William Powell had co-starred before at Paramount. Oddly enough, that studio put them not into the luxurious romantic films they did so well, but instead into seedy crime and sex melodramas like *Ladies' Man* and *Street of Chance*—

A parallel scene from the remake, TILL WE MEET AGAIN: George Brent and Merle Oberon

90

The stars of the remake: Geraldine Fitzgerald, Pat O'Brien, Merle Oberon, George Brent

both good pictures, but a sad waste of their co-starring magic. Ironically, it was Warner Bros., specialists in taut, zippy crime films, that had the wit to team the two stars in the lushly romantic vehicles that their faces and screen persona almost demanded: *Jewel Robbery,* an excellent romp in the Lubitsch manner, lightheartedly directed by William Dieterle, and at the other end of the spectrum, the tragic *One Way Passage.*

Powell is a convicted murderer being taken back to the United States to face execution in the electric chair. Francis is dying from one of those ambiguous movie diseases that leaves no tell-tale signs other than an occasional shortness of breath and a decorous cough or two. The two meet and fall in love, neither—at first—knowing the other's secret. Powell is in the custody of a detective who is basically quite decent, and does his best to make his captive's last journey as pleasant as possible. Powell also has two underworld friends on board who are helpful in lifting handcuff keys and otherwise trying to aid in his escape plans when the ship makes a brief stopover. His freedom is already a fait accompli when he learns of Kay's condition—and voluntarily goes back on board ship with her. Eventually she too learns his secret, but neither lets on to the other, and at journey's end, they part, each vowing to keep a date to see in the New Year at Caliente, each knowing that they will both be dead by then. A very brief epilogue follows in a cocktail lounge at Caliente, on New Year's Eve. As the bartender talks to a customer, they hear the sound of two glasses clinking and breaking—and turning to the sound, see only the broken glass on the bar.

One Way Passage whips along at the usual Warner pace, and its 68 minutes aren't even devoted exclusively to Powell and Francis, since a secondary love interest develops between the detective and a female crook (Warren Hymer and Aline McMahon respectively) and there's even time for a little traditional Frank McHugh comedy. But

somehow the accelerated pace seems appropriate for the story of the doomed lovers with so little time —and Powell and Francis play their scenes in a leisurely manner, as though savoring each moment. If there's no time for deep emotion to develop, then at least that serves the end of the tragic parting, since they are torn away from the audience, as well as from each other, just as we are getting to know them.

In later years, Warners never seemed to learn that so many of these films worked *because* they were so short. If they didn't allow for gloss or acting showcases, nor did they allow for cliches, unnecessary complications or slow wrap-ups, because there just wasn't time for them. Frequently they remade these incisive little pictures, padding them to "A" length and reshaping them for newer stars. Loretta Young's *Life Begins,* also a short film, was remade as *A Child Is Born* and expanded considerably. One of the many added ingredients was the blinding, in a laboratory mishap, of the only doctor qualified to handle the heroine's complicated pregnancy—*exactly* the kind of plot contrivance that smacks of studio hack writing, and robs the original of its unpolished power. *One Way Passage* was similarly expanded in its remake, *Till We Meet Again* (1940), with Powell and Francis appropriately but somewhat mechanically replaced by George Brent and Merle Oberon. One of the padding devices in this version was to glamorize and stretch out the secondary love theme, only sketched in in the original, into a romantic subplot that, in the hands of Pat O'Brien and Geraldine Fitzgerald, was almost equal in importance to the main plot.

Despite the added care, length and money that went into *Till We Meet Again,* nobody remembers it any more. But the rough-hewn *One Way Passage,* achieving its poetry and sensitivity from the story itself, and from the beautifully controlled playing of its two stars, is a haunting film that nobody can forget.

A Farewell to Arms

Paramount, 1932.

Directed by Frank Borzage. Scenario by Benjamin Glazer and Oliver H. P. Garrett from the novel by Ernest Hemingway. Camera: Charles Lang.

With: Gary Cooper, Helen Hayes, Adolphe Menjou, Mary Phillips, Jack LaRue, Blanche Frederici, Gilbert Emery, Henry Armetta, George Humbert, Fred Malatesta, Mary Forbes, Herman Bing, Tom Ricketts, Robert Couterio, Peggy Cummingham, Augustino Borgato, Paul Porcasi, Alice Adair, John Davidson, Doris Lloyd, Georges Regas, Reinhold Schunzel.

Hemingway wrote *A Farewell to Arms* in 1930, and this film was in fact the first Hemingway story to be filmed at all. Hemingway purists may argue that it is too romantic an interpretation and that, even if less interesting filmically, *The Snows of Kilimanjaro* and *For Whom the Bell Tolls* are more authentic Hemingway. But it is probably still the best *film* to be made from a Hemingway novel, and considering how young the art of screenwriting for the sound film was in 1932, the screenplay is reasonably faithful and sophisticated. (Compare for example, the far more naive and simplified adaptation of Somerset Maugham's *Of Human Bondage* two years later.)

Although a handsome production with big sets, plenty of extras and outstanding camerawork, *A Farewell to Arms* carefully remains non-epic in scope, thus avoiding the dreadful pitfalls that made the overblown Selznick remake with Jennifer Jones and Rock Hudson such a disaster. It is "emo-tionally big" in the way that few movies are any-more, yet director Borzage could get away with scenes and even cliches that would seem absurd from other directors. Ricardo Cortez battling the waves in a small rowboat to get to Greta Garbo in *The Torrent* was merely ludicrous—yet one accepts an almost identical scene here without question. Similarly, the very last, ultratheatrical shot of the film remains tender despite its size, music and sweeping camerawork.

There's just no explaining how Borzage could exploit yet control sentiment at one and the same time, yet he did it over and over, even in such unlikely films as *Flirtation Walk* and *China Doll*. There's no question but that Sidney Franklin's 1932 version of *Smilin' Through* is superior to Frank Borzage's overproduced Technicolor remake in 1941. Yet the latter seemed to wring more emotion out of its highlights. In the famous wedding death scene, Borzage did nothing differently other than to reverse the camera positions and angles, yet of the two, his is by far the more moving.

Gary Cooper's performance—comparatively early in his career—is, apart from being relaxed and naturalistic, surprisingly mature. It quite steals all the thunder away from Helen Hayes's theatrically efficient but mannered and self-conscious acting. Considering that it is such an important role, it is more than ever a tribute to Borzage's skill that one *cares* about the outcome of her love story, despite the Hayes interpretation. One can't help but wonder how much more effective Ruth Chatterton, originally slated for the role, might have been.

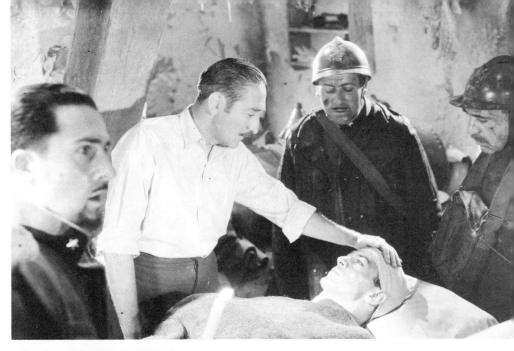

Wounded in the fighting, Lt. Henry (Gary Cooper) is reassured by his friend Major Rinaldi (Adolphe Menjou) before Rinaldi operates.

Rinaldi introduces his friend to Nurses Ferguson (Mary Phillips) and Barkley (Helen Hayes).

Rinaldi is none too pleased to find Lt. Henry and Nurse Barkley striking up a firm friendship.

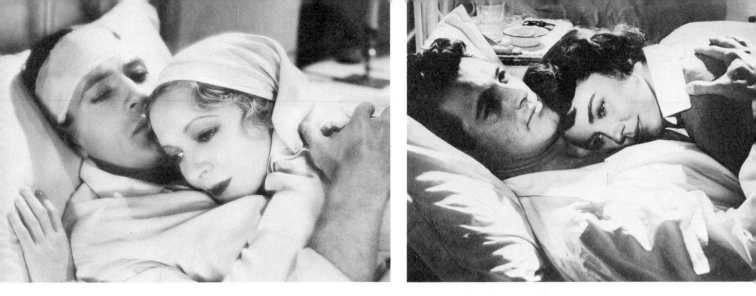

Equivalent scenes from the two versions: left, Cooper and Hayes; right, Rock Hudson and Jennifer Jones in the fifties remake.

Much was made of Hemingway's "disgust" with the "happy ending" tacked on for the American release, but actually this has been somewhat exaggerated. The American ending was merely ambiguous; although the dialogue and narrative buildup made it quite plain that Nurse Barkley had no chance of surviving, she *seemed* to rally as the armistice bells pealed out. Thus the fadeout was on an embrace, with Miss Hayes still alive—but it was the kind of gutless ending that allowed the audience to make up its own mind as to whether she lived or died, and was by no means the traditional happy ending. Its major drawback was that it forced the excision of the final extremely powerful climactic shot (Cooper with the body of Hayes in his arms), a shot that was of course retained for the European release.

Curiously, although it was in reissue distribution until the early 50s, *A Farewell to Arms* then became a virtually lost film for twenty years, to reappear in the 70s when it had entered the public domain. Bootleg prints then began to proliferate, to be shown at small 16mm theatres—and to do the film considerable harm. For one thing, most of these prints were copied from reissue material from the 30s, and those reissue prints had been cut substantially to conform to current Production Code standards. The film was originally tight and compact, with no wasted footage. When cuts are made in such a carefully structured film, the balance and pace are bound to suffer. Too, most of the cuts were made in the love scenes, so that it became more of a war film, less of an emotional story. More important still, the 16mm prints were of decidedly inferior quality. With no disrespect to either Hemingway or his adaptors, this *A Farewell to Arms* had something of the quality of a glossy magazine romance. It was neither particularly realistic nor particularly profound (though it *was* honest); for its emotional impact, it needed all the gloss and veneer of Charles Lang's magnificent camerawork. One of its highlights was a brilliant, Germanic montage of the horrors of war, done in stylized expressionist form, with stark blacks and whites. In most of the circulating prints of the 50s, this sequence was so dark as to be almost undecipherable.

In some cases, it's hard to understand why one generation reveres a film, while the next reacts to it with apathy. Sometimes of course a film *does* date, and the second generation recognizes why. But in many cases—too many, alas—cuts and inferior prints mean that later audiences just aren't seeing the same film. *A Farewell to Arms* is very much a victim of this.

Unaware of how deeply they are in love, Rinaldi does his best to break up their romance.

Hot Saturday

Paramount, 1932.

Directed by William Seiter. Scenario by Seton Miller, Josephine Lovett and Joseph Moncure March from a novel by Harvey Ferguson. Camera: Arthur L. Todd.

With: Nancy Carroll, Cary Grant, Randolph Scott, Edward Woods, Lilian Bond, Grady Sutton, William Collier, Sr., Jane Darwell, Rita LeRoy, Jessie Arnold, Oscar Apfel, Rose Coughlan, Marjorie Main, Dave O'Brien.

Hot Saturday was an interesting and mildly offbeat little novel dealing with the romantic and sexual frustrations of a small-town girl. Much of it is told in time-consuming (and now overfamiliar) semi-stream-of-consciousness internal dialogue. In the novel, Ruth is engaged to Bill, but he calls it off when he believes unsavory gossip about her and Romer, dilettante playboy. Entirely innocent and in a fit of pique, Ruth rushes to the likeable (but, as she knows, not serious) Romer and surrenders her virginity to him. The next day, a crestfallen Bill tells her that he's sorry, that he knows the gossip couldn't be true, proposes marriage again—and she accepts. The movie shifts this around somewhat:

Ruth (Nancy Carroll), likewise rejected by Bill (Randolph Scott), also rushes off to Romer (Cary Grant)—with the same results. The next morning, however, on the appearance of a contrite Bill, Ruth tells him that what he believed yesterday wasn't true then—but it is *now*. She leaves the small town for a more liberated big-city life with Romer, who, slightly more sensitive and serious than in the novel, does then propose marriage, though only at the last moment.

What impresses most about *Hot Saturday* is its relaxed sophistication. Sophistication on the screen was certainly not new or rare in 1932, the year of *Trouble in Paradise* and *Love Me Tonight*, but it was (in those films) a rather *conscious* sophistication. In its own less ambitious way, *Hot Saturday* is a film of equal maturity, full of assured playing and excellent dialogue, so naturalistically welded that many pungent lines are almost lost because of the offhand way that they are delivered. Good taste was always a keynote of director William Seiter's work, both in his silents and in his very prolific sound career too, and it is a constant factor in *Hot Saturday*. It is a pre-Code movie, and makes no bones about sex in a couple of sequences, but it never

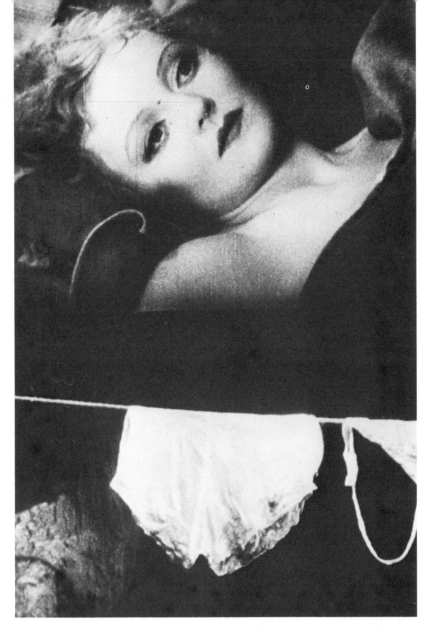

Rescued by Bill (Randolph Scott) from a torrential downpour, Ruth regains consciousness and sees her clothes—*all* of them—hanging up to dry.

The first meeting, at the town dance, of Nancy's two admirers: Cary Grant and Randolph Scott.

strives for shock or tries to prove how "adult" it is by hitting us over the head with its implications. Although like many Depression-era movies it has its Cinderella aspects, it's not really an "early 30s" movie in the accepted sense. The fashions, the cars, the remarks about Hoover and Prohibition, all place it clearly in the pre–New Deal era, but essentially it's a picture about youth and comparative innocence. It's undated by period in the sense that its characters and attitudes are still valid—somewhere, if not in Hollywood or New York—and that we can all of us recognize in it something of our own years of growing up.

One of its charms is that its "ordinary" people have none of the excesses of virtues and vices that Frank Capra's stereotypes possessed in the 30s; the worst vices of its "villains" are petulance, childishness and shrewishness. Its basic overall cheerfulness is enhanced by liberal pillaging of the Rodgers-and-Hart and Strauss melodies owned by Paramount. ("Isn't It Romantic?" must have been used more times throughout the years as theme music than any other single melody, sometimes used as ironic counterpoint, more often to sound just the right note of light romantic optimism.) The love scenes, dominated more by disappointment and yearning than by passion, have an honest ring to them, and are helped by the pleasing playing of Cary Grant and Randolph Scott (rivals in love at the *end* of the 30s too, in *My Favorite Wife*) and most especially by the utterly winning elfin charm (and solid dramatic ability) of lovely Nancy Carroll.

Bill is a solid, idealistic type and deeply in love with Ruth.

Quite incidentally, William Seiter used the film as the basis for a loose (and uncredited) remake in 1940—the delightful Deanna Durbin vehicle *Nice Girl?*

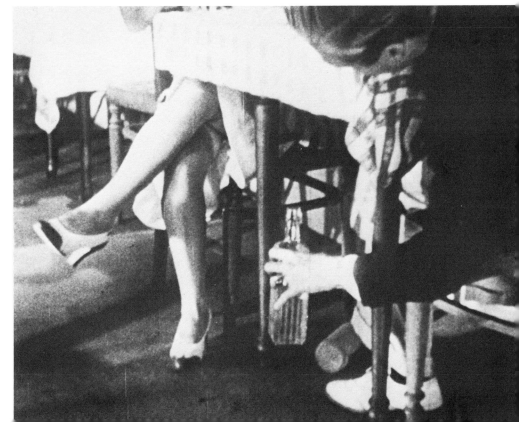

The film is full of quick establishing shots like this one, which in a second or two sum up the small town's weekend preoccupation with sex and liquor.

Halliwell Hobbes, George Marion, Edwin Maxwell and Dewey Robinson conduct the experiment that will bring murdered diplomat Warner Baxter back to life.

Six Hours to Live

Fox, 1932.

Directed by William Dieterle. Screenplay by Bradley King from the play *Auf Wiedersehn* by Gordon Morris and Morton Barteaux. Camera: John Seitz.

With: Warner Baxter, Miriam Jordan, John Boles, George Marion, Beryl Mercer, Irene Ware, Halliwell Hobbes, Edwin Maxwell, John Davidson, Dewey Robinson, Edward McWade, Hans von Twardowski, William von Brincken.

Although still extant, *Six Hours to Live* is virtually a lost film in that it is almost never shown, and has little reputation to spur revivals. Which is a pity, for it is one of the most elegantly and wholly romantic films from a period in Hollywood history when the German influence was still at its height. "Influence" is almost too weak a word to use in this case, since it was directed by the German William Dieterle, as one of his earliest Hollywood movies, and was done at the Fox studios, whose directors, cameramen and art directors were still somewhat under the spell of the late F.W. Murnau.

Six Hours to Live is a decidedly unorthodox welding of Gothic romance with science-fiction—the latter an element surprisingly prevalent in many now-forgotten early 30s movies. Its plot has Warner Baxter playing Paul Onslow, delegate to a political Geneva conference. Onslow, weary of the constant struggle in political life, wants to retire and marry the girl he loves (Miriam Jordan), but first must

make sure that his much-exploited country is not taken advantage of in the treaty under discussion. He is the lone holdout to the signing, despite assassination threats. Eventually, he *is* assassinated. But his associates have been experimenting with a scientific device that can bring the dead back to life (so long as the manner of their death did not destroy vital organs)—but only for six hours. Paul is brought back, and in the six hours allotted to him, manages to conclude the treaty negotiations, and also to ensure that his fiancee is safely ensconced in the arms of another man who loves her, and who in the long run will make her happier.

Such a story obviously cannot be taken too seriously, and Dieterle does not approach it on realistic terms, but as larger-than-life theatre. For a relatively unimportant film, it is quite unusually handsome in its sets (the scenes of the political conference, and of mob unrest in the streets are quite spectacular) and makes the most of Fox's impressive array of standing street sets. The laboratory scenes are excitingly done, full of *Frankenstein*-inspired machinery, flashing lights and humming electricity. They might even be considered a trifle on the grisly side for what is neither a horror film nor a science-fiction thriller. John Seitz's camerawork is, as always with that fine cinematographer, quite outstanding, and recreates exactly the moody mysticism of the silent German fantasies. One sequence has the newly revived Bax-

98

Police chief Edwin Maxwell shows Baxter the form of garotte with which he was murdered.

Dorothy Jordan, object of romantic rivalry between Warner Baxter and John Boles in the film.

ter taking off on a mad dash through the countryside in an automobile, surviving a wreck at top speed (''Only the devil could live through that!'' comments an amazed witness) and then entering a candle-filled church to comfort a grief-stricken bereaved mother (Beryl Mercer) and to assure her that her son is happy, and waiting for her. The bizarre automobile dash recalls the two similar scenes in Fritz Lang's *Dr. Mabuse* films, while the expressionism of the church sequence is a direct throwback to Lang's silent *Destiny*.

Even this early in the return-from-the-dead game, certain clichés have already emerged. The living dead man has acquired quite remarkable insights and wisdom in his brief visit to the other side, knows the secrets of all about him, including the identity of his murderers, and—like Boris Karloff in *The Walking Dead* and others after him—will tell

science nothing of the life beyond, other than uttering a few platitudes about peace and serenity. Seeing the scientific apparatus about to be commercially exploited, he destroys it, commenting on the futility of interfering with God's plan.

Although there is enough plot in *Six Hours to Live* for three films, and it covers a lot of ground in only seven reels, it is the romantic aspect of the film that dominates. The scenes wherein Baxter tries to persuade his fiancee that she really loves the other man more, even if she doesn't realize it, are quite touchingly done, tinged with the sense of desperation that Baxter was able to bring to his acting in films like *42nd Street* or *The Prisoner of Shark Island*. The fact that the romantic rival is played by John Boles, a Baxter look-alike, will presumably make the girl's adjustment a little easier. The final scene is especially moving. Just before Baxter had been revived, the equipment and the process have been tested with a rabbit. The animal reappears as Baxter waits alone in the garden, its own death signifying that Baxter's will follow in a few minutes. His work done, the woman he loves protected, he awaits death, while a sad little romantic melody serves as his requiem. It's all very artificial and theatrical, yet because of the film's brevity and abundance of incident, to say nothing of the overall romanticism of its design, one can accept it and be touched by it.

John Boles, Miriam Jordan and George Marion.

The film's major set and the scene of its climax: the zoo interior.

Zoo in Budapest

Fox, 1933.

Directed by Rowland V. Lee. Presented by Jesse Lasky. Screenplay by Dan Totheroh, Louise Long and Rowland V. Lee from a story by Milville Barker and John Kirkland. Camera: Lee Garmes. Edited by Harold Schuster.

With: Loretta Young, Gene Raymond, O.P. Heggie, Wally Albright, Paul Fix, Ruth Warren, Russ Powell, Roy Stewart, Murray Kinnell, Frances Rich, Lucille Ward, Niles Welch, Tom Ricketts.

What a pleasure it was to find that this long lost "classic" was in fact every bit as unusual and as magical as had been claimed for it. However, it would be a disservice to the film to wax too enthusiastic about it to those who have not seen it (but hopefully will, one day). Like *Broken Blossoms*, it is an innocent and fragile film, a fairy story that can really exist only in the now faraway Europe of the early 30s. Like Shangri-La, one has to *want* to believe in it.

There is almost no story. Loretta Young plays an ophan approaching the age when she will be bound out as an apprentice, sentenced to years of hard work before she attains legal adulthood and freedom. She decides to make a break for freedom while she still has the chance, and does so during the orphanage's weekly outing to the zoo. Gene Raymond plays Czarny, an animal handler at the zoo whose love for animals is getting him into more trouble than the sympathetic zoo superintendent (O.P. Heggie) can cover up. His latest escapade has been to steal the fur from around the neck of the wife of an officious politician—after she has asked him to arrange for the purchase of one of the animals so that she can have its skin turned into another adornment. Czarny is on the loose too, avoiding the zoo officials and the police, and he joins forces with the young orphan, helping her to hide.

Melodrama tends to pile up in the latter portions of the film: the girl is nearly raped by a lustful animal keeper (Paul Fix), and a lost child is trapped in one of the animal cages. In trying to rescue the child, other animals are allowed to escape, and the big cats fight among themselves; with the help of an elephant Czarny is able to rescue the child from a tiger, and order is finally restored. In an ultra-happy ending, the grateful parent arranges to adopt the orphan just as she is about to be hauled off to virtual slavery, and in addition puts Czarny to work as gamekeeper and horse trainer on his estate. The final shot shows boy and girl happily riding through

Czarny, the animal handler, has helped the escaping orphan (Loretta Young) to elude her pursuers.

The orphans on their regular tour of the zoo.

their new home, gaily garbed in peasant costume, and planning an early marriage.

There are very clear definitions between good and evil. The "good" superintendent is almost saintly, and the voice and face of O.P. Heggie (the blind hermit in *The Bride of Frankenstein*) suit the role admirably. The "bad" Paul Fix is even given Wagnerian musical motifs and a physical makeup that, oddly, is rather like that of the confessed murderer in *The Cabinet of Dr. Caligari*. Musically, it is overscored, but that too is justified in stressing the film's fairytale quality. The camerawork by Lee Garmes has a deliberately mystical quality to it—particularly in the shots of the young fugitives hiding in the deserted zoo at night. Eerie bird cries punctuate the still air, and mist drifts over the man-made lakes; at night, and deserted by visitors, the zoo takes on the look of an unexplored Eden that will hide and support its modern Adam and Eve. Many individual shots look for all the world like illustrations from children's books, while one brief but lovely vignette of the troop of orphans marching over a little foliage-surrounded bridge seems to anticipate exactly the scene from Disney's *Snow White and the Seven Dwarfs* of the little men marching homeward over a rock bridge.

Cameraman Lee Garmes once mentioned that there were very few real sets in the film, and that most of the atmosphere was evoked by merely arranging as much green shrubbery and foliage as possible around the camera—and the actors. When one studies the film with that in mind, it is surprising how economically designed the film is. What design

As the mist rises, he carries her through the zoo's flamingo pool to a safe hiding place.

The story's villain, none too subtly named Heinie, is played by Paul Fix.

In a sudden switch to all-out melodrama, Heinie tries to rape the orphan.

of the zoo one really sees seem to have been suggested by the Tivoli Gardens in Copenhagen. However, economical or not, the sets stayed around for use in subsequent Fox movies; the flamingo pool was put to more exotic use in *Hoopla* when it gave Clara Bow a chance to cool off and take a nude swim!

The original prints in the early 30s (one of these still survives) were released with rich tones and tints, as in the silent period. It was generally speaking not a very practical procedure in sound films, since different color stock had different densities which affected sound reproduction. Moreover, since, despite its beauty, it was not particularly realistic, most directors wouldn't have used it even if it had been practical. Pictorially, it still is a magnificent film, even in black and white. Since Garmes was frequently a co-director of the films he photographed and is responsible for some of the very

finest cinematography of the 30s and 40s, he must obviously share in the credit for the film's beauty. Directorially too, it is almost certainly Rowland V. Lee's finest film. Adept and expert at imitating the style of others, he wrought many of his films in the image of Lubitsch, Lang, Erich Pommer or James Whale, and perhaps because of that has been a little underappreciated. Here, since the film is so unique, he has nobody to imitate—and the results make one wish that he hadn't so often been content to emulate others. (*Zoo in Budapest* was so well-liked that Lasky engaged Lee and Garmes to do a follow-up film, *I Am Suzanne*. It was likewise a childlike romance, starring Lilian Harvey and Gene Raymond, and blueprinting much of the charm and plot of the substantially later *Lili*. However, impressive though it was, it was clearly pursuing charm rather aggressively, and it lacked the casual spontaneity of *Zoo in Budapest*.)

The only criticism one might make is that the film really doesn't need its exciting and admittedly showmanlike climax. The whimsy and sentiment would have been quite enough without the hero dangling from a rope above snarling tigers. But Fox had a rather consistent policy of slapping surefire hoke and action climaxes on to films that otherwise might have seemed a bit slow, so that the customers always went home feeling they'd had their money's worth. They're not necessarily wrong here. The climax is good, vivid, spectacular stuff. But *Zoo in Budapest* is really *Babes in the Wood* mated with a happy-endinged *Romeo and Juliet*. All it really needed was a final "And they all lived happily ever after" farewell title.

For the happy ending: adoption, marriage, and good jobs handling the animals on a rich man's estate.

Queen Christina

MGM, 1933.

Directed by Rouben Mamoulian. Produced by Walter Wanger: Screenplay by H. M. Harwood and Salka Viertel, with dialogue by S. N. Behrman, from a story by Salka Viertel and Margaret Levin: Camera: William Daniels: Musical Score: Herbert Stothart.

With: Greta Garbo, John Gilbert, Ian Keith, Lewis Stone, C. Aubrey Smith, Reginald Owen, Elizabeth Young, Lawrence Grant, David Torrence, Gustav von Seyffertitz, Ferdinand Munier, George Renevant, Fred Kohler, Akim Tamiroff.

Of all the Garbo films, many of them fascinating, all of them worthwhile if only for the Garbo mystique, *Queen Christina* is perhaps the only one with sufficient artistry of its own to match her unique presence, and to warrant the term "classic." It has the nobility and intelligence of *Conquest*, but far more passion; it is as perfect a showcase as *Camille*, but avoids that film's tableau-like construction. Most of Garbo's directors—even the exceptional ones like Clarence Brown—were

aware that they were making Garbo *vehicles*, and tended to sublimate their own talents in order to emphasize, sustain and further develop the Garbo image. Rouben Mamoulian, on the hand, was in 1933 riding the crest of critical prestige. Acquiring him was quite a coup for MGM, and he did not operate under the status of an MGM contract director. Moreover, *Queen Christina* was clearly a perfect vehicle for Garbo, and since she had been off the screen for more than a year, was more than usually presold in terms of audience anticipation.

Mamoulian had the wit to tailor much of the film's style to set off Garbo's unique appropriateness for the role of Sweden's somewhat masculine seventeenth-century queen, and to incorporate certain devices that had always proven successful. But he had no need to cheapen the innate strength of the story by making it merely a framework for Garbo, and certainly no intention of sacrificing his own ornately visual style in favor of a series of set-pieces and stunning closeups. While the success of the film is inextricably bound up with the Garbo performance and mysterious presence, it is *one* Garbo film

103

Queen Christina (Garbo) is envious of her lady-in-waiting's secret love.

Former lover Ian Keith has now become one of the chief conspirators against Christina.

Lewis Stone in one of his traditional roles as wise court counsellor and friend—and the one who must constantly remind her that duty must take precedence over love.

that—given its existing script and direction—*could* have worked with another actress. One can envision Brigitte Helm, Louise Brooks, Diana Wynyard or even Katharine Hepburn in the role; or in later years, Ingrid Bergman or Micheline Presle. It would have been less perfect without Garbo, but it would still have worked, whereas many of the Garbo films (*Wild Orchids, The Kiss, Mata Hari*) would have collapsed without her persona to give them unity and dignity.

Garbo obviously *respected* the role, and it shows through in the strength of her performance. (Not that her contempt for certain other roles was equally apparent; she was too much of a professional for that.) The last-minute replacement of Laurence Olivier (already a good actor, but still weak in the elusive matter of screen presence) by John Gilbert may initially have been a gesture of friendship and support on Garbo's part to her former co-star and lover, but it adds—subliminally, as well as obviously—to the emotional power of the film. The well-known frustration and ultimate sadness of the Garbo–Gilbert love affair—helped along its road to destruction by MGM studio head Louis B. Mayer—could only nourish emotional rapport with the doomed love affair of the story. (It seems doubly poignant in retrospect, since *Queen Christina* did re-establish John Gilbert in talkies and demolished the myth of his weak speaking voice. Yet his spirit had been shattered beyond repair, and he died one picture and three years later.)

Queen Christina impresses on so many levels: its baroque and ornate sets and design, the uniquely visual style of its director, the tower-of-strength ensemble acting from a predominantly male cast of venerable veterans, and the many flourishes of theatrical bravura. Writers and directors seemed to vie with each other in dreaming up dynamic entrances for Garbo—appearing out of a cloud of steam as she alights from a train was one memorable example—but she seldom had a more impressive (or more appropriate to the mood of the narrative) introduction than in this film, where after a hard horseback gallop across country, she reaches her palace, alights, and strides through anterooms and up stairways until she reaches her private chambers, the camera initially picking her up in extreme long shot, maintaining a discreet but decreasing distance, establishing her virility, her masculinity and her truly kinglike qualities before moving in close enough, at the end of the sequence, to reveal that she is also a woman.

Rightly, much has been written—even rhapsodized—about the film's classic love scene between Garbo and Gilbert. So hypnotic is the spell of the scene that no one has ever been appalled by, or seen fit to comment on, the way all the mystery and beauty of that scene is suddenly wrenched away at the end, the sublime replaced by the banal, in a resolution so unnecessary as to be insulting. One can only assume that at a screening of rushes, Mayer or Thalberg must have felt the scene too ethereal in its appeal, and tacked on an ending so that all the lunchroom attendants and garbage collectors (supposedly insensitive souls, though it has never been effectively proven) would get the point too.

But up until the sellout, it's a magnificent

John Gilbert, as the Spanish envoy, is rather easily taken in by Christina's disguise as a boy.

Tunic removed, however, Christina's femininity is more easily recognized, and . . .

scene. Garbo, as the queen, is dressed as a man for one of her hunting forays, and happens to come across John Gilbert, as an emissary from the King of Spain, actually on his way to meet her. By chance, the two are forced to share a room and a bed at an inn that has no other accommodation available. The delicate scene is first played for comedy, some of it veering on the outrageous, but always remaining within the confines of good taste so that it is comedy tinged with a kind of wistful charm. Then when Garbo's sex (though not her identity) is revealed the mood changes subtly, signalled by an incredible expression of mixed shyness, happiness and anticipation on Garbo's face— the kind of expression that seems to come about once in a decade in movies, obviously cannot be scripted or directed, *has* to come from within the player, and when it does come, lights up the entire film. (Jean Gabin achieved a similar miracle of subtle facial expression in one of the very few romantic scenes in *La Grande Illusion*.)

The consummation of their love is not even

hinted at by the usual overt means; there are no pans to symbolic fireplaces or across blank ceilings. All we get is the establishment of the passage of time, and with it the realization that these two people are completely and passionately in love. As the sequence nears its close, the still incognito queen— inwardly planning to see that she never loses this love, but knowing that there will be almost insurmountable problems at court, and above all realizing that even if it is allowed to continue, can *never* again be as perfect as it has just been—begins to walk around the room, touching and memorizing the look and feel of every object in the room that has become so dear to her. She seems to glide and drift rather than walk (the camera rarely shows her feet, concentrating on her hands and face). She is accompanied by a lovely, wistful little romantic

. . . she and the envoy fall deeply in love.

melody, so soft and muted that it too seems to be drifting rather than orchestrated. It has neither passion, nor foreboding for the future, merely an expression of total contentment with the present. It is one of the most felicitous pieces of theme music ever written. The scene itself is perfect, wordless since no words are needed, and the meaning of the scene conveyed with utmost delicacy. Then, the sensitive character played by Gilbert is forced to ask, ''What are you doing?''—and as if he and the audience were total idiots, Garbo is made to tell him. Even if that concluding dialogue had been in the original script, Mamoulian's exquisite handling of the scene, and Garbo's superb playing of it, rendered it redundant. If ever there was a case to be made for a finished work being taken to the editing table—even now, nearly fifty years after it was made—and shortened by a few feet, this is one of them. For a moment we are back to earth again, taken out of a dream, out of a moment of unutterable beauty, and reminded that this is after all just a Hollywood movie aimed at a mass audience. But up until that moment, what a scene it is—and fortunately Garbo and Mamoulian are able to rekindle the magic once our outrage has subsided.

The duel between Ian Keith and John Gilbert.

Leslie Howard and Heather Angel, the lovers born centuries apart, who meet only briefly.

Berkeley Square

Fox, 1933.

Directed by Frank Lloyd. Screenplay by Sonya Levien and John L. Balderston from the play by Balderston suggested by an original story by Henry James; Camera, Ernest Palmer.

With: Leslie Howard, Heather Angel, Valerie Taylor, Alan Mowbray, Irene Brown, Beryl Mercer, Colin Keith-Johnson, Juliette Compton, Betty Lawford, Ferdinand Gottschalk, Samuel S. Hinds, Olaf Hutten, David Torrence.

Only one or two prints are known to have survived of *Berkeley Square*, and thus, apart from isolated archival screenings, the film has been unseen for some forty years. As often happens, a kind of legend has grown up around it. This is partly because its romantic theme is so appealing, and, as with *Lost Horizon*, grows more wistfully attractive (and pertinent to contemporary life) as the years go by. Secondly, a Tyrone Power remake in the early 50s (*I'll Never Forget You*) was sufficiently good on its own (largely because it was an easy-going, nonprestige production) that we all automatically upgraded the original a few notches higher. Unfortunately, it just isn't as good as we remembered—or assumed—but its playing, its dialogue and its civi-

lized tone still entitle it to be something of a landmark in the romantic film.

The plot tells of one Peter Standish, living in 1933 London in a Berkeley Square mansion. Even on the eve of his wedding he is distracted, morbidly obsessed with the past—though to him it is merely a romantic absorption with a gentler time. He is convinced that somehow he can transport himself back to an earlier age—1784, to be exact, a date that old diaries have shown to have marked the arrival of one of his ancestors from the Americas. The transformation does in fact take place, and he finds himself as his own ancestor, having to tread warily when his knowledge of the future—the immediate future as well as the distant—suggests to his hosts that he may be in league with the devil. In the original play, his disenchantment with the past is more emphasized and better motivated: he is appalled by the squalor and poverty, and by the barbarism of public executions. In the film this is modified to a gentler level, having most of its outlet in comedy: for example, he astounds everyone by his insistence on bathing *daily*. His dramatic outburst against the bigotry and narrow-mindedness of the day seem rather intolerant, in view of the limited exposure that the film gives him to eigthteenth-cen-

Peter Standish (Leslie Howard) is obsessed with the past, and with the people who lived in his house 200 years earlier.

tury England. On a romantic level however, the film works rather well, and the love that develops between him and his Helen (Heather Angel) is touchingly and delicately handled. He finally explains why their love is doomed: he must go back to his own world, and she will die before he is born. She understands, and tells him that they *will* be together, ". . . not in my time, nor in yours, but in God's." When he returns to the present, he immediately seeks out Helen's grave—which tells him that she died young, and unmarried. He breaks off his own wedding plans, and withdraws into the life of a recluse—awaiting death, and reunion with Helen.

The film has a great deal going for it: elegant production mountings, great care paid to costuming and other period details, distinctive writing, and some fine acting, with Howard and Valerie Taylor repeating their stage roles. Taylor, who made a handful of British films including *Went the Day Well?* and was later quite active in both television and as a screenwriter, was a major theatrical talent. Her career was quite remarkable, embracing everything from Chekhov and Shaw to Lillian Hellman and A. E. W. Mason. She launched a long· and highly successful U. S. tour with *Berkeley Square* at the Lyceum in New York in 1929, and switched roles periodically, playing both Helen, the romantic lead opposite Leslie Howard, and the larger role of Kate.

There are two areas wherein the film does *not* work, however. First, Frank Lloyd, despite his commercial success (and British birth which, by Hollywood logic, frequently caused him to inherit the direction of British-locale stories), was not a particularly skilled director, and certainly not one who was able to *add* to what was already provided by cast and scenario. In *Cavalcade*, made just a few months earlier, he hardly had to; the film succeeded beautifully just on its acting and the Noel Coward writing, just as Lloyd's *Mutiny on the Bounty* worked more from writing and playing than it did from direction. But *Berkeley Square* is a ticklish subject, and needs inspiration, warmth, nuance —none of them qualities that can easily be built into a script, but which directors like Frank Borzage, James Whale or Clarence Brown would certainly have added, instinctively, during shooting.

Secondly, it is a very theatrical property and needs to be wholly theatre, or wholly film. There are elements of the supernatural in the story, and screenwriter Balderston, adapting from his own play, and also being somewhat of a specialist in horror films, does occasionally try to turn the narrative into a semi-horror film. The flashforward sequence (Peter *thinks* of the future and Helen, peering into his eyes, is given a horrifying newsreel montage of war, death and destruction) is a device that could never work on stage (unless film were utilized) and it is a powerful and chilling highlight—

After his return from the past, he tells his fiancée (Betty Lawford) that he can never marry and will await death to be reunited with Helen (Heather Angel).

but these moments of pure film do tend to throw into stark relief the theatricality of the rest of the film, so that it doesn't really work on either level.

Rather appropriately, an anecdote from the cameraman of the film, Ernest Palmer (not nearly as well known as his superb photography entitles him to be) sums up one of the basic problems of the film. Having worked on early sound musicals, science-fiction films, and under such demanding masters as F. W. Murnau, he still felt that this film presented him with the greatest single photographic problem he had ever faced. The script called for this specific image: "A *closed* door which *looks* as though it is *about* to open." The italics are mine, but the problem was Balderston's—and the film's!

110

A deleted scene (or possibly a publicity still) illustrating the husband's wedding night apathy.

Extase

Elektra Film, Czechoslovakia, 1933.

Directed and written by Gustav Machaty. Camera: Jan Stallich.

With: Hedy Kiesler (Hedy Lamarr), Albert Mog, Jaromir Rogoz, Leopold Kramer.

Throughout the 30s and 40s one of the most notorious of films (especially in the United States), *Extase* acquired a totally undeserved reputation for salaciousness. U.S. mutilation of, and sensational advertising for, the film, and a long string of censorship battles didn't help. In order to placate censors, dialogue was inserted indicating that the two lovers had been married before the famous seduction took place (although since the girl's visit to the man's hut was entirely unplanned, and his surprise at her entrance quite obvious, this was a little hard to justify). In certain states where censorship was less rigid and distributors thought they could get away with it, the limited nude swim sequence was expanded via new footage. In some such versions, *two* nude ladies splash about together! And all the time one heard reports, probably the result of wishful thinking, of fully unexpurgated versions, with far more explicit sex and nudity, playing in always remote areas—the Philippines was one location so

blessed. However, the likelihood of this seems very slim. Later, fully complete versions revealed but little more of the sexual material—and substantially more of the rest of the film, which had been trimmed down drastically to focus attention on the two sequences of well-publicized notoriety.

In any event, director Gustav Machaty had never set out to make a cheap exploitation movie, and the taste and imagination with which he sets up his sex encounters show no need or inclination to become explicit. He was a past master of eroticism by symbol and implication; perhaps the most genuinely sensuous shot he ever filmed (depending of course on the degrees of eroticism that "turn on" the individual spectator) was one of a pair of nude legs walking across the deep, comfortable, expensive white fur rug on a bedroom floor—in the German *Nocturne*. Far from seeming tame today, the symbolic and implied sex of *Extase* remains strikingly stimulating. Film students of the 70s, inured to total nudity and explicit sexual acrobatics in current porn movies, have been heard to gasp the traditional "Oh, wow!" at scenes in *Extase* that express sexual desire solely through lighting and symbols.

When *Extase* finally reached American release in 1940, seven years after its production, Hedy La-

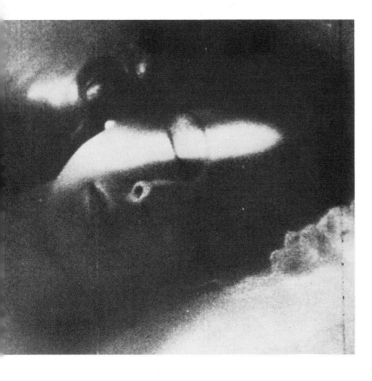

Examples of the phallic symbols that are scattered throughout the film.

marr was a well-established Hollywood star, and in fact *Extase* had its New York premiere the same month as the Gable–Lamarr *Comrade X*.

Talkies came slowly to the smaller European countries. They knew they had more chance of retaining a tenuous hold on outside markets if they stuck to the "universal" style of the silent film. While Hollywood films employed more and more dialogue, many an early European sound film was virtually silent, telling its story almost wholly by images and music. Carl Dreyer's *Vampyr* was such a film, and *Extase* must surely hold some kind of record for being the talkie with the least amount of talk. There is only one brief direct-dialogue sequence, and even that is hardly necessary. Otherwise the film limits itself to the occasional odd line of dialogue where lip-synchronization is not needed. One would think that this procedure would have eliminated any need for alternate foreign versions, yet incredibly there *is* a separate French version with its own leading man. Albert Mog, the Czech male lead, has a solemn sensitivity, while the French lead had a mild Chevalier leer through much of the film, indicating that no matter how seriously everybody else took sex, to the French it was still a matter for fun and relaxation!

Extase has less of a plot than a single situation. A young bride, virginal and flushed with the excitement of love, is sadly disillusioned in her marriage to an older man. He is dull and undemonstrative, businesslike and unwittingly cruel. (Without thinking about it, he goes out of his way to crush a bumblebee beneath his chair as he sits in an outdoor restaurant; later, in contrast, the young hero "saves" a bee and places it on a leaf of grass). After weeks of frustration and boredom, the wife goes home to her father's estate and files for divorce. While she is enjoying a nude swim in a forest pool, the horse on which she has left her clothes ambles off to answer the mating call of another horse, and in pursuing it, she encounters a young engineer, working with his men on an outdoor project. He returns her clothes, makes no advances, and she is impressed with his sincerity and friendliness. Later, frustrated and starved for affection, she seeks him out at his cabin, and they make love. They plan to run away together, and she is to await him at a hotel. En route, he picks up her husband— clearly an ill and defeated man—and, not knowing who he is, gives him a lift. After they reach the hotel, the husband commits suicide. The lovers leave for the railway station, but there is a long wait for the train, and the young man falls asleep. As he sleeps, the girl leaves him.

The concluding passages of the film are some-

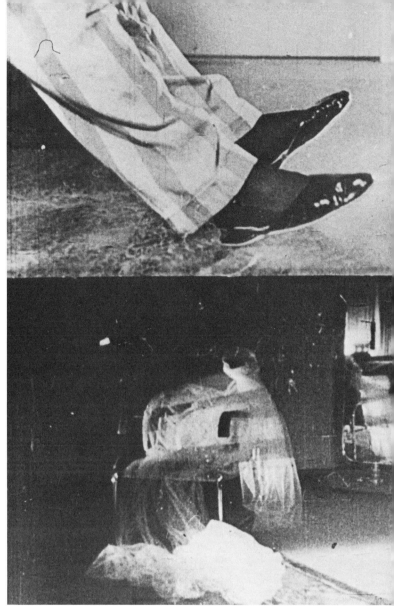

Blow-ups of two adjacent frames from the wedding night sequence. Top, the husband stretches lazily and delays, which then cuts directly to a shot of the discarded, phantom-like wedding gown.

what ambiguous. Has the girl left him because he has merely fulfilled a need for her, and she can now move on to other men and other adventures? There is an Eisensteinian montage designed to show not only the passage of time, but also the jilted man's absorption into his work—although the technique-conscious flow of images is so absorbing in itself that one tends to forget why it is there.* Towards the end are intercut images of the girl with a baby, clearly enjoying the fulfillment of motherhood.

*This Eisenstein influence is equally apparent in the divorce sequence, a satiric montage of speeded-up typewriters and bureaucracy in motion, paralleling the sequence in Eisenstein's *The General Line* in which the governmental bureau finally authorizes the release of a tractor to a group of farmers.

113

After the divorce, the first kiss of real love—and the symbolic release achieved via superimposition.

The love scene that follows.

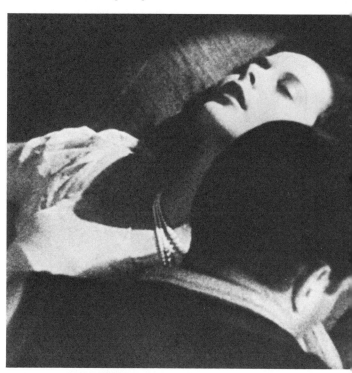

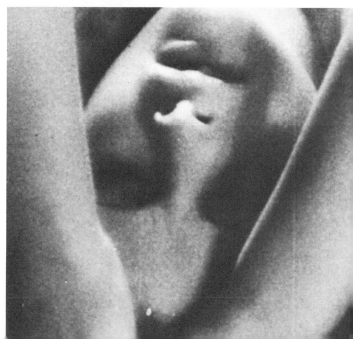

Again, the intent is not altogether clear: Is the child the result of their union, has she finally found happiness elsewhere, or—as seems most likely—is the engineer merely daydreaming sadly about the home and family life that *might* have been his had she not left him?

Meaning and logic are not terribly important to *Extase*, however, since its appeal is wholly emotional and its style wholly visual. The latter is often extremely Freudian in its imagery, and frequently boldly erotic. Water images abound throughout. As the girl sleeps, the light of the morning sun shining through her window forms a phallic sunburst across her face that seems to penetrate her brain. The urgency of sexual desire is frequently expressed by cross-cutting between a rearing stallion and a mare, elementary symbolism that was repeated in a like context in Stanley Kramer's *Not as a Stranger*. The girl's first kiss from the stranger ''releases'' her quite literally, with her ghost image flowing through his body while the kiss continues. Following intercourse, a single drop of dew falls from the bud of a plant just outside the window. Passion and sexual urgency are frequently expressed via closeups of the girl's mouth, her panting breast, and by smoothly circuitous camera movements especially

114

The wife is distraught when she learns of the suicide of her former husband in the same hotel where she is staying with her lover.

in voyeuristic situations, such as the girl waiting on her marriage bed for the husband who is more interested in adjusting his pince-nez or placing his shoes neatly beneath a chair.

The emotional quality of the camerawork is enhanced by the music, which breaks up long stretches of romantic themes with occasional Mickey-Mousing effects that comment on, and sometimes ridicule, the husband's nonsexual pettiness. (The excellent, important and virtually nonstop score was the work of a Dr. Becche, an operatic

The husband's vanity expressed through multiple mirrors, many years before Orson Welles used the same shot in *Citizen Kane*.

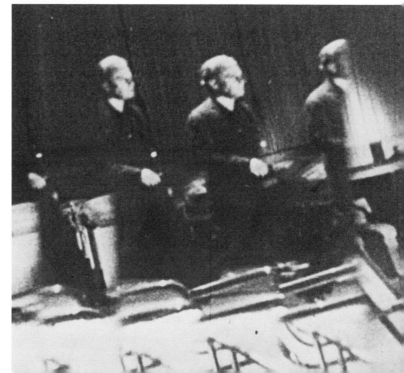

Although copied from a badly scatched print, this composition —the lovers framed by wine glasses and the shadow of a musician—is a perfect example of the rich chiaroscuro style of director Machaty.

The same style transferred to Hollywood: Machaty's first American film, the 1938 "Crime Does Not Pay" short, THE WRONG WAY OUT.

composer, who had done the music for a number of similarly almost silent early talkies, including Leni Riefenstahl's *The Blue Light*.)

Although the film's concentration on imagery, erotic and otherwise, is admittedly somewhat self-indulgent, it is entirely consistent with the style of the film, and at no time a lazy escape from traditional professionalism. In fact, some shots would do credit to the most highly equipped Hollywood studio. The sequence of the honeymooning couple having a meal at a seafront restaurant has a remarkably elaborate crane shot which rises from ground level to dizzy heights. When the girl goes to visit her potential lover in his cabin at night, the urgency of her journey is emphasized by the rapid jump-cutting of the lighted window of his cabin—from extreme long shot to long shot, to medium shot, to closeup—while the music underlines the feeling of desperation, and as she stands in the open doorway, a sudden change of focus *within the shot* draws attention to the hand that falls limply, in supplication, by her side. *Extase* is full of the most sophisticated if self-conscious film technique, and it is a pity that Machaty never had the opportunity (as did Murnau, Lang and Ophuls) to take full advantage of Hollywood equipment and expertise. (Machaty did come to Hollywood, where his work—on *Crime Does Not Pay* shorts and an interestingly erotic Republic melodrama, *Jealousy*—was stylish, but short-lived and unrecognized.)

Hedy Kiesler (Lamarr) is beautiful (without being overpoweringly so) and a surprisingly good actress, especially in view of the limited opportunities that a nondialogue script provides. In her early Hollywood days she claimed that she was not acting at all in the closeups of sexual ecstasy, merely performing facial pantomime to a tune called by the director, but this seems unlikely and merely a typical Hollywood ploy to whitewash a big star, and remove some of the "stigma" of having appeared nude and displayed sexual awareness. In any event, it's a remarkable performance—even if the credit does have to be shared rather more than usual with the director, the cameraman and the musical composer.

While its love scenes are highlights, they occupy a relatively small portion of *Extase*. Nevertheless, its aura of romanticism is present throughout. When the husband shoots himself and dies (an episode drawn out beyond probable medical lengths) his death is equated by an intercut with the struggles of a fly caught on flypaper. When he has died, the young lover downstairs (not yet knowing the facts) sticks a daisy on the flypaper, its petals suddenly transforming that graveyard-in-miniature into something offering hope and beauty, beneath which the young lovers dance. If Machaty hadn't decided on his ambiguously downbeat ending, it would have been an ideal—and dazzling—shot on which to end *Extase*.

Hallelujah, I'm a Bum

United Artists, 1933.

Directed by Lewis Milestone. Screenplay by S. N. Behrman from a story by Ben Hecht. Songs by Richard Rodgers and Lorenz Hart. Musical Direction, Alfred Newman. Camera: Lucien Andriot. Reissued under the title *Heart of New York*.

With: Al Jolson, Madge Evans, Frank Morgan, Harry Langdon, Chester Conklin, Tyler Brooke, Edgar Connor, Bert Roach, Dorothea Wolpert, Louise Carver, Harold Goodwin, Burr McIntosh, Tammany Young (and Rodgers & Hart in bits as bank tellers).

There are many musicals that might well classify as potential "great love stories," since in many cases the boy-meets-loses-gets-girl is the simplest framework on which to hang the songs. Rodgers and Hart's previous *Love Me Tonight* is perhaps a leading contender, since it is all about love, and has one particularly touching love scene. But *Love Me Tonight* is too elegant and perfect a musical merely to be regarded as a love story. Take away its scintillating score and its sparkling comedy—to say nothing of its brilliantly stylized technique (it is almost certainly director Rouben Mamoulian's finest film) and what would be left could hardly hold its own on a purely romantic level.

On the other hand, *Hallelujah I'm A Bum* could. While its Jolson songs are important, and are undoubtedly what helped sell the film (not that it sold well, more's the pity), the songs *could* be deleted and the film could more than hold its own as a love story.

Oddly enough, its basic appeal is to the losers of the world—those who have searched for love and never found it, or perhaps those who have found it briefly, and lost it. It is a film of wish-fulfillment and yearning, and ultimately it is a rather sad film. That, coupled with its Depression background, and its unpopular innovational style—rhyming dialogue was used a great deal of the time—contrived to make it a largely unsuccessful film at the time of its release. It probably enjoyed greater popularity in the mid-40s when, drastically cut and shorn of some of its best numbers, it was revived to cash in on the new Jolson interest and popularity spawned by *The Jolson Story*. Jolson himself went on record as saying that it was easily his *worst* film, though to Jolson's show-biz mind, success was automatically equated with money at the box office.

Since this film failed at the box office, to him it undoubtedly failed in all other areas too. Certainly it is the least typical Jolson film, but in many ways it is probably his best—not least because his bombast is tamed to a remarkable degree by one of the few Jolson directors with enough clout to overrule him. The expected Jolson dynamism is still there in the musical numbers, but in the dramatic scenes there's a poignancy he never achieved in other films.

Like many Depression-era films, such as *Man's Castle* and *One More Spring*, it adopts an unrealistic, fable-like stance, as if to suggest that blind faith in a general "happy ending" can bring that about when no really practical solution is in sight.

Al Jolson plays Bumper, a happy bum who lives in Central Park, doesn't work, never needs money—and fortunately enjoys the friendship of the Mayor of New York, who gives him an occasional handout. The Mayor is played by Frank Morgan, and his mistress, June, by Madge Evans. When he surmises, unjustly, that she has been unfaithful, they have a scene, and she walks out. In a daze, she wanders through Central Park, and tries to commit suicide by jumping into the lake. Bumper rescues her, but the shock has brought on an attack of amnesia. Her mind is a total blank, and she falls deeply in love with Bumper, her only protector. Equally in love himself, he decides to mend his ways, gets a job, and moves June—whom he calls Angel—into an apartment. They are totally happy, and plan an early marriage. But inadvertently the drunken and distraught Mayor confides in Bumper, tells him of his need for June, and shows him June's picture.

Frank Morgan as the Mayor of New York (a character based somewhat loosely on Jimmie Walker), Edgar Washington and Al Jolson.

Bumper brings them together again. The shock restores June's memory, but erases all knowledge of what has happened in between. She looks around her at the shabby rooming-house with disdain, and is frightened and repelled by Bumper himself. After they leave, Bumper returns to his old life in Central Park.

As with most fairy stories, in bald outline it does not sound very logical—or very impressive. The Central Park sequences embrace most of the songs, these often making social or political—or just philosophic—comments on the Depression. But it's the love story—or stories—that occupy must of the footage, and a major reason for their success is the incredibly "right" casting of Madge Evans.

Without ever being a great actress, Madge Evans was always a good one. Moreover she was

Edgar Washington, Al Jolson and Harry Langdon enjoy a meal of leftovers at the Central Park Casino.

beautiful, cool and elegant without being so to an overpowering degree, so that she was not an unattainable ideal. In *Hallelujah I'm a Bum* she's the perfect dream girl for each of the two men in her life: for the Mayor, she's glamorous, a bought-and-paid-for decoration, and initially at least, little more than a sex object. To Bumper, she's innocence, youth and love. When he sings one of the loveliest Rodgers and Hart love songs to her—"You Are Too Beautiful"—we envy him his good luck, yet also fear that it cannot last. Sex is much more involved in her relationship with the Mayor; even a (tastefully done) nude scene with Bumper is used to define her new innocence rather than her sensuality. We can be sorry for her too, when she regains her memory: although she does love the Mayor, and there's a subtle suggestion of marriage via a musical hint (although it's never actually mentioned), she's also lost the companionship and joy in simpler things that she had shared with Bumper. As for Bumper, his ending is the saddest of all: although he goes back to his carefree life as a bum, it won't be the same now that he has had the emotion of deep love. Nor will his newfound ambitions stand him in good stead, since he now has no one to work hard for.

The film is too whimsical in detail to be regarded in entirely realistic terms. Apart from one or two establishing scenes actually shot in Central Park, most of it seems to have been shot in the quite different Griffith Park in Los Angeles. Although the Mayor is clearly based on Jimmy Walker, *no* Mayor who did nothing but have a good time could last long in any city. The Central Park idyll could only be remotely feasible in good weather. June's amnesia is like none in medical history, wiping out not only memory but all sense of morality as well. Perhaps that is why it works its magic best on those who can see it in either dream or wish-fulfillment terms—not only the losers and the loners, but perhaps too those for whom marriage has became a matter of contentment and security, but not of romance.

Madge Evans and those haunting Rodgers and Hart melodies and lyrics make the major contribution to the film, but Frank Morgan's performance as the Mayor—only gradually realizing how desperately in love he is—is an intensely moving one too, reminding us what a first-class dramatic actor he was before MGM typecast him as a comic buffoon. Jolson, remarkably under control, manages to

Madge Evans as Angel . . . anybody's Dream Girl

prove himself quite an actor too, even in scenes where his body is motionless and his voice stilled. The eloquence of these few pantomimic moments is a far cry from the lugubriously overflorid acting of sentimental scenes in such earlier films as *The Singing Fool*. If Harry Langdon's delightful and affecting comic touches have been overlooked in this appraisal, it is only because his relationship to the romantic core of the film is minimal. The wistful pathos he adds does, however, make itself felt in the cumulative effect of the film's many lesser strands and characters.

Maskerade
(Masquerade in Vienna)

Tobis-Sascha, Vienna, 1934.

Directed by Willy Forst. Screenplay by Walter Reisch. Musical score by Willy Schmidt-Gentner, played by the Vienna Philharmonic Orchestra. German Dialogue. U.S. release, 1937.

With: Paula Wessely, Anton Walbrook, Olga Tschekowa, Peter Petersen, Hilda von Stoltz, Walter Janssen, Julia Serda, Hans Moser; and the voice of Enrico Caruso.

Although *Maskerade* has many of the trappings of romantic farce and at times seems not too far removed from René Clair's silent classic *The Italian Straw Hat*, its plot—dealing with the catapulting of a virtuous young Austrian girl into a liaison with a notorious libertine/artist whom she eventually reforms—is actually based on a well-documented turn-of-the-century incident. With its plot complications and misunderstandings, and its unpredictable mixture of comedy and warm romance with sudden stark drama, it also at times takes on the surface look of an Erich von Stroheim film.

While in the 70s *Maskerade* doesn't entirely live up to its near-legendary reputation, it's easy to understand its huge popularity in 1937, when it benefited from a kind of double nostalgia. Its release had been held up for some years so that MGM could use the property as a remake with which to introduce Luise Rainer to American audiences, under the title *Escapade.* Thus not only was it about a vanished way of life (which many in the 30s could still recall) but it was also virtually an echo from a vanished way of movie life too. European films were harder and less romantic by the mid-30s: German films now made under the Nazis, the French, exemplified by *Pepe Le Moko,* specializing in a kind of lyrical defeatism. Small wonder that the warmth and charm of this period romance—an art film that was not an "arty" film—found a ready audience.

MGM's *Escapade* had copied it meticulously, even to specific camera movements, and recast it flawlessly (with William Powell, Reginald Owen and others) but in changing the emphasis so that it became rather aggressively a showcase for Luise Rainer, it lost much of the original's spontaneous charm. Even apart from the freshness of its story, however, the original was an infinitely superior work. Today, admittedly, when comparisons with Schnitzler's writing and Max Ophuls' many films in a like tradition are inevitable, it loses just a little. Former actor Forst doesn't have quite the panache of Ophuls, and the once creative and satiric use of sound as counterpoint is no longer new. But its charm, elegance and unerringly accurate depiction of the last years of an aristocratic Vienna certainly remain. Paula Wessely, then fresh from a major

Anton Walbrook with Olga Tchekowa. Walbrook plays a notorious painter; Tchekowa a countess whose reputation is above suspicion. In order to protect her reputation and explain away the "mystery woman" who was in his apartment, he fabricates a fictitious name.

triumph on the Berlin stage in *Rose Berndt*, was both a unique actress and a refreshingly different personality, and her performance is as appealing as ever. Peter Petersen's restraint and subtlety are a joy to watch, and Anton Walbrook (he diplomatically changed his name from Adolph during the Nazi period), though criticized at the time for too *much* restraint, is likewise excellent. At the time Hollywood proudly boasted that both stars, director, and screenwriter has been signed to Hollywood contracts, but ultimately only screenwriter Reisch made the transfer.

With Max Ophuls gone, few directors even try this kind of film any more, and none pull it off as successfully as he did—or as Willy Forst did in this lovely minor masterpiece.

However, a girl with that fabricated name does exist—and their lives are intermingled. Ultimately she falls in love with and reforms him, though not until after he is almost killed by an irate husband. Paula Wesseley gave a charming performance as the innocent reformer.

The perfect wife (Myrna Loy), the perfect executive (Clark Gable) and the perfect secretary (Jean Harlow) in a movie equally perfectly tailored to popular taste.

Wife Versus Secretary

MGM, 1936.

Directed by Clarence Brown. Produced by Hunt Stromberg. Screenplay by Norman Krasna, Alice Duer Miller and John Lee Mahin from a novel by Faith Baldwin. Camera: Ray June.

With: Clark Gable, Jean Harlow, Myrna Loy, May Robson, James Stewart, George Barbier, Hobart Cavanaugh, Gilbert Emery, Margaret Irving, William Newell, Marjorie Gateson, Gloria Holden, Tom Dugan.

Although it is hardly a classic or even a major romantic film, *Wife Versus Secretary* is such a marvelous barometer both of public taste and of MGM's application of surefire formula methods of

One of Harlow's relatively few "sweet, simple, nice girl" roles, her Whitey was not called on for sultry sex or fast-paced wisecracks. It was to remain one of her most appealing roles.

catering to that taste, that it deserves to stand almost as the definitive Gable vehicle of its period.

Clark Cable, in 1936, was at the very peak of his popularity. Behind him was a long, unbroken chain of successes covering melodrama, romance and adventure, and successful teamings with the biggest feminine stars at MGM: Garbo, Myrna Loy, Joan Crawford and Jean Harlow. His two films immediately prior to *Wife Versus Secretary* were his biggest hits yet, *China Seas* and *Mutiny on the Bounty*. At the box office he could do no wrong, and *Wife Versus Secretary* was carefully calculated to showcase Gable with *two* of his regular co-stars, to keep the fans happy, to appeal to the sophisticates but more especially to the working girls who read Faith Baldwin novels and dreamed of falling in love with their boss, and most of all, not to rock the boat in any way. There *is* nothing in *Wife Versus Secretary* to offend public *or* censors. In fact there is nothing in *Wife Versus Secretary* at all except its stars (which was quite enough), the typical MGM gloss, and the usual tasteful direction by Clarence Brown which managed to make it all look more intelligent than it really was.

The plot consists of nothing more than Gable being happily married to Myrna Loy, but also maintaining a pleasant (and strictly platonic) business relationship with secretary Jean Harlow—who admires him, *could* love him, but is too decent to do so, and anyway has a likable boyfriend (James Stewart) in tow herself. A business trip to Havana for Gable contrives a somewhat unlikely situation where Harlow has to join him to help push a big

deal through, and wife Loy happens to call late at night and find Harlow on the other end of the phone. She walks out—Harlow convinces her that she's wrong—Gable and Loy are reunited, and Harlow reconciles with mildly estranged boyfriend Stewart to provide a happy ending all around.

Had the film been made in 1932, before the Production Code cast its baleful glare on public morality, the film might have been somewhat livelier, played for all-out drama or piquant sex comedy. One can well imagine Gable having a harmless affair with his secretary then, or even deciding she was preferable to a somewhat stuffy wife. And the business deal would undoubtedly have been peppered by wisecracking stenographers and oily speculators. But in 1936, all was decorum and even-keel respectability. So little really happens in the film that one tends to remember it not for incident, but for its mildly offbeat locations—an ice-skating rink, for example.

One has no reason to be unduly critical of *Wife Versus Secretary* purely because it is a formula picture. Jean Harlow, domesticated and tamed more and more with each picture (though the jump from the hard-boild adventuress of *China Seas* to the sensitive, heart-of-gold secretary here was quite a spectacular one to take place in a period of only six months), was totally charming and stole both the picture and audience sympathy. And formula picture or not, one can still recall it with affection more than forty years later. How many "formula" films of the 70s can we expect to be likewise remembered in the year 2010?

Une Partie de Campagne

1936; final editing and release 1946.

Written and directed by Jean Renoir, from the story by Guy de Maupassant. Camera: Claude Renoir. Music: Joseph Kosma. Assistant directors include Jacques Becker, Yves Allegret, Henri Cartier-Bresson, Lucino Visconti and Jacques Brunius.

With: Sylvia Bataille, Jeanne Marken, Gabriello, Georges Darnoux, Jacques Brunius, Paul Temps, Jean Renoir, Fabrielle Fontan, Marguerite Renoir, Pierre Lestringuez.

Fate seemed to conspire to make this vignette the perfect little film that it is. Initially, Renoir was unable to complete the film—nor was he even sure *how* he wanted to complete it. With the Nazi occupation, the first negative was lost to the Germans, and a second one constructed without Renoir, who was by then in Hollywood. When the film was finally prepared for release after the war, it was too late to do anything about missing scenes, since even those players who might still have been available—

to say nothing of the location itself—would have been ten years older. The decision was made to release it as it stood, a forty-minute vignette. And it was perfect the way it was.

It's a delicate little tale of a city family's day in the country. The men go fishing, the wife enjoys the comic flirtations of a local Lothario, and the daughter, Henriette, a young innocent in love with the very idea of love, is seduced by a serious young man who takes her rowing down the river. Years later, the family returns for another day in the country. Henriette is now married to a boorish oaf of a husband, obviously condemned to a life of drudgery. Accidentally, she meets her previous lover. Embarrassed, sad for the things that might have been, their lives cross again only for a moment or two, before her husband arrives to take her back to the city.

So many things about the film are just exactly right. Sylvia Bataille is both lovely and gauche, per-

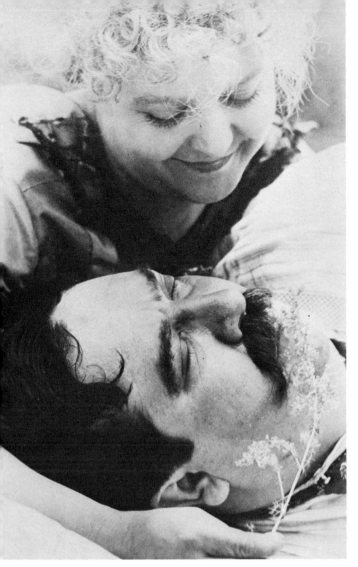

Mother and father relax in the afternoon sunshine (Gabriel and Jeanne Marken).

following Henriette's seduction, to the return, years later, is all the more effective because we see drudgery and monotony replacing love and beauty immediately.

Several of the scenes in the film are clearly based on specific paintings by Renoir's famous father Auguste. And nature herself seems to have conspired in the creation of this little masterpiece. The sun shines when it is needed, casting light on the leaves and reflection on the water. While Henriette asks her mother about the yearnings for love that she feels that Spring day, a butterfly—its own beauty and happiness to die that day—flits in and out of the scene, a piece of naturalistic symbolism far too fragile (and technically difficult) ever to have been planned. And when sadness descends, the rains come—again unanticipated, blocking out the sun, falling into the river like a million tears.

Few seduction scenes have been as sensitively handled as the brief yet exquisitely done sequence

fect for the young Henriette, while as her mother Jeanne Marken can be both foolish and wise, depending on the circumstances. Joseph Kosma's score, even at its most joyful somehow suggesting the sadness that is to come, is of itself one of the most romantic pieces of music ever designed for a filmic love story. Despite all of director Renoir's own skill, sensitivity and humanity, the film would be only half the thing of beauty that it is without that score.

The unfilmed sequences, dealing with the interim years and the family's life back in the city, while possibly of more importance in de Maupassant's original story, matter not at all on film. In fact the sudden abrupt jump from the end of the day,

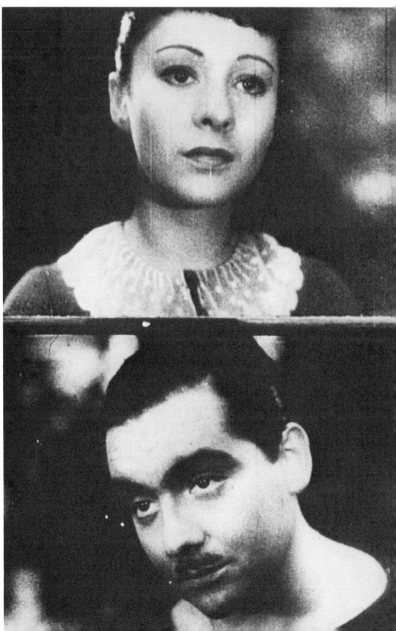

Frames direct from the film: the exchange of yearning glances that precedes the seduction (Sylvia Bataille and George St. Saen).

A detail closeup from one of the tenderest love scenes ever put on film.

here, little more than a rush of music, and Henriette's face turned sideways to reveal a single ambiguous tear.

In America, *Partie de Campagne* isn't nearly as well known as it deserves to be. European distributors had the wit to release it as it was, a work of art on its own that could only enhance any film it was paired with. In the United States, however, it was combined with two other off-feature-length movies (*Jofroi* and *The Miracle*) to form a composite film known as *The Ways of Love*, which by virtue of its Rossellini component (*The Miracle*) went on to a storm of precedent-shattering censorship battles. Poor *Partie de Campagne* was lost and wasted in the middle, denied to those wo were turned away by the notoriety (and the Cathlolic Legion of Decency ban on the film), and being far too sensitive a film to satisfy those who came to it looking for salaciousness and sex.

Nevertheless, in four reels, plus a river bank, some trees and sunshine, a superb musical score, and the skill of the whole company in front of and behind the camera, it says—feelingly—more about love than almost any other film ever made.

Back to the city with the boorish oaf who will soon be Sylvia's husband.

126

Before leaving on a European vacation, engineer Tom Bradley (Gary Cooper) is asked by his boss (William Frawley) to do a little free advertising from his car.

Desire

Paramount, 1936.

Directed by Frank Borzage. Produced by Ernst Lubitsch: Screenplay by Edwin Justus Mayer, Waldemar Young, Samuel Hoffenstein, from an original story by Hans Szekeley and R. A. Stemmle: Music and lyrics by Frederick Hollander and Leo Robin. Camera: Charles Lang.

With: Marlene Dietrich, Gary Cooper, John Halliday, Ernest Cossart, William Frawley, Alan Mowbray, Akim Tamiroff, Zeffie Tilbury, Charles Davis, Marc Lawrence, Stanley Andrews, Alden Chase.

What a felicitous team this film created in the collaboration of Frank Borzage as director and Ernst Lubitsch as producer. Lubitsch, normally his own director, sets the mood and style. His wit and elegance are ever present. As has also been said of Hitchcock, most of Lubitsch's "direction" is performed in the preshooting stage, when the film is planned and storyboarded. Apart from correcting or otherwise guiding the performances of the actors, shooting the film is virtually an anticlimax. On the other hand, as has been proven on at least two occasions when Otto Preminger took over the directorial reins on a Lubitsch film, the actual director can still wreak changes—and damage—if he is not totally in tune with Lubitsch's mood. Frank Bor-

zage is not only in tune here, but is able to bring about subtle and helpful improvements through his own innate good taste. Even at his best, there was a certain vulgarity and heaviness to Lubitsch, a reluctance to let a scene play without all the ammunition possible behind it, a need to underline certain scenes. Perhaps Germanic "thoroughness" might be a better description of it, and in view of the virtuosity of his films, such criticism seems picayune indeed. But when a film that is wholly his, by design, such as *Desire,* is handled by as appropriate a director as Borzage, the added lilt merely increases the pleasure. The only, and very minor, strikes against *Desire* are its somewhat heavy title, and a slightly overlong running time.

Its plot is pure froth and frou-frou, about a Riviera-based jewel thief (Dietrich) who is reformed by the love of a straightforward American (Cooper). It's another fairytale, and at that one made at the height of the movies' Cinderella years, when the self-imposed censorship of the Production Code frowned on the mention of sex, and disapproved almost as much of the sympathetic depiction of criminals. Yet Lubitsch was adept at sidestepping such restrictions—much more so than directors like Raoul Walsh, who found themselves totally hamstrung with their freewheeling style hog-

Madeleine (Marlene Dietrich) and Carlos (John Halliday) are high-class jewel thieves and confidence crooks.

tied by the Code. Lubitsch got away with murder in *Bluebeard's Eighth Wife* merely by having his sexual combatants married and therefore perfectly legal. Here, with impeccable taste, he sidesteps anything that might cause censorial alarm while at the same time making it abundantly clear what is going on. Gary Cooper clearly has an "illicit" sexual liaison with Dietrich at one point—yet the only indication of it is a delicious line which makes the situation crystal clear to the sophisticates, yet at the same time also has such a totally innocent secondary meaning, and one quite within the context of the story, that any censors would merely have looked foolish had they sought to remove it.

The climax is a mild compromise, it's true. In 1932, Lubitsch's *Trouble in Paridise* let its jewel thieves escape scot-free, rich from their larceny, and decidedly unmarried. Here the Code demands a wedding and "moral compensation," but the obligation is met rather neatly in a trick fadeout which seems to poke fun at such prudish idiocy. But this thumbing of the nose at the Code at the *end* of the film was nothing compared to what Lubitsch pulled off at the beginning of the film. Despite a Code ruling that crime must never be shown in an attractive manner, or so as to inspire imitation, Lubitsch outlines in meticulous detail just how to carry out a totally bloodless and seemingly foolproof jewel theft!

Few films of the 30s ever surpassed this one in sheer visual elegance. The sets and decor, all white marble and filmy drapes, gleam and glisten; the camera glides smoothly over polished floors and up luxurious stairways; and Dietrich, sumptuously gowned in flowing white creations, has seldom been more attractively photographed. She may have looked more exotic in her earlier von Sternberg films, but never so ravishingly beautiful as here. Too, the deftness of dialogue and the directorial skill turn this goddesslike creature into a human being too, though perhaps not one that we are likely to meet, more's the pity. The luster of the film's photography is matched by the charm of its musical background, and by the impeccable performances right down the cast.

While the film is funnier in its first half, turning more to being a serious love story in its second half, the elegance of performance throughout provides the even keel that prevents that division from becoming disturbing or even noticeable. What a pleasure it is to see John Halliday, that perfectionist at gentleman crooks, turning from suave charm to genuine menace with the subtlest change of expression of voice. "Are you trying to double-cross me?" he asks Dietrich at one point, in an astonishing lapse from his customary savoir-faire, and quite rightly she rebukes him with a scornful "Don't be vulgar!" (One can almost trace the influence of the Production Code just through a scrutiny of John Halliday's roles. By 1940, and such films as *Escape to Glory*, while his roles were essentially the same characters, he was no longer allowed to be charming or gallant, but merely a rat with a smooth exterior.)

If there is a lapse of taste *anywhere* in the film, it is only in the traditional use of American speed-cop sirens for Spanish motorcycle policemen—a typical example of Hollywood's egomanic urge to reshape the rest of the world to its own image. For the rest, it is sheer unadulterated delight. Looking at it today, it's hard to believe that almost all of its principals—Lubitsch, Borzage, Cooper, Halliday, Cossart, Frawley, Tamiroff, Tilbury—are gone. *Desire* is a more than fitting memorial to all of them.

By chance Tom falls in with the thieves —and in love with Madeleine—in whom he effects a reformation.

The Prisoner of Zenda

Selznick International–United Artists, 1937.

Directed by John Cromwell. Produced by David O. Selznick. From the novel by Anthony Hope and the dramatization by Edward Rose: Screenplay by John Balderston, adaptation by Wells Root, with additional dialogue by Donald Ogden Stewart. Camera: James Wong Howe. Music: Alfred Newman. Additional direction (action scenes): W. S. Van Dyke.

With: Ronald Colman, Madeleine Carroll, Douglas Fairbanks, Jr., Mary Astor, Raymond Massey, C. Aubrey Smith, David Niven, Montague Love, William von Brincken, Philip Sleeman, Torben Meyer, Byron Foulger, Ian McLaren, Lawrence Grant, Ralph Faulkner, Howard Lang, Ben Webster, Boyd Irwin, Evelyn Beresford, Emmett King, Al Shean, Charles Halton, Francis Ford, Spencer Charters.

One can almost pin down *The Prisoner of Zenda* as being the last (and best) of the great romanticist adventure films—and with no snub to Errol Flynn's later *The Sea Hawk,* a superb swashbuckler but lacking a love story with the emotional

values that make *Zenda* succeed on levels other than those of derring-do.

From the start, *The Prisoner of Zenda* was conceived to cash in on the worldwide excitement generated by the coming coronation of Britian's King Edward VIII. The phrase "cash in" is perhaps too crassly commercial a term, in view of the impeccable taste of the whole film; nevertheless its first third—with tourists and diplomats alike converging on the small kingdom to witness the ceremony, or just to be a part of the excitement—would not have been so carefully developed had the coronation itself not been of such topical and all-consuming interest. The excitement surrounding the coronation may well have been a deliberate if unwitting mass attempt to blot out the rising war fears, as though tradition itself could keep world affairs on an even keel and keep disaster at arm's length. Ultimately of course Edward's coronation did *not* take place, and the film was confronted with the tricky problem of maintaining a duty-before-love climax without in any way seeming to be condemning the conduct of the abdicated King or of the American divorcee, Mrs. Simpson, whom he subsequently married. (To have followed their example and concluded with a love-before-duty climax would have been flying in the face of public opinion, and would have opened the film up to accusations of cashing in. Had British law permitted the King to ascend the throne *and* marry Mrs. Simpson, doubtless *The Prisoner of Zenda* would have joined in the celebration by changing its ending to accommodate those circumstances.)

The Prisoner of Zenda is virtually the "definitive" Ruritanian romantic adventure, dealing with the efforts of plotters to remove King Rudolph from the throne before his coronation, and pave the way for the country's takeover by his evil and power-hungry brother, Black Michael. They are thwarted by the fortuitous arrival of Rudolf Rassendyll, a distant cousin and an exact double, who is persuaded to impersonate the missing King at his coronation and help in his recovery. This Rassendyll does, despite the delemma of falling in love with the real King's bride-to-be, and being unable to explain why he does not reciprocate her own quite obviously genuine love for him. With the King finally rescued, proven to be a better man than anyone expected by virtue of his ordeal, Rassendyll bids farewell to his Princess—who now knows the truth, but turns down his plea to find happiness with him, choosing instead to follow the dictates of duty and stay to rule her new country with a man she does not love, but at least can now respect.

From the opening titles, which have a romantic flavor all their own, neatly placing the whole film in the context of a disappeared age of chivalry and courtliness (although no dates are ever given, there are clear hints that it is set in the late 1800s, close to the time of Queen Victoria's jubilee), everything about the film is just right. The cast is hand-picked and its equal could never have been found in a later period. The staging is sumptuous, the sets and decor stunning, and one never has the feeling, as one does with so many spectacles, that the palaces and ballrooms disappear immediately outside camera range. On the other hand, the lavishness of production is limited to scenes where it really counts: The king's arrival at the station, en route to his coronation, is a necessary transitional scene, but not one on which to squander production values, and so it is treated with remarkable economy. James Wong Howe, a superb cameraman, creates some magnificent images, sharp, beautifully lit, and employing one of the longest and most spectacular pullback shots in the whole history of cinema for the scene where the substitute King and his Princess descend

Ronald Colman, as Rudolph Rassendyll, has substituted for the missing King Rudolph at the coronation, and he and Princess Flavia (Madeleine Carroll) receive the cheers of the populace.

130

Even villainy has its romantic side in this elegant swashbuckler: Black Michael (Raymond Massey) with the mistress that he loves but cannot marry, played by Mary Astor.

the long marble stairway into the ballroom. Alfred Newman's score, like Tiomkin's for *Lost Horizon* the same year, is yet another reminder of how much the movies have lost musically. It's a sweeping, virile, melodic score which particularly emphasizes the big romantic scenes. Director John Cromwell, who invariably showed his allegiance to the theatre in most of his movies, might seem an odd directorial choice in the face of a Curtiz or a Mamoulian, and indeed, did prove a little disappointing in his handling of the few but important action scenes to the extent that MGM's action maestro, W. S. Van Dyke, was brought in to beef up these sequences. But basically it is *not* an action film, telling its story more in terms of people and dialogue, and in that respect Cromwell gets far more out of it than Curtiz —or Van Dyke, if he had been hired to do the whole film—would have done.

As for the rather talkative screenplay by John Balderston, as also in his screen treatment of *Dracula* it tends to stay largely within four walls and to downplay vigorous action until its rousing climax with its splendid duel sequence and exciting stunt horse falls as the villain's castle is attacked. But with such literary dialogue, and such marvelously theatrical (in the best sense of the word) interpretations of the roles, the concentration on talk is a decided asset in this case. Even in the heat of the duel to the death, the choice lines never let up. In magnificent old theatrical tradition, one blockbuster line follows another, rolling romantically from the

lips of Colman and Carroll and venomously from those of Massey. ("It's the day, the hour, and very nearly the moment!" he hisses early in the coronation ceremony, unaware as yet that his little world is about to crumble when the twin Colman shows up to replace the kidnapped King.) Douglas Fairbanks, Jr., in the performance of his life, is so absolutely right in the role of the dashing, likable yet thoroughly unscrupulous villain, Rupert of Hentzau, that one regrets all the more that Selznick never followed through with his announced plan to star him in a sequel. (One even wonders whether that announcement was perhaps a ploy to defeat the Production Code? Lovable rouge or not, Rupert *does* commit two cold-blooded murders onscreen, is responsible for others offscreen, and yet is allowed to escape scot-free at the end. Even with the promise of retribution in a sequel,* it's incredible that Hollywood's own censorship allowed his villainy to triumph in that excessively moral period.)

This version is without doubt the best of the five Zendas to be filmed since 1915. In Rex Ingram's ornate but rather stodgy version of 1922, Lewis Stone played the dual Rudolph/Rudolf role, Alice Terry was Flavia, Ramon Novarro was fine as Rupert, and Stuart Holmes—of course—was Black Michael. MGM's version in the 50s was handsome and surprisingly good, maintaining a far higher batting average than most remakes, but Stewart Granger was never able to do justice to some of the retained Colman lines. Colman, hard-pressed to explain his actions to Princess Flavia, has one line— "Then will you believe *this*, with*out* understanding —I *love* you!"—which he breaks up into four phrases, with appropriate pauses and emphases. Granger repeats it vebatim as a single, styleless line, and its poetry is gone. However, Deborah Kerr was a good Flavia, James Mason an excellent if somewhat humorless Rupert of Hentzau, Robert Douglas a satisfying successor to Massey as Black Michael, but Jane Greer hardly as effective—and certainly not as touching—as Mary Astor had been as Michael's mistress. In keeping with the times,

Rupert of Hentzau was made in 1923, but not by Rex Ingram, and with Lew Cody rather than Ramon Novarro as Rupert. It was produced by Lewis Selznick (father of David, who produced the Colman film) and brother Myron. Rupert returns, more villainous than ever, murders King Rudolph, and is himself killed by Rudolf Rassendyll. Possibly the distinctly unsympathetic turn that the character takes is the reason why the sequel was never made by Fairbanks, Jr., as it would have been most unsatisfactory to find a lovable scoundrel coming to such a bad end. For the record however, Flavia abdicates when Rudolf refuses the throne, and both finally achieve marital happiness in England.

Sir C. Aubrey Smith, as Colonel Zapt, whose love of King and Country provides a touching subplot.

sentiment and patriotism were played down as being "square"; Rudolf has no chance to remember dreamily that "trout stream near Aylesbury," and Colonel Zapt is deprived of that "I have a feeling for my King" speech done so movingly by C. Aubrey Smith.

When Colman's *The Prisoner of Zenda* opened at the Radio City Music Hall, it was an enormous critical and popular success, as it subsequently proved to be all over the world. The critics didn't take it too seriously and some even poked fun at its grand-manner dialogue, but all appreciated its style and exuberance.

As with the same year's *Lost Horizon* (what a banner year for Colman!) it is the love scenes that survive best on a serious level. *None* of *The Prisoner of Zenda* dates; indeed its production elegance and craftsmanship, and almost unmatched ensemble playing, can only increase its values through the years, as such qualities become rarer. But while the film as a whole is a zestful romp, its love scenes are rather more than that, and despite the artificial quality of the plot, there is an earnest and sincere feel-

ing to the romantic exchanges. Even the climactic renunciation scene, with theatrical-tableaux staging in the Queen's bedchamber and frequent long shots to enable the beams of sunlight through the window to suggest a halolike effect, becomes intensely moving. Madeleine Carroll, relatively passive throughout the film, is permitted to make the scene hers rather than Colman's with her impassioned "Oh, if love were all . . ." speech. Unreal or not, with so much happiness within reach—and still possible, if love were placed before honor—we feel for both of these larger-than-life—but at the moment very human—people. As Rudolf finally rides off into the sunset, sped on his way by Colonel Zapt's parting compliment that, Englishman or not, he's the finest Rassendyll of them all, it might even have destroyed our romantic glow to know that eventual happiness *did* await Rudolf and Flavia. Fortunately, in 1937, Anthony Hope—never considered a serious literary figure anyway—was so forgotten and outdated that audiences did *not* know about events in the sequel.

A decidedly Beverly Hills concept of a Tibetan monastery.

Lost Horizon

Columbia, 1937.

Produced and directed by Frank Capra. Screenplay by Robert Riskin from the novel *Lost Horizon* by James Hilton. Camera: Hoseph Walker. Aerial photography: Elmer Dyer. Musical Score: Dmitri Tiomkin. Musical Direction: Max Steiner.

With: Ronald Colman, Jane Wyatt, Thomas Mitchell, John Howard, H. B. Warner, Edward Everett Horton, Sam Jaffe, Isabel Jewell, Hugh Buckler, David Torrence, John Miltern, Lawrence Grant, Leonard Mudie.

Lost Horizon was one of the major Hollywood films of 1937, bowling audiences over with both its novelty and its sumptuous staging, winning two Academy Awards (though in relatively minor categories) and being nominated for five others. Certainly for a still relatively small company like Columbia, it was an incredible achievement—and easily Frank Capra's most ambitious production to date.

In many ways it was almost archetypically a "Hollywood" production. It was based on a popular best-seller, and it had air-tight box-office insurance in the star persona of Ronald Colman. To make certain that its philosophic undertones didn't overbalance the purely entertainment values, a character (not in the book) was provided to create sustained comedy relief—a role excellently handled by Edward Everett Horton. Although its art deco design was far more Beverly Hills than Tibet, the film was lushly impressive to look at. And to top it off, there was one of Dmitri Tiomkin's most romantic scores.

It was also a film that made few demands on its audience. There was plenty to look at and listen to, and there was no arguing with its philosophic pleas for peace and love as opposed to war, greed and chaos. With the world rushing headlong towards World War II (or to be accurate, with some of the world rushing headlong, and the rest of the world sitting passively by) it was immensely topical too. Subsequent world events—the Cold War, Korea, Vietnam—have merely reinforced its kind of universal topicality.

Its humanity is all on the surface, however—which is undoubtedly why the film was so popular. The mid-30s in Hollywood were somewhat of a wasteland. Movies strove to entertain all members of the Great American Family, and to avoid harsh realities, unpopular themes, or controversial issues. That is why the few strong films of the period, such

In a sequence deleted from the released version, Robert Conway (Ronald Colman), on board ship, plays a Chopin melody that has never been published. It stirs memories of Shangri La, where he heard it, and the film then goes into flashbacks to tell his story. Listening are Hugh Buckler, John T. Murray and Lawrence Grant.

as Lang's *Fury* or LeRoy's *They Won't Forget* seem even more powerful than they actually are. In a desert of pure escapism, *Lost Horizon* seemed to be saying something profound. Audiences found themselves thinking—if only on a surface level—and went home happy, feeling they had undergone both an emotional and an intellectual overhaul. And all credit to the film for that: Capra was a cunning director who knew his audiences and was skillful at using sentiment rather than logic to pound his message home.

If one accepts the basic concept of *Lost Horizon* at face value, its story of a superior civilization, cut off from the rest of the world, where a lack of strife promotes happiness, honesty, health and long life, is naive in the extreme. In all fairness, the character played by John Howard—who is meant to represent all the materialistic qualities of the world—makes by far the most sense. But of course in a romantic sense, he is no match for Ronald Colman —and by making his character entirely physical and unreasoning, by making him insensitive and crude, Capra virtually succeeds in turning him into a near-villain.

If the film has flaws on a philosophic level, it has quite a few (though less importantly) on a filmmaking level too. Apparently on its initial previews, reception was unfavorable to its earlier sequences, so Capra jettisoned the establishing episodes, and totally reshaped the structure of the film (which was originally in flashback). Capra, in his autobiography *The Name Above the Title* (eminently readable, though highly suspect in detail) oversimplifies this

editing process, admits only to junking the opening reels, and feels that the film plays much better in its present form (which has also been subject to minor cuts and trims throughout its reissue career). The later portions of the film too, in which Robert Conway (Colman) stumbles blindly through the mountain wilderness and is finally rescued by tribesmen, show a certain editorial carelessness. This episode is bolstered by the odd stock shot from earlier films, and in particular by scenes from a Andrew Marton–directed circa 1930 adventure-documentary, which are none too carefully matched. (Columbia used much more from this older film in a 1952 release, *Storm Over Tibet*, and it is quite fascinating to see the extended sequences from which this *Lost Horizon* episode was extracted and built). There is nothing particularly unusual about the extensive re-editing of a film, or about the use of stock footage, but both of these particular instances did result in damage to the overall film—in one case by reducing a complex structure to a much simpler narrative, and in the other by somewhat jarringly taking one "out" of the film by calling attention to the editing process.

It is difficult to regard *Lost Horizon* as a classic (either in terms of theme or of filmmaking) except in the purely commercial sense. It *is* a most entertaining film, a showcase for Hollywood gloss, and for fine ensemble acting, with H. B. Warner's work standing out. The war turmoil at the beginning, and the flying scenes, are excitingly done. And some moments have tremendous power—although the death of the High Lama is a chilling sequence rather than the "beautiful" experience as described by Conway to his colleagues.

But thanks to the dash and flair of Colman, and the intelligent playing of Jane Wyatt, the film does achieve a classic stature in a way that probably neither Capra nor (especially) James Hilton really wanted. Many reviewers at the time were critical of the romantic subplot, feeling that it got in the way, and was merely a sop to the Colman fans. Their irritation often took the unfair tactic of attacking Jane Wyatt, calling her "dull" and the role "silly." Since Jane Wyatt was relatively new to film, and her stage record not especially outstanding, she was fair game. Some critics even confused her with another newcomer, Jane Wyman. Yet it's the love story of *Lost Horizon,* regarded at the time as an intrusion, that stands the test of time best. It's late in developing, and never allowed to dominate. Too, it's a little one-sided in giving Colman the bulk of the dialogue, but it's good dialogue and he makes the most of it. There's one particularly well written (and spoken) scene in which Colman compares himself to the shadow of the airplane—rushing headlong over mountains and rivers, covering ten times the distance of the plane itself—only to find, on landing, the plane itself (with which he has compared his Sondra) waiting to greet him. It would take the eloquence and the musical diction of a Colman to compare his lady love to an airplane and *still* make it sound poetic and a compliment—and he pulls it off beautifully. Jane Wyatt remains silent through this fairly long speech, but in the embrace that follows, the camera angle favors her, and the kiss itself, one that suggests both supplication and total love, is one of the emotional highspots of the film—perhaps because it is relatively underplayed, given minimal backup from Tiomkin's score, and fades out as soon as its point is made.

Other love scenes in the film exploit the idyllic backgrounds of forest and waterfall, and even include a charming and tastefully done nude bathing scene, played for light comedy rather than sensuality. It's actually a totally unnecessary scene, but the relaxed playing from Colman and Wyatt, and the refusal to turn it into a heavy-handedly suggestive scene, make it a pleasant escape from the portentiousness of the surrounding philosophic discussions.

Jane Wyatt's casting opposite Colman in *Lost Horizon* was quite as felicitous as Edna Best's

The finely handled mob turmoil scenes in the Far East, with which the film now opens.

teaming with Ralph Richardson in the same year's *South Riding* in Britain. Wyatt had a classical kind of beauty and a directness in her acting, plus a crisp, clear diction, which made her unique among Hollywood leading ladies. She was seldom used to her best advantage by Hollywood, and never became the major star that she deserved to be. From her point of view, the *Lost Horizon* role isn't even particularly demanding, calling for little more than beauty and a sensible, straightforward performance —to which she adds the indefinable quality of sensitivity. Colman, however, was doing little more than going through his customary paces with aplomb and style in a role absolutely made to measure for him. But it wouldn't have worked nearly as well as it did had in not been for the intelligence of Jane Wyatt's performance, since by her very demeanor she has to suggest all the qualities which would cause a man like Conway to fall in love with her, and which the script itself doesn't altogether spell out.

Lost Horizon is a typically escapist Hollywood film of the late 30s, and in some ways, despite its pretensions, a surprisingly formularized film. But it is also one of the most satisfying romantic films of the period, enriched as it is by the Colman–Wyatt teamwork.

With Jane Wyatt, as Sondra.

At Shangri La, Chang (H.B. Warner) explains the community's philosophy to Conway.

Linden Travers, Paul Lukas

Brief Ecstasy

Phoenix Films–Associated British Film Distributors, 1937.

Directed by Edmond Greville. Produced by Hugh Perceval. Written by Basil Mason. Camera: Ronald Neame.

With: Paul Lukas, Linden Travers, Hugh Williams, Marie Ney, Renee Gadd, Fred Withers, Howard Douglas, Fewlass Llewellyn, Peter Gawthorne.

Entirely coincidentally, this film's title reveals exactly what it is: a combination of *Extase* (the Czech film, which clearly influenced some of it) and the still eight-years-away *Brief Encounter*. Directed by Frenchman Edmond Greville, whose European films always dealt fairly openly with sexual matters (the Charles Boyer *L'Orage* before the war, the adaptation of Zola's *Passionelle* after the war), its bluntness and honesty was quite rare in British films of the 30s. Since it was not a film of major importance, few critics noted it—but Graham Greene was one that did, and applauded it for dealing openly with lust rather than love. His own critical descriptions of the visual style—he referred once to "buttocks on the billiard table"—suggest that he rather enjoyed the rare opportunity to write about the application of sex to a British movie!

Phoenix Films was a small company set up to make intelligent "B" and programmer-level pictures in England. Unfortunately (in a commercial sense) they spent so much on production values that there was little left for stars. They were in the awkward position of turning out films that were too good and usually a little too long to fill the supporting slot—but too lacking in star value to play top of the bill, except at the smaller halls. Their struggle was a gallant but vain one; after a dozen or more really worthwhile little pictures, they went out of business. *Brief Ecstasy* is quite the best film of their short but distinguished existence.

It's a simple little tale of a "good girl" who is seduced, quite with her own acquiescence, by a philandering adventurer who only the next day is to leave for an assignment in India. She has no regrets, even though she realizes that she does love him sincerely. He, on the other hand, has definite regrets and wants to marry her. He cables her a proposal, but the telegram is lost. She returns to her studies at the university, is made an assistant to her professor, and ultimately marries him. Years later the young man returns, and, not unexpectedly, movie contrivance being what it is, is the house

Emotions captured and conveyed via tight closeups: the initial approach to seduction. Hugh Williams, Linden Travers.

Hugh Williams and Linden Travers in a romantic interlude in a café, where the compositions and lighting are again borrowed from *Extase*.

guest of the professor. At first he does not recognize his former conquest, and when he does, seeks to resume the relationship.

Circumstances put the opportunity for a rekindling of their romance in front of them when they are forced to spend the night at an inn. The wife resists all temptations, although her desire is clear, but she is finding it all too easy to lie to her trusting

husband. A jealous housekeeper, who has always loved the professor and has resented his marriage, tries to implant in him the idea that his wife is being unfaithful. Morose and brooding, he acquires a gun —not sure whether he plans murder or suicide, or both. Finally the housekeeper's schemings are revealed, and the wife's innocence—in deed if not in thought—established. The interloper leaves once again, and wife and husband resume their rather unexciting but somehow now more solid relationship.

The story, as can be seen, is not markedly original, nor is it helped by the Mrs. Danvers-like presence of the housekeeper. In a longer film, there would have been time to make her role more subtle. In a "B"-length film such as this, there is virtually no time for niceties with a supporting character, and baleful glances and cutaways to heavily-shadowed reaction shots fill in her motivations and actions far too obviously. But she is the only real weakness in an otherwise striking little film, unusually well acted by Linden Travers as the wife, Paul Lukas as her husband, and Hugh Williams (the Steerforth of *David Copperfield,* frequently cast as a good-looking cad) as the slightly more-sympathetic-than-usual other man.

What really sets the film apart, especially for one in its limited budgetary classification, is the remarkable collaboration between the writing, directorial and photographic aspects. The cameraman,

Triangle: husband (Paul Lukas), wife (Linden Travers) and former lover (Hugh Williams).

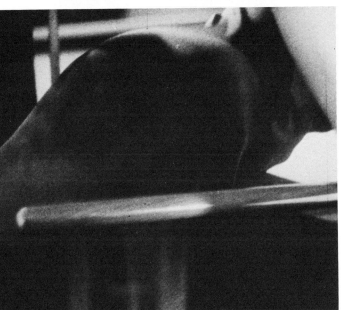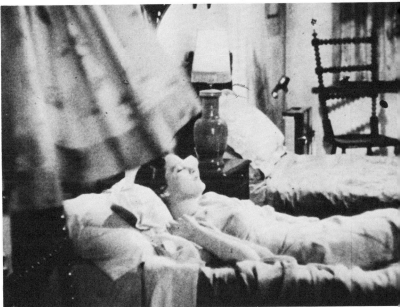

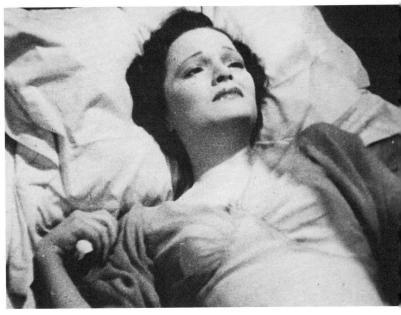

Erotic and symbolic detail shots.

Sexual frustration symbolized by a violent storm; a sequence copied intact from *Extase*.

Two frames from the film, indicating how the director constantly cuts to and fro between tight closeups.

Wife and former lover enjoy a quiet idyll in the country, an innocent jaunt that assumes serious overtones when they are accidentally stranded overnight.

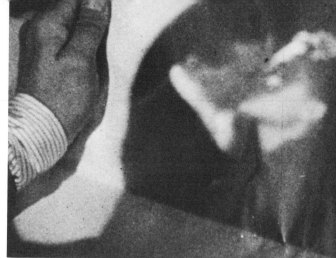

The husband visualizes his wife and her lover in a passionate embrace.

Ronald Neame, was always an excellent cinematographer (especially in Technicolor, later on) and would ultimately become a good director too. But here he handles the black-and-white camerawork almost like Lee Garmes in a von Sternberg movie. In fact, Linden Travers, here at the *beginning* of her career, was never (despite bigger budgets and Technicolor in later years) to look more beautiful. In framing and lighting her face and body, Neame lavished on her all the meticulous and loving care that Garmes and Bert Glennon devoted to Dietrich in her Sternberg films. There are lyrically composed shots of the young lovers in the countryside, beautifully lit interiors full of menace and suspicion. One sequence during a storm, in which the woman locks herself in her bedroom (the husband is absent) while the lover pounds in frustration on the door, and the wind causes the curtains to billow through the windows as the wife lies rigid on the bed, manages, through sheer pictorial and editing virtuosity, to suggest the whole wretchedness and misery of sexual frustration.

Throughout the film the camera constantly seems to pick out casual sexual detail, as though through the suddenly excited eye of an onlooker: the wife's tight bodice as a jacket is zipped up to her neck, a glimpse of immaculately stockinged leg. Much of the phallic symbolism of *Extase* is repeated, particularly in the use of a billiard cue as wife and lover spar verbally and make polite conversation. Another distinct echo from *Extase* is the pre-bed ritual of the husband, meticulously folding his trousers, the careful arrangement of brushes and combs. The camera picks out these details as still-lifes, telling us in effect that that is what the devoted but unromantic husband is, too.

In the end, duty wins out over lust. But this is *still* a love story if not a highly romantic one—a uniquely British approach that will be returned to, and discussed at more length, in the pages devoted to 1945's *Brief Encounter*.

A romantic meeting between the Squire and the schoolteacher: Ralph Richardson and Edna Best

South Riding

Korda–London Films–United Artists, 1937.

Produced and directed by Victor Saville. Supervised by Alexander Korda. Screenplay by Ian Dalrymple and Donald Bull from the novel by Winifred Holtby. Photographed by Harry Stradling. Art Direction: Lazare Meerson. Music: Richard Addinsell.

With: Ralph Richardson, Edna Best, Ann Todd, Edmund Gwenn, John Clements, Marie Lohr, Milton Rosmer, Glynnis Johns, Herbert Lomas, Lewis Casson, Edward Lexy, Jean Cadell, Peggy Novak, Josephine Wilson, Laura Smithson, Florence Gregson, Joan Ellum, Arthur Hambling, Gus McNaughton, Skelton Knaggs, Ralph Truman, Felix Aylmer.

Certain films, in retrospect, quite transcend their narrative, artistic and entertainment values to become invaluable, if unwitting, mirrors to attitudes of their times, and *South Riding* is such a film —especially as one can find equally representative films from other countries. In 1937, the war scare was beginning its inexorable buildup. In France, Jean Renoir's *La Grande Illusion* faced the threat head on, and tried vainly to oppose it on purely humanitarian grounds. In America, Frank Capra's *Lost Horizon* was a rationale for literal escape, and a justification for extending America's isolationist policy. In Britain, *South Riding* reflects a typical head-in-the-sand attitude. It totally ignores even the possibility of war, and seems to suggest that by concentrating on internal problems, the bigger external ones will somehow solve themselves and go away.

English novels of the 30s, and the movies based on them, rarely came to serious grips with the social problems of the times. The approach was usually "polite," with the rather superficial probing of housing and other problems masked by a romantic facade. The American treatment of its social problems was more dynamic, but only slightly more honest in its reliance on a melodramatic rather than a romantic framework. Only in the 1940s did both countries begin to make social essays without sugar-coating the pill: *The Grapes of Wrath* in the U.S., and *Love on the Dole* in Britain.

South Riding is one of the best and one of the

most typical of England's polite social pictures of the 30s. A big popular success, not least because of a Hollywoodian production gloss then rare in British movies, and also because of the strong literary flavor behind its romance, it had the curious effect of seeming very old-hat and dated just a few years later, when revived during the war, but of reverting to its former stature some years later. In its own way, it's as valuable a film as *The Grapes of Wrath*. The Steinbeck film is an uncompromising record of events; *South Riding*, by its very evasions and compromises, is an equally valid record of attitudes. However, perhaps I overstress its "social" label, for it is as a romance and as a drama that it holds up best. Based on an extremely popular novel by Winifred Holtby, who died prior to its release, the film was subtitled "An English landscape." But though land is important to the story, if only in a symbolic sense, it actually displays little real feeling for the land—far less certainly than in such wartime British films as *Tawny Pipit* and *A Canterbury Tale*, where the beauty of the land and the need to uphold its traditions were used as a propaganda tool and to stimulate a sense of national pride. Were it not for the huge estate and manor house, so impractical in the 30s and representing a withdrawal from the old aristocratic way of life, just as Tara did in *Gone With the Wind*, the film could tell its tale just as effectively in a London slum suburb. There were stronger *Gone With the Wind* parallels in later British films, most notably in the 1947 *Blanche Fury*. With a little more sex, *South Riding* wouldn't be too far removed from *Peyton Place* either. Surprisingly though, its more obvious parallel was not cited by reviewers at the time—perhaps out of respect for

the deceased author, and the fear that such comments might be misconstrued as accusations of plagiarism. The whole interweaving of tormented aristocrat, insane wife (incarcerated in an asylum), high-strung daughter, and frustrated romance with a sensible and wholesome young teacher is of course a blatant borrowing from Brontë's *Jane Eyre*. Since Brontë was, like Holtby, a Yorkshire-woman, it is not at all surprising that Holtby should have seen fit to draw upon her for inspiration in penning a tale of modern Yorkshire, and in any case the Gothic tradition and characters of *Jane Eyre* have long been a major influence on modern novelists—and filmmakers.

Because *South Riding* does borrow so openly, its final outcome is never too much in doubt, although the film actually takes more from Brontë than the book did. In the novel of *South Riding*, the character that derives from Mr. Rochester does ultimately commit suicide, making it look like an accident, in order that his insurance money will continue to provide for his daughter's education. The film leads up to that point, but manages to avert tragedy, and arrive at an extremely dramatic and satisfying (if somewhat improbable) climax in which political corruption is punished, social reform achieved, and the romantic alliance between squire and schoolteacher not only bespeaks happiness for them personally, but suggests a crumbling of class distinction barriers generally.

If it's a trifle too tidy in its climax, the film more than makes up for it in other ways, not least in its deft juxtaposition of Lazare Meerson's sets and much location photography (the South Riding of the title is nonexistent, and the film was shot in the

A temper tantrum by daughter Midge (Glynis Johns, on stairs) raises fears in the Squire (Ralph Richardson) that she may have inherited a streak of the insanity that has confined her mother to an asylum. At left, Marie Lohr.

Yorkshire territory known as the *West* Riding) and in the unusual accuracy of many of the geographic and other details. One Depression-affected family lives in an abandoned double-decker bus, a relatively familiar sight during Britain's Depression years, so familiar in fact that the movie doesn't take particular pains to stress it. On another occasion, a couple out joyriding in a car pass a sign that informs them that the road is "unsuitable" for traffic—a typical British understatement that means, in fact, that the road will soon disappear into a river—even in the 30s, still a fairly common transportation "inconvenience" in Britain.

Another major asset is the expert photography of Harry Stradling; in fact it was this film, and the French *La Kermesse Heroique*, that established Stradling's reputation as a cinematographer. Here the camerawork has a pleasing Hollywood professionalism to it, yet it manages to avoid the *ultra*-gloss of Stradling's Hollywood and Sam Goldwyn years. A simple love scene in a hotel lobby, framed by and photographed through palm fronds, is both romantic and yet devoid of artificiality—a virtue of course that is not wholly Stradling's, but must also be attributed to the unerring good taste of Victor Saville, one of Britain's best directors.

One unexpected asset was the inspired teaming of Ralph Richardson and Edna Best. This was Richardson's tenth film since his debut in 1933, but apart from a traditional hero role in *The Return of Bulldog Drummond* and a lesser romantic role in one of the separate stories of the omnibus film *Friday the 13th* he had been largely limited to villain and bizarre character support parts. And Edna Best, despite some good roles here and there, had hardly been used to advantage by British films; her immediately prior film had been Hitchcock's *The Man Who Knew Too Much*, three years earlier. Both of these players were taken for granted as "fixtures" in British movies, but no more. They thus seemed to arise naturally out of their environment, reasonably familiar faces, but with no star images or stereotypes to combat. Both were good-looking individuals without being strikingly handsome in a film-starry way; both too, had flawless diction and delivered good dialogue beautifully. In their own unique way, they gravitated together as naturally as Bogart and Bacall, although it would have been far more difficult to find for them a series of follow-up vehicles.

John Clements as the socialist/reformer tries to sell his ideas to the schoolteacher.

(Quite coincidentally, Ann Todd, who played Richardson's insane wife, had earlier played his romantic interest in *The Return of Bulldog Drummond*. Later they played father and daughter in *Breaking the Sound Barrier*.)

South Riding isn't the kind of film one thinks of automatically in recalling the screen's great love stories, and perhaps it isn't "great" in that sense. But it is entirely reflective of its period, and a solidly satisfying—and durable—film that deserves to be better known than it is.

Slumdwellers living in an abandoned bus; this is one of several similar scenes deleted from the American release version.

Algiers

United Artists, 1938.

Directed by John Cromwell. Produced by Walter Wanger. Screenplay by John Howard Lawson and James N. Cain from the novel *Pepe Le Moko* by Detective Ashelbe. Camera: James Wong Howe. Art Direction: Alexander Tuluboff and Wade Rubottom. Music: Vincent Scott and Mohammed Igorbouchen.

With: Charles Boyer, Hedy Lamarr, Sigrid Gurie, Joseph Calleia, Alan Hale, Gene Lockhart, Johnny Downs, Stanley Fields, Nina Koshetz, Joan Woodbury, Claudia Dell, Robert Grieg, Charles D. Brown, Ben Hall, Armand Kaliz, Walter Kingsford, Paul Harvey, Bert Roach, Luana Walters, Gino Corrado, Stanley Price.

Usually Hollywood remakes of French classics are a disaster, as witness Fritz Lang's reworking of Jean Renoir's *La Bête Humaine* and Anatole Litvak's vulgarization of *Le Jour Se Leve* as *The Long Night.* However, *Algiers*, from Julien Duvivier's *Pepe Le Moko*, is an outstanding exception. It is perhaps not coincidental that all of the three French originals just cited starred Jean Gabin. The two remakes that failed starred such essentially American actors as Glenn Ford and Henry Fonda respectively; the one success starred another Frenchman, Charles Boyer, and did *not* seek to translate and transplant the story into an American idiom and locale.

In many ways, though not all, *Algiers* might even be considered superior to its inspiration. It goes the usual Hollywood route of course; it is overproduced, too glossy perhaps, rather too full of familiar Hollywood faces that just don't seem to belong in the seedy Casbah. But emotionally it works: it becomes a kind of lush Greek tragedy which one can appreciate and enjoy as from a distance, without really believing in it or becoming too involved with its characters.

Its plot by now must be quite well known; cut down to its barest essentials, it deals with one Pepe Le Moko, refugee criminal from Paris, who reigns as a kind of uncrowned king of Algiers' Casbah section—from which the police cannot and dare not try to remove him. The only way to bring about an extradition is to tempt him out of his exile—and an opportunity arises when the police get wind of Pepe's infatuation with a beautiful tourist, who reminds him of the Paris he loves. Through a complicated series of machinations and misunderstandings, Pepe is tricked into leaving the Casbah, and

Pepe (Charles Boyer) and his under-world mistress (Sigrid Gurie).

rushes to the docks where his love is leaving on the boat for France. The blare of the ship's foghorn drowns out his shouts to her as she stands on the deck—and as the ship steams out of the harbor, Pepe commits suicide.

The two versions, seen side by side, offer a fascinating illustration in the artful shifting of emphases. The American remake was shot with a print of the original film on the set, for constant reference. Superficially, it is an *exact* copy in content, characters, continuity, editing, even the design of the sets. Much of the footage from the original film was incorporated into the remake, sometimes as back projection. And the marvels of the optical printer, plus James Wong Howe's skill as a camera-man, result in some quite remarkable effects, the climactic scenes especially being a neat amalgamation of old footage and new. As Boyer dies in the American version, the camera pans up from his body to the ship steaming away from the French version.

The original musical score is used virtually intact, though with some additions. Yet despite the incredible fidelity of the new film to the old, it is a totally different film. And most of the differences are crystallized in the two leading roles. Jean Gabin (though not yet typed as a doomed ''loser'') is tougher than Boyer, less romantic. There is slightly less tenderness in his relationship with the woman from Paris, and considerably less in his dealings

Pepe Le Moko's Casbah headquarters: in left background, Charles Boyer and Sigrid Gurie; in right foreground, Alan Hale and Stanley Fields.

The girl from Paris (Hedy Lamarr), who reminds Pepe of all that he has lost.

with other women. As a gang leader, Gabin is more ruthless and brutal. Boyer, not only playing the role in keeping with his now well-established screen image, is also forced by the Production Code to tone the character down. When he beats up an underling, it is realitvely brief, totally lacking the prolonged fury of the same scene in the original. Since "suicide in plot solution" was an absolute taboo in Hollywood films of the 30s (though the Code would occasionally turn a blind eye when it was perpetrated offscreen or ambiguously) Pepe cannot slash his wrists as he does in the French version. Instead he runs along the dock, calling after the ship, and a detective shoots him. Joseph Calleia, as the inspector in charge, and a somewhat more sympathetic character than his French counterpart, apologizes sadly. "He thought you were trying to escape," he explains. "But I *have* escaped," replies Pepe, turning the despair of the original film into a kind of sad truimph.

The differences in interpretation are even more marked in the case of the woman from Paris—played in the original by Mireille Balin, a beautiful Marlene Dietrich look-alike who was frequently cast in Dietrich–von Sternberg roles in France's many homages to Hollywood style. Balin certainly suggests the glamour, the excitement of Paris, the elegant sex that means so much to Pepe. But there's a kind of coldness too; there's no vulnerability to her, and when, believing Pepe dead, she continues on her journey as the mistress to an older man, the audience can't feel too sorry for her, as she's certainly quite capable of looking after herself.

Hedy Lamarr, on the other hand, in her first American film, at the peak of her youth and beauty —and breathtakingly photographed and lit by James Wong Howe—is more than just Pepe's ideal. Like Elizabeth Taylor in *A Place in the Sun* she becomes the unattainable ideal of everyone in the audience. There is a languid quality to her acting (quite possibly the result of inexperience, but effective nonetheless) which suggests that she has been ill-used and has given up trying; there is pain in her eyes even in her love scenes, as though she knows that happiness can never be. Reason tells us that *any* woman possessed of such stunning beauty could call all the turns herself, yet when she follows in the less explicitly spelled-out footsteps of her predecessor, taking off with the dull, boorish businessman, emotion rules out any thought of escape for her— and her plight seems perhaps even more tragic than that of Pepe. Hedy Lamarr was never a great actress, but here, a symbol as much as an individual, she had the perfect screen role for her—and was never again to get one even remotely as good.

The original *Pepe Le Moko* undoubtedly had more raw honesty, but it was so much tied to the pessimism of the French cinema of the 30s that, if not as dated as *Quai des Brume*, it does seem almost as contrived in its own way as the average Hollywood product of the day. The romanticism of *Algiers* is timeless, however; its tragedy can never move us quite the way *Of Mice and Men* does, but it will always beguile and move us with its beauty and sheer technical and artistic expertise. It has Boyer at his peak; Gene Lockhart cringing as only he could; Hedy Lamarr, obviously supremely confident of her youth and beauty, yet quite relaxed; and

146

a wonderful gallery of underworld types who behave like Fritz Lang characters as they might have been rewritten by Damon Runyon. (One wonders whether Duvivier, or the author of the original, ever saw Sam Goldwyn's 1931 *The Unholy Garden,* a Ronald Colman vehicle written by Ben Hecht and Charles MacArthur. Although not a very good film, and climaxed by an unlikely happy ending, its similarities to the Pepe Le Moko story are quite remarkable.)

Despite the excesses of back projection, a common drawback in Hollywood films of the 30s here heightened by the use of footage from the original, *Algiers* is visually a most exciting film. The camera is constantly (but purposefully) mobile, as it had been in John Cromwell's previous film *The Prisoner of Zenda* (also photographed by Howe) and has some elaborate silhouette and gauze work. In a scene that improves on the original, the camerawork even uses back projection creatively at one point. As Pepe rushes through the Casbah streets, and down the steps that lead to the sea, the images of the Paris that he is trying so desperately to escape to are superimposed in front of him, while the evocative music surges in tempo to match his own pace.

Much of the appeal of *Algiers* depends on one's mood of the moment; it is easy to be entirely capti-

Pepe dies as the steamer that would have taken him back to Paris sails away behind him. Left, Joseph Calleia as the local police inspector and, right, Sigrid Gurie.

vated by it if one is in the right emotional frame of mind. Younger audiences, on the other hand, with the pressures of modern living upon them, and oriented to the grammarless "now" movie with its passionate and often obscure personal statement, might find this bridge to the traditional old Hollywood difficult to cross.

Algiers incidentally, was later given another going-over, this time in 1948, with Tony Martin and Yvonne de Carlo—not quite as bad as one expected, but hardly to be considered as any kind of competition to this definitive 1938 version.

An informer (Gene Lockhart, left) is about to be executed by Pepe's gang.

On a visit to an island, the star finds a message he had hidden in the rocks, years ago when he was himself a struggling young actor in that little seaside community. Anna Lee, Clive Brook.

Return to Yesterday

Capad-Ealing, 1939.

Directed by Robert Stevenson. Screenplay by Stevenson, Angus MacPhail and Roland Pertwee from the play *Goodness, How Sad!* by Robert Morley. Camera: Ronald Neame. Music: Ernest Irving. Produced by Michael Balcon.

With: Clive Brook, Anna Lee, Dame May Whitty, Hartley Power, David Tree, Milton Rosmer, Olga Lindo, Garry Marsh, Arthur Margetson, Elliot Mason, O. B. Clarence, David Horne, Frank Pettingell, Wally Patch, Alf Goddard, John Turnbull, Mary Jerrold, H. F. Maltby, Ludwig Stossell, Molly Rankin, Patric Curwen, Peter Glenville.

An extremely pleasing trifle that was rather lost in the shuffle, even in England where its release coincided with the outbreak of war, *Return to Yesterday* is yet another reminder of the compact and tasteful films that Robert Stevenson directed with such regularity in his pre-Hollywood years. Its plot is little more than a vignette: a successful Hollywood star (Brook), seeking escape and relaxation, returns to the little British seaside town of his youth, and there joins up with a struggling troupe of actors. He

falls in love with the company's young ingenue, and she with him—but finally, aware of their age difference and feeling that she'll find greater happiness with the young man to whom she was formerly engaged, he pretends that his "love" is only transitory and superficial. Giving up his one chance for real happiness, he returns to what is for him the empty life of a star.

Despite its slightness, the pleasant evocation of a prewar British seaside town, the rich gallery of characters, the neat interweaving of pathos and comedy, and the theatrical yet witty dialogue all make it a thoroughly enchanting film in a minor key, with the credit due as much to the original author (Robert Morley) as to scenarist-director Stevenson. It is extremely well cast and acted, and Anna Lee (Mrs. Stevenson), a charming player, manages to keep her one occasionally irritating mannerism (a sunny smile, normally an asset, that she tended to overuse until it became artificial) well under control. Her performance here is quite one of her best. Moreover, although a few years older than the nineteen allocated to her screen character, she was at just the right age to suggest the fresh youth and

An interesting camera angle that tells its own story: seeing the reflection of the youngsters (David Tree and Anna Lee) in a dressing room mirror, the older star realizes that he is an interloper.

beauty that so enchant the Hollywood star, and at the same time the maturity to weigh the problems and accept a role as his mistress, thanks to a wife who will never divorce him.

No great dramatic heights are scaled or plumbed, but the film builds steadily in its dramatic pitch, moving from lighthearted comedy at the beginning, to the star's initial joy as he begins to recapture his youth, disillusion when he realizes how much pettiness and struggle had actually marked that earlier day, and then a genuine happiness when love finally comes. Although not an expensive film,

The star deliberately sets out to disillusion the young girl who is in love with him.

149

As he leaves the little town, en route to Hollywood, he is thanked by the company's character actress, Dame May Whitty, for his sacrifice.

it does allow for sets and locations which establish a realistic background and thus make the somewhat novelettish story more plausible. The cast helps too, particularly Dame May Whitty, as a wise old actress, and O. B. Clarence as her husband—the latter a particularly well etched portrait of an ineffectual old man who takes delight in standing up to the bullying and cheating manager, or in trying to establish himself as the social equal of his "betters," even though such efforts only result in his being rebuffed or ignored despite his courage. And when it eventually moves into the basic age-youth conflict of the final reels (and that age gap seems far less pronounced today, particularly with Brook, an exceptionally handsome fifty playing a man in his forties) the film achieves emotional effects that are quite moving.

Not the least evocative of the film's sentimental qualities is a musical score that makes good use of such traditional and plaintive English and Scottish songs as *Will Ye No Come Back Again?* and *Barbara Allen,* both dealing with a romantic but unrecapturable past.

The final scene—another British railway station farewell—is quite poignantly underplayed, and has much of the sensitivity of the final scene of Barrie's *A Kiss for Cinderella.* Approving of his "renunciation scene," Dame May Whitty tells Brook: "Thank you for doing it the David Garrick way—and I don't suppose she saw the play." And Brook, as the train steams out, taking him back to Hollywood, a new film, and a loveless future, calls to her: "Give her my love—but only when she can't hear you."

150

Love Affair

RKO Radio, 1939.

Produced and Directed by Leo McCarey. Screenplay by Donald Ogden Stewart from a story by Leo McCarey and Mildred Cram. Camera, Rudolph Mate. Editors: Edward Dmytryk and George Hively. Music: Roy Webb.

With: Charles Boyer, Irene Dunne, Maria Ouspenskaya, Lee Bowman, Maurice Moscovitch, Astrid Allwyn, Scotty Beckett, Joan Leslie, Tom Dugan, Frank McGlynn, Sr.

Although the film itself is a total Cinderella fable fully in keeping with the morality of the Production Code that so dominated Hollywood in the late 30s, the title *is* a little surprising since its connotation, at the time, was suggestive of something slightly illicit. Doubtless RKO gambled on the well-established images of the stars, and on the kind of reviews it was bound to get (and did) to offset any possible misinterpretation.

In a kind of happy reversal of the *One Way Passage* situation, Michael (Charles Boyer) and Terry (Irene Dunne) meet aboard ship and a casual flirtation develops into something much deeper.

Since both are engaged to marry (and in both cases for affection plus money, not for real love) they agree to meet in six months, atop the Empire State Building, when they feel they will have had enough time to analyze their feelings—and test their love through absence. In the intervening months, Michael goes to work as a sign painter, while Terry encounters somewhat unexpected success as a nightclub singer. On their separate ways to their rendezvous, however, Terry is struck down by a car—and seemingly crippled for life. When she doesn't appear, Michael, after waiting for hours, assumes she has decided to go through with her former marriage. Later, they do meet by chance, and Michael's opinion is confirmed. Then, by a combination of chance and coincidence, he learns the truth, and they are reunited.

The story is the least important part of *Love Affair.* What matters far more is the deft way that Leo McCarey (with superb collaboration from his two stars) keeps it all bowling along merrily within the structure of a comedy, yet constantly pulls drama and pathos from thin air. Little gems of comedy, often totally unrelated to the basic storyline, constantly act as punctuation and prevent the honest sentiment from ever becoming sticky—though there are one or two very narrow escapes, as in the scenes where the crippled Terry gives singing lessons at an orphanage, "Wishing" being the song she falls back on most. (Hollywood has always had a kind of cheerful sadism about such things; one recalls the inmates of the insane asylum in *The Snake Pit* joining in a rousing rendition of "Going Home"!)

Love Affair in some ways finds itself in parallel circumstances to *Berkeley Square*. It was extremely well received at the time of its release, garnered rave reviews on its premiere at Radio City Music Hall, and did exceptionally well in England. It has had no TV release or theatrical reissue, and its reputation was further heightened by a 1957 remake, *An Affair to Remember*. Too wide (in Cinema-Scope) and much too long, it was still a warm and charming film. Leo McCarey again directed, retaining many of the virtues of the original (except brevity), and in Cary Grant and Deborah Kerr had entirely worthy successors to Boyer and Dunne. However, unlike *Berkeley Square*, *Love Affair* not

only retains its initial qualities, but because it was always a good film, seems to have increased them through the years.

At the time, its warmth, sincerity and charm—to say nothing of its overall elegance—were its mainstays. But it is so firmly entrenched in the Hollywood tradition of the late 30s—resolutely turning its back on the Depression and reflecting that time when going to Europe on a luxury liner was a normal pastime for the rich and a once-in-a-lifetime means of escape and possible romance for the not-so-rich—that today it takes on an added sociohistorical dimension as well. It's purely a trifle, and perhaps works so well because it never tries to be more than that. The opening is gay and witty, perfectly exemplified by the montage of international radio broadcasts in which newscasters announce the coming marriage of Michael. The crusty old British announcer, nattily attired in dress suit and monocle, recites the story as the major news event of the day, followed by a long silence as he shuffles through a sheaf of notes looking for some other story worth relaying. Finding none, he signs off lamely but still cheerfully with "Well, that seems to

Despite its posed look, this *is* a scene from the film—an elegant bit of comedy business where potential lovers Irene Dunne and Charles Boyer try to create the impression that they are not together.

152

be all. Goodnight!'' Considering the upheaval that Europe was in at the time, and the horror stories converging from all sides, that little scene in itself sets the tone of the solidly escapist romance that follows.

In terms of film technique *Love Affair* is a strange mixture. From its opening titles—a gift box being opened, and layers of tissues removed to reveal the titles, embossed on satin, beneath—it is pictorially a sumptuous film, with Rudolph Mate's photography and RKO's battery of art directors ensuring that it remains so throughout. McCarey himself is not much of a technician, and is often clumsy in the way he arranges people, cuts between them, or sets up exits. Yet McCarey's shortcomings there are overcome by his writing skill, and the skillful way he works with his actors, and somehow that clumsiness becomes a kind of spontaneous artlessness that works very much to the film's advantage. Irene Dunne's underplayed farewell to Maria Ouspenskaya (as Michael's dying mother) is a suddenly tender and poignant moment, as it would be in life, but as such moments all too rarely are in film. McCarey, like Frank Borzage, has the knack of wring-

A farewell to Michel's grandmother, played by Maria Ouspenskaya.

Subdued moments of religion and well-controlled sentiment, such as this scene in the private chapel of Michel's home, add much to the overall warmth of the film.

153

As their ship arrives back in New York, the lovers agree to wind up their affairs and meet again in six months atop the Empire State Building.

ing real emotion from minor incidents, and never quite showing us how he did it.

Another major factor in the film's favor is the likable quality of the two losers. Life may not be very full of good losers—but neither is it full of ordinary characters who suddenly become semivillains in order to make things easier and tidier for the principals. So many Hollywood love stories introduce us to entirely decent and worthwhile characters such as Robert Cummings's fiancee in *It Started With Eve,* before the advent of Deanna Durbin, or Lyn Bari as John Payne's fiancee in *Sun Valley Serenade* before Sonja Henie comes along to quite ruthlessly steal him away. Then, in order to make the hero sympathetically available to the star and heroine, the scenario quite arbitrarily distorts the fiancee into a scheming shrew. In the unreal but very civilized world of *Love Affair,* Lee Bowman remains very appealing in the kind of role that would normally turn Ralph Bellamy into a buffoon, while as his feminine counterpart, even Hollywood's supreme (on film!) bitch Astrid Allwyn is sensible and likable, and the corn and near-syrup pay off because the sensitivity outweighs the obviousness.

Love Affair doesn't display great passion, and apart from those orphanage scenes, is almost British in its subtle restraint. The greatest compliment one can pay it is that if this survey were limited to ten films, it would still incontestably be among them!

Injured in an accident en route to their meeting, Irene Dunne drops out of sight to work at an orphanage—with a happy ending all the more welcome for its delays.

First Love

Universal, 1939.

Directed by Henry Koster. Produced by Joe Pasternak. Screenplay by Bruce Manning and Lionel Houser. Musical Director: Charles Previn, with orchestrations by Frank Skinner. Camera: Joseph Valentine.

With: Deanna Durbin, Robert Stack, Helen Parrish, Eugene Pallette, Leatrice Joy, Lewis Howard, Marcia Mae Jones, June Storey, Frank Jenks, Kathleen Howard, Peggy Moran, Thurston Hall, Samuel S. Hinds, Doris Lloyd, Charles Coleman, Jack Mulhall, Mary Treen, Dorothy Vaughn, Lucille Ward.

Although perhaps a trifle formularized, and lacking the genuine freshness of the very first Deanna Durbin vehicles, *First Love* is still

"vintage" Durbin. The Durbin career* is rather neatly split into two halves. The first ten films—all produced by Joe Pasternak and directed by a handful of particularly felicitous directors headed by Henry Koster, Norman Taurog and William Seiter —were beautifully designed to showcase the unique Durbin personality, and to provide the "family entertainment" dictated both by the box office and by the Production Code strictures of the period. On all counts, and with understandable though relatively minor fluctuations in quality, these ten films delivered the goods admirably—a remarkable series of

*For a complete survey of all the Durbin films and their ingredients, reference can be made to the author's "The Career of Deanna Durbin" in the November 1976 issue of *Films in Review.*

Boy meets girl: Robert Stack (left) was invariably interested in horses or automobiles, so Deanna had to be a good ''pal'' with like interests before the romantic element took over.

films cut to a pre-established formula pattern, and yet still seeming quite spontaneous as well as gay and charming, funny and musical. The second eleven films—admittedly increasingly difficult to produce, with Deanna maturing so rapidly and thus presenting both script and ''formula'' problems, were far less successful. The elements of charm contributed by the Pasternak–Koster team were less evident, and with an occasional highspot, the Durbin films did spiral downwards.

One or two critics in 1939 tended to sneer at *First Love* for being little more than a Cinderella story—but they missed the point, for the film is a *deliberate* (and subtle) modernization of Cinderella, complete with single slipper abandoned at the height of the ball as the clock strikes midnight, and the abusive ugly sisters magnificently compressed into one supremely bitchy in-law, well played (against type) by Helen Parrish, who had only just played Deanna's sister in *Three Smart Girls Grow Up*.

First Love, like all of the *best* Durbins, directed by Henry Koster, a filmmaker who always seemed to combine those rare (in one man) qualities of craftsmanship, charm and good taste, was the film that finally allowed Deanna to grow up. It was much publicized at the time for giving her her first screen kiss—from Robert Stack. Although a good gimmick, it was also a rather saddening reminder that Deanna had to grow up, and accordingly the film

A final song from Deanna Durbin to fellow students before graduating; the particularly attractive young lady leaning on the piano is Peggy Moran, soon to be the wife of the director.

156

Henry Koster, right, director of the best of the early Durbin vehicles; in rear, assistant director Frank Shaw.

either seriously or realistically, Universal was nevertheless canny enough to realize that Depression-era audiences might find it a little hard to sympathize with a girl who seemed surrounded by luxury, as Deanna invariably was. But though affected *by* society, she was only rarely *of* it; she usually won over (or defeated) the rich snobs, and had a much closer relationship (especially in *First Love*) with the hired help—butlers, cooks, chauffeurs.

Although, as its title implies, not dealing with *great* love, the romantic elements of the film are so deftly handled by director Koster that they are often extremely touching. Particularly effective is a scene (that could so easily have been nawkish in other hands) wherein a disillusioned Durbin goes back to her old school, wanting to bury herself in work and become a teacher, and is talked out of it by Kathleen Howard (the old curmudgeon who was W. C. Fields's wife in *It's a Gift*), who tells her that *that* was the mistake *she* made. It's a beautifully underplayed scene that has surprising emotional depth.

was received with some reservations. This is a pity since today the film can be seen as perhaps the *definitive* Durbin vehicle, combining the pleasing naiveté of the earlier ones with the sophisticated charm of those immediately coming up. (It was # 6 in that magical first ten grouping.) Both as entertainment on its own level, and as a mirror to the innocence of the day (it was a prewar film by the skin of its teeth) it holds up beautifully today, and seldom was Durbin to be the beneficiary of such sumptuous settings and elegant decor. The old *Phantom of the Opera* set was re-dressed and given added splendor for the ballroom scene, and Joseph Valentine's camerawork gleamed. Moreover, the "pain" of Deanna's growing up was considerably lessened by the fact that she had grown into an unusually beautiful young lady. Moreover, she had made considerable strides as an actress, and her superb singing voice seemed to be taking on a new richness.

Not content merely to pillage Cinderella, Universal did a lot of borrowing from their own folklore. Eugene Pallette virtually repeated his *My Man Godfrey* role and performance, and daughter Parrish getting her comeuppance at his hands was one of the film's highlights.

Although *First Love* was not meant to be taken

Cinderella meets her Prince Charming at the ball.

A graphic contrast: certainly no remake, and a considerably less innocent FIRST LOVE from the seventies, with William Katt and Susan Dey.

It's interesting—and perhaps a sign of the film's maturity—that it is on Kathleen Howard that the film in fact closes. All of the earlier Durbins had climaxed on a radiant closeup of Deanna beaming or singing, an image of absolute happiness. Here, however, though Deanna's romantic problem is neatly solved, she is almost unceremoniously pushed off-screen, with neither closeup nor embrace. It is on a strangely touching closeup of Kathleen Howard, barely able to control her emotions over the happiness of *others*, that the film fades out. Such subtleties abound in *First Love*, not least in the way it drags its Cinderella construction out into the open and *exploits* it (Deanna is told that she will be escorted to the ball by six white mice—which turn out to be six uniformed motor cycle police-men!) as opposed to the earlier films which glossed over the Cinderella undercurrents and probably hoped that audiences wouldn't recognize them.

What is particularly surprising about *First Love* is that it is also an outstanding comedy. The Durbins were always intended to amuse, but it is doubtful if Pasternak and Koster, back in 1939, could have anticipated the gales of joyous laughter that greet the film today. There is the same kind of mathematical formula involved in the film's laughter quotient as in its charm—and it creates the same illusion of total spontaneity, as well as catering totally to audience hopes and expectations. Unsympathetic or pompous characters are magnificently set up to be deflated, both by situations and by sparkling one-liners. Lewis Howard spends most of the film in a lethargic stupor, every nuance, gesture and lazily delivered line of dialogue exactly on target. He tops it all with a beautifully delivered speech on his theory of energy conservation—that perpetual inertia *stores up* energy for times of crisis—and *this* comic highlight is topped when his father (Eugene Pallette), finally driven to despair, boots him across the room and through the French windows. While comedy one-liners have a way of dating, in *First Love,* if anything, they get funnier. Sometimes by accident they take on a new topicality. Charles Coleman, the butler who becomes Deanna's Fairy Godmother, is asked by her why he is always so serious, and he replies that "Gay butlers are *extremely* rare!" It's hard to pinpoint the exact magic that makes *First Love* such an entrancing and endearing film, but whatever that magic is, it seems to replenish and double itself every few years.

In terms of movie chronology, *First Love* is useful too; it could hardly be further apart in content, morality and style from a 1970s *First Love* in which Susan Dey (a nonsinging contemporary equivalent to Durbin) enjoys a *dual* first love, living with both an older man and a fellow college student, playing much of the film in the nude, and chattering endlessly and explicitly about the anatomical characteristics of lovemaking! Even though it was glossily and dreamily lit, and photographed in color like a TV perfume commercial, it never once suggested the joy—and pain—of first love as did the Durbin film, which probably had no such intentions either, but found that kind of honesty somehow just came naturally.

The Forties

John Wayne and Marlene Dietrich livened up the early forties in a trio of romantic adventures at Universal; this is the first, 1940's SEVEN SINNERS.

The second version of BACK STREET (1940) with Charles Boyer and Margaret Sullavan.

Few ten-year spans have encompassed as many dramatic events and sweeping changes in lifestyles as the 40s, a decade already fragmented (in America at least) into three sections prewar, wartime, and postwar.

In Hollywood, 1939 saw the beginning of the change. Movie audiences were clearly beginning to tire of the innocent Never-Never Land imposed on it by the Production Code in 1934. Even before war became an unavoidable reality, Hollywood was trying to get back to the gutsier fare of an earlier day. 1939 saw restoration of the Horror and Gangster cycles, and the transference of the love story from lighthearted, often semicomic romance to a return to the more full-blooded emotional fare of *When Tomorrow Comes, A Letter of Introduction, Dark Victory* and *The Rains Came.*

Although America assumed it could avoid involvement in any coming war, still it sensed that war was inevitable. This meant not only that the face of Europe would change, but that Europe would be lost to America as a market for Hollywood films. The gay, carefree romances, comedies, and light dramas set in a prewar Riviera milieu—films like *Bluebeard's Eighth Wife* and *I Was An Adventuress*—began to disappear just as that world itself would soon disappear. Forced to deal with themes that were both more American and more contemporary, Hollywood grew up quickly—or, to be fair, reverted to a maturity and sophistication it had been forced to abandon during the later part of the thirties.

Once involved in the war, the impact on Hollywood was felt in all areas of production, and certainly not least in the love story, which fed on both the emotionalism and the patriotism of the period to produce such films as *Remember the Day, Since You Went Away* (both with Claudette Colbert), *The*

161

Preston Sturges' THE LADY EVE (1941) managed to be not only a zany screwball comedy spoofing classic romance, but also a pretty good romantic story on its own terms, beautifully team-acted by Henry Fonda and Barbara Stanwyck.

Clock, an unusually sensitive story of a wartime romance with Judy Garland, *One Foot in Heaven* (unrelated to the war, but one of many films stressing the values for which the war was being fought) and, in a totally different vein, drawing romanticism out of the war, *Casablanca.* Many of the films of this period were of course spurious and dishonest, unable to survive past the emotionalism of the moment. Yet oddly enough, some of the most

touching material can be found in some of the worst and most dated 40s films.

Stage Door Canteen, released early in 1943, was one of many propagandist, morale-boosting all-star revues through which the entertainment industry patted itself on the back for the valuable job it was doing. Even in its day, its acts and turns seemed mediocre, the hobnobbing between theatrical greats and humble servicemen both condescend-

A subsequent romantic comedy by Sturges even topped *The Lady Eve*; Veronica Lake and Joel McCrea in SULLI-VAN'S TRAVELS (1941).

PENNY SERENADE (1941): Cary Grant and Irene Dunne in a funny and often very moving, if overlong, story of the tribulations of a young married couple.

ing and embarrassing. Only slightly more stomach-turning than a scene of an unconvincingly accented British sailor murmuring "Just like Christmas, ain't it?" after being given an orange by Katharine Cornell, was the unlikely spectacle of thousands of servicemen standing reverently with bowed heads while Gracie Fields sang *The Lord's Prayer*, and then immediately launching into a spirited ditty about killing Japs! Linking this farrago—and designed as no more than a link—was a simple little love story about three soldiers finding romance with three canteen girls. The footage devoted to this story was minimal, probably no more than a fifth of the entire running time, yet somehow director Frank Borzage—the maestro from *Seventh Heaven* and *A Farewell to Arms*—worked his old magic.

BLOOD AND SAND (1941) was a pretty turgid story, but its dynamic use of color by director Rouben Mamoulian and the torrid playing of Rita Hayworth and Tyrone Power made it work.

SMILING THROUGH (1941) was an overproduced remake of the old tear-jerker, with the Frank Borzage directorial magic pulling it off despite its often maudlin qualities; Brian Aherne and Jeanette MacDonald.

163

One of the most popular and long-running romances in the late thirties and early forties was that of Dr. Kildare (Lew Ayres) and his nurse, Mary (Laraine Day)—whom MGM finally had to kill off in a traffic accident, just before her wedding, in order to pave the way for plot and character changes in the series.

FELICIE NANTEUIL (1942): Two up-and-coming French players, Micheline Presle and Louis Jourdan, both of whom would be working in Hollywood after the war.

Sentimental, corny, obvious though it may have been, this part of the film worked superbly well. The men playing the soldiers were all young new faces—Lon McAllister, Bill Terry, and western-star-to-be Sunset Carson, not yet using that name—while Marjorie Riordan stood out among the three girls for her simple, direct, naturalistic quality. Few American movies captured the spirit of wartime romance as effectively or as emotionally as this segment of *Stage Door Canteen*, and the cunning use of the song "Don't Ever Say Goodnight" as a romantic motif was almost inspired. Of all the "big name" entertainment in the film, only a couple of the Big Band specialties (Benny Goodman's in particular) really impress, and of course the bands were an integral part of the wartime scene. If one could cut most of the "acts" and *all* of the propaganda (especially Sam Jaffe's emotional and flag-waving introduction of a Russian sniper!) and somehow build up the story element, one might have quite a picture. Even as it is, those story elements do represent some of the most affecting moments that Hollywood produced on wartime love.

RANDOM HARVEST (1942): An obvious but tastefully and meticulously produced tear-jerker with Ronald Colman and Greer Garson.

THIS ABOVE ALL (1942): WAAF on leave (Joan Fontaine) and deserter Tyrone Power begin a wartime idyll.

Dialogue makes it abundantly clear that their great love does not include sharing a room. . . .

. . . and a last-minute marriage by Arthur Shields pacifies the Production Code.

More Code restrictions and concern about its political content removed most of the literary guts from Ernest Hemingway's FOR WHOM THE BELL TOLLS (1943) but left it as an interesting romantic vehicle for Ingrid Bergman and Gary Cooper.

The very climate of World War II—separations, disrupted families, sudden marriages, death —was conducive to the contemporary love story. However, romantic and patriotic fervor rarely go hand in hand with a sense of perspective. Just as the very best films about World War I—in varying ways, *All Quiet on the Western Front*, *A Farewell to Arms* and *Paths of Glory*—came well after the war (in fact, the last-named and best came well after World War II)—so the best and most honest of the World War II love stories, such as *The Americanization of Emily* (1964), only appeared many years later.*

While many of the World War II romances, often beautifully produced, had an extremely strong emotional impact at the time, they have dated rather badly because of a basic dishonesty which, if not exactly unnoticed at the time, was nevertheless accepted as a condition of moviemaking under the restrictions of the Production Code. A typical case in point is the Tyrone Power–Joan Fontaine movie, *This Above All* (1942), directed by Anatole Litvak from the Eric Knight novel. Handsomely produced, its many studio "exteriors" less jarring then than now, it tried hard to be more than "just" the love story of a deserter from the army and a sheltered society girl enjoying her first real freedom as a member of the women's forces. The novel made much of the social upheaval that came

*Certain World War II movies, most specifically the British *Millions Like Us*, were honest mirrors of their time. But they were essentially documentarian in flavor, and while they sometimes contained romantic elements, they could not accurately be classified as "love stories."

LOVE STORY (1944) was a big boxoffice morale booster in wartime Britain. Margaret Lockwood was a dying pianist who falls in love with Stewart Granger, RAF pilot going blind.

with the war, and the apparent abolition of class distinctions—or at least, the idealistic need for such an abolition—and to its credit, the movie didn't sidestep these issues. On the other hand, the couple were obviously drawn together initially by pure physical attraction, if not downright lust. Love came later. The movie has the heroine turning her back on family and social obligations and, on her first leave, rushing off to a seaside rendezvous with her soldier—where they chastely occupy separate rooms, and do no more than share platonic walks along the seafront. Since moral values underwent a tremendous shift during those war years, and people in their position would "live for the moment" without considering their actions immoral, this whitewashed quality struck an immediately artificial note, a note underlined by dialogue obviously included at Production Code insistence. When a soldier friend (Thomas Mitchell) calls on Power, Joan Fontaine is at pains to stress that they have separate rooms. Later, in an emotional outburst, she insists: "We've done NOTHING to be ashamed of!" (Poor Miss Fontaine was doomed to unconsummated love affairs during the 40s: she was given the same identical line of dialogue to purify her long association with pirate Arturo de Cordova in *Frenchman's Creek*.)

In the original novel on which *This Above All* is

Another far less pretentious but thoroughly pleasing British wartime romance—this time with more emphasis on comedy—was DON'T TAKE IT TO HEART (1944), starring husband-and-wife team Richard Greene and Patricia Medina.

Wartime movies saw the emergence of the boy-and-girl-next-door romantic team. Van Johnson and Phyllis Thaxter in THIRTY SECONDS OVER TOKYO (1944).

Although essentially a war action movie and a good one, John Ford's THEY WERE EXPENDABLE (1945) included a brief, touching, and unresolved front-line romance: John Wayne and Donna Reed.

based, the Fontaine character had entered into a sexual liaison with the hero from the beginning. At the novel's end, the hero dies, and the pregnant heroine is looking forward proudly to unwed motherhood. The film cops out rather spectacularly here; the seriously wounded Power may live or die (though the script angles towards an optimistic interpretation), but there is no doubt at all about the heroine's status. Still entirely pure, she nevertheless is married to Power before there is any chance of his expiring!

Coupled with such basic dishonesties are rather surprising lapses into inaccuracy of detail. At one point, the heroine decides to buy her boyfriend a dressing gown to greet him when he awakens, and going out early in the morning, accomplishes her mission. Quite apart from the fact that clothing was severely rationed, and that as a member of the forces she probably wouldn't have had sufficient spare ration coupons to buy a dressing gown in the first place, the chance of finding a clothing store open before breakfast in a tiny seaside resort, would be virtually nil. It's a minor point in itself, but a point that would not be lost on wartime British audiences. Lapses such as that (and there were others), combined with the Hollywood-dictated morality, do tend to make *This Above All* seem unreal today, a mirror not of its time but of Hollywood's

enforced attitude to those times. As such it has more value to the social historian than to the romantic devotee of great love stories. And it's a pity, because in many ways Hollywood made these films extremely well. The sense of urgency, the fervor of emotion, was somehow communicated even by directors six thousand miles from the scene of their

167

PERFECT STRANGERS (1945), known in the U.S. as *Vacation from Marriage*, was another unusual wartime romance about a drab married couple who find themselves revitalized through the separations and dangers of war; superbly acted by Robert Donat and Deborah Kerr

James Mason and Margaret Lockwood made a popular British team in often quite torrid period romances and melodramas. WICKED LADY (1945), if not the best, was the most profitable— and the one most severely mauled by U.S. censors.

story. *This Above All* has many touching moments, the best of them when it is on the safer censorial ground of dealing with love of country rather than with physical love. Joan Fontaine's little speech about *why* she loves England and what the country means to her is beautifully done, the formal structure of the words quite overcome by the sincerity and seeming spontaneity of her delivery.

With most of Hollywood's big male stars either in the armed forces or concentrating on war films, a major void presented itself. America was adopting the moviegoing habit as never before, and many of the wartime entertainment-seekers were women— either separated from their men or working alongside them. They were ripe for rich emotional entertainment, and with most of the male stars unavailable, the women took over. Vehicles designed for stars like Bette Davis, Greer Garson, Olivia de Havilland and Barbara Stanwyck brought the stylish soap opera to a new level of elegance and box-office importance. Even pin-up queen Rita Hayworth, in films like *Tonight and Every Night*, was part of this emotional renaissance, and virtually performed solo in that film, without the benefit of a male co-star (Glenn Ford or Gene Kelly) of equal magnitude. Helping the women to dominate the screen was the emergence of a new wartime phenomenon—the shy, guileless "boy next door" type

as exemplified by Robert Walker and Van Johnson, big at the box office perhaps, but in terms of screen presence, no match for the female superstars they played opposite.

One additional and perhaps accidental assist to the Hollywood love story of the period was the paring of budgets, the rationing of gasoline, and the concentration on studio shooting as opposed to location shooting. This meant a wholesale return to atmospheric and evocative if not always convincing Hollywood sets. MGM in particular created some stunningly picturesque sets for its big love stories such as *The White Cliffs of Dover* and *Random Harvest*.

In Britain, the war had a rather different effect on the love story. Initially, as Britain settled down to an all-out war effort, virtually every film—even if not a war film per se—reflected a war-oriented milieu. Period stories disappeared totally, not only because they were expensive (a major consideration in the early days of the war, when films could count on only the home market, and when costly sets were a risk, since they could be obliterated in bombing raids) but because they would seem trivial in the face of the realities of war. Too, filmmaking was becoming so increasingly influenced by documentary styles—documentaries now came into their own for training and informational as well as propagandist purposes, and were shown widely— that all films were taking on a realistic, underplayed look. Film stories deliberately played down romance, taking the attitude that love and marriage should wait until after the war—or, if it was permitted, as in a documentarylike film such as *Millions Like Us*, then at least it should take second place to the demands of war. By 1943, however, the public desperately needed escapism in its movie entertainment, and was proving it by flocking to the Hollywood films of Esther Williams and Bob Hope. Taking the hint, British production tentatively explored an ambitious costume love story with *The Man in Grey*. Based on a popular period romantic novel by Lady Eleanor Smith, it even stressed its determination to be escapist by setting its opening (and its epilogue) in contemporary wartime London, but telling its basic story in flashback. It was an overwhelming success—as much because of the need for such a film as on its own individual merits. Its four stars—James Mason, Margaret Lockwood, Phyllis Calvert and Stewart Granger—were immediately launched on big romantic star careers (soon to be joined by Patricia Roc and Dennis Price), and while they appeared in various combinations thereafter, no subsequent film ever had the temerity to co-star all four at one time! Mason's role in *The Man in Grey* established a unique blend of romantic fascination with sadism which was to continue to dominate most of his British films. In this film, he beats his mistress to death with a riding crop, while in his Svengali-like role in *The Seventh Veil*, he created the most famous piece of romantic savagery since Cagney pushed the grapefruit into Mae Clarke's face, by smashing his cane down upon Ann Todd's hands as she plays the piano—thereby destroying her career as a pianist, but somehow automatically ensuring his ultimately happy union with her.

Another *film noir* about sex rather than romance: the powerful THE POSTMAN ALWAYS RINGS TWICE with Lana Turner and John Garfield, released in 1946.

CHRISTMAS HOLIDAY (1945): An unusual entry in the prolific group of *film noir* melodramas, this somewhat white-washed version of a strong Somerset Maugham story cast Deanna Durbin as the young wife of a hoodlum and killer, played by Gene Kelly. It was very much of a love story despite the grim theme and was surprisingly well acted by Durbin.

169

Yet another *noir* entry, with the violent and masochistic, but nonetheless genuine, love of Joan Bennett for Dan Duryea as one of its strong plot elements. 1946's SCARLET STREET, directed by Fritz Lang.

Film noir in the Old West—and in color. DUEL IN THE SUN (1946) with Joseph Cotten loving Jennifer Jones, and Gregory Peck merely lusting after her.

In THE BEST YEARS OF OUR LIVES (1946) the problems of the reestablishment of family life after the war were discussed. Left:

Harold Russell and Cathy O'Donnell; right, Fredric March and Myrna Loy.

The success of *The Man in Grey* spawned a whole series of period romances, none of them needing the excuse of a contemporary flashback framework. They are an interesting group, extending into the early 1950s, varied in style, encompassing tongue-in-cheek melodrama (*Caravan*) as well as deadly serious if somewhat class-conscious romantic drama (*Fanny by Gaslight*), and including a number of films done in Technicolor. Interweaving with the film noir cycle towards the end of the 40s, they became progressively better as films, but sadly, increasingly less profitable. Their escapist approach, especially during the war years, quite certainly extended to their treatment of women. Al-

though during the war years in Britain women had certainly achieved—and earned—a greater sense of equality than ever before, these period romances maintained the attitudes of old. The women in them were wholly innocent and virginal, or wholly evil—but in either state, decidedly subservient to the male. When, in *The Man in Grey*, Phyllis Calvert complains to Stewart Granger that she cannot bear a year's enforced separation from him, he chides her sternly with the comment, "If you're to become my wife, you must learn to obey me"!

With the end of the war, there was a big upswing in love stories in British cinema. It was as though emotions that had been held in check by the

MARGIE (1946): Jeanne Crain in one of the loveliest of forties films. It was also one of the most romantic, though its love was directed mainly at a bygone period.

Jane Wyatt rivalled Myrna Loy as the perfect movie wife in picture after picture, though too often her role was as a stable anchor rather than as a romantic ideal. Nevertheless, her beauty, grace and intelligence made such roles stand out far beyond the often brief limits of their footage. With Dana Andrews in BOOM-ERANG (1947).

war were now being released as a catharsis. Moreover, it was a kind of therapy to pause briefly and pat oneself on the back for a job well done—as *The Way To the Stars* and *Brief Encounter* did—before returning to a life that was still difficult and austerity-laden. The love stories in those two films might well seem models of typical British decorum and restraint to non-British eyes, but by British standards they almost wallowed in sentiment and affirmed both the importance of love and the nobility of its denial.

Hollywood, with its big stars back in the fold, had no intention of losing the huge new audience it had built up during the war years—although of course it ultimately did, to television. But initially it tried to maintain the momentum it had achieved, both by continuing to use big female stars like Joan Crawford in elaborate emotional vehicles, and—despite the still fairly rigid structures of the Production Code—by striving for a continued and increased maturity of content.

There were changes elsewhere in the world too. Sweden entered into a stimulating period of renaissance, and France—perhaps the one country in the world whose intellectuals and poets have been instinctively attracted to and accommodated by film—likewise stimulated us with films from works by Jean Cocteau and Jean-Paul Sartre.

All told, the 40s was to be one of the most satisfying periods in all film history. Despite the initial problems caused by the war, it was a period

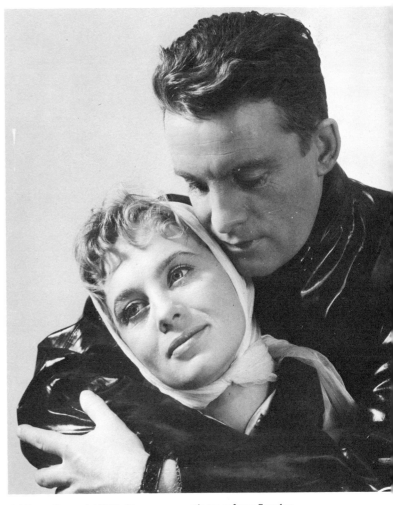

Mai Zetterling and Alf Kjellin, new romantic team from Sweden, seen in such outstanding forties films as IRIS and TORMENT.

171

TASK FORCE (1949): One of the better retrospective looks at the war, with Jane Wyatt again the perfect wife—to Gary Cooper.

ADAM'S RIB (1949): Spencer Tracy and Katharine Hepburn in one of their battle-of-the-sexes comedies.

THEY LIVE BY NIGHT (1948): Story of a doomed romance; another powerful *film noir*; with Cathy O'Donnell and Farley Granger.

in which the audiences created for film were so large that commercial risks were lessened. A lot of mediocre junk made money merely because there was an audience—but a lot of praiseworthy and mature and offbeat material was offered because of that same audience. Perhaps the basic honesty of many of the love stories produced, and the lyricism or poetry of others (Britain's *I Know Where I'm Going*, France's *Sylvia and the Phantom* and *Le Diable au Corps*) are the qualities that most endure. Honesty is not quite the same thing as realism. In the 50s, realism, or an attempt at realism, came to be regarded as increasingly important and necessary in a commercial sense—and the image of Love in Film began to change again, and change drastically.

Beulah Bondi, Fred MacMurray, Barbara Stanwyck, and
Elizabeth Patterson.

Remember the Night

Paramount, 1940.

Produced and directed by Mitchell Leisen. Screen-
play by Preson Sturges. Camera: Ted Tetzlaff.
Music: Frederick Hollander. Art Directors: Hans
Dreier and Roland Anderson.

With: Barbara Stanwyck, Fred MacMurray, Beulah
Bondi, Elizabeth Patterson, Sterling Holloway,
Willard Robertson, Charles Waldron, Paul Guil-
foyle, Charles Arnt, John Wray, Thomas Ross,
Snowflake, Tom Kennedy, Georgia Cane, Virginia
Brissac, Spencer Charters.

Most people who saw *Remember the Night* recall it
fondly, yet never remember the title, perhaps because of a plethora of similar titles (*Remember?,
Remember Last Night?, Remember the Day* and
many others). Yet as soon as one describes the plot,
memory—and affection—return immediately. It's
the tale of a down-on-her-luck girl, in court on a
shoplifting charge. It's just before Christmas, and
in order to get the case disposed of quickly, the
prosecuting attorney finds a legal technicality to

have the hearing delayed until after the holidays.
He wants to get away early—and doesn't feel that
he has been unduly harsh on the girl since she'll at
least be fed, and have a place to stay (albeit in jail)
over the holidays. Circumstances cause her to be
paroled in his care however, and since he's going tp
spend Christmas with his family he agrees to drop
her off at *her* mother's home, which is on the way,
and collect her on the way back. The mother, however, is a bitter harridan who feels disgraced by her
daughter, and rejects her. The attorney, now feeling much warmer to the girl, whom he previously
regarded only as an imposition, decides to take her
along to spend Christmas with his folks. They fall in
love, despite the girl's fear that it cannot work. Ultimately, although she had at one time thought of
skipping out, she decides to return to New York to
face her trial and sentence—and then face a happy
future.

This storyline of course is the merest of bare
bones, and it is the meat of those bones that gives
this film its delicate charm and warmth. A great deal

Barbara Stanwyck and Joel McCrea.

of the credit must inevitably go to screenwriter Preston Sturges (on the verge of becoming a director himself). In some ways it is a typical Sturges film, skillfully interweaving drama, pathos and wildly zany comedy as only he could, throwing in a gag every time the sentiment threatens to get sticky, or returning to reality and a hint of sadness every time a particularly good comedy sequence seems about to upset the balance and turn the film from a love story into something far more lightweight. This ability to change horses in midstream—dynamically, yet without a jolt—was a talent almost unique

to Sturges. Other directors, like Arthur Penn, pulled it off occasionally, but never with Sturges's consistent skill. Reportedly the original script was much too long and had to be drastically cut during shooting. But the gaps don't show, and the highest compliment one can pay the film is that one would like a little more of everything in it.

With all due respect to Sturges's fine script, however, in this case it is very much director Leisen's film. It is very easy to downplay and minimize his whole body of work. A former art director he always seemed far more concerned with how his

174

films *looked* than in how they played. Too often, decor and sets swamped people. A film like his *Death Takes a Holiday* cried out for a dramatic stylist, wheather it be Lang or Borzage—who would have made a very different film out of it. Too often —*Midnight* (written by Brackett and Wilder) and *Easy Living* (written by Sturges) are typical examples—his films were as good as his scripts but no better, lacking the additional sparks that one suspects that their writers (and directors-to-be) could have brought to them had they been allowed to direct their own material. But Leisen was a man of taste and sophistication, and occasionally did bring off a beauty. His later *Kitty* was a remarkable film, quite one of the best of its kind, and for once decor and costumes (it was a period piece) were an important adjunct to the story, and with superb lighting and sweeping camera movements Leisen made them an integral part of his story. But *Remember the Night* is almost certainly his best film.

Preston Struges's forte, as in *Christmas in July*, was the comedy with sudden moments of warmth and humanity; Leisen's strength was in just the opposite approach, emotional material highlighted and punctuated by inventive comic moments. Leisen and Sturges *share* the highlights of this film. The magnificent comic bravura performance of Willard Robertson as Stanwyck's theatrical defense attorney (an exact opposite of the tight-lipped prosecutors and judges he usually played) is *pure* Sturges, depending only on his writing, a good character actor given his head, and a director who'll (in this instance) stand by and just record, without interfering. But on the other hand, the unexpectedly touching "End of Perfect Day" sequence (the family grouped around a fireplace, lazily and contentedly singing that song), honestly sentimental, carefully lit and composed, yet seemingly casual and spontaneous, is pulled off almost wholly by Leisen. Its appeal is both emotional and visual, al-

though Sturges's writing is cunning in the way it seems to shoot the sequence down in flames *before* it starts, almost ridiculing the sentiment and at least one of the participants.

The handling of comedy in an essentially romantic film can be very tricky. Leo McCarey's *Love 'Affair* has no really funny gags or sequences, but the odd lines of dialogue here, or the odd character there, keep it constantly amusing. *Remember the Night* has two or three sequences that would not be at all out of place in a wacky screwball comedy; they have deliberately not been described here, as the way they burst absurdly yet somehow naturally into the narrative flow is one of the joys of this film, and to discuss them would be to remove one of the film's assets, that of surprise. The film is a model of using vignettes and incidents, sometimes just details, and building them so that they help the story— and especially the characters—to grow, develop and change in ways that are both dramatically and emotionally satisfying. Even Fred MacMurray, going through his (for him, in that period) rather typecast paces, is given the chance to make his role three-dimensional, and rises well to the occasion.

Sentimental, funny and not *too* dramatic, *Remember the Night* is almost a model of how good and mature films *could* be made during a period when the strictures of the Production Code and the requirements of the box office often forced films into sterile, predictable, assembly-line channels. One can recognize certain moralities there to placate the Code, but they're subtly done. And the happy ending is muted, implicit rather than explicit. With all the "freedom" possible on the screen today, a remade *Remember the Night* (perish the thought) could never hope to equal the grace—or the maturity—of the original. It's not only Leisen's best film, but it also gave Barbara Stanwyck one of the best *roles* she ever had, and she responded in kind with one of her best performances.

Charlotte (Bette Davis) with the man she loves but cannot marry (Paul Henried), and the man who wants to marry her, but whom she does not love (John Loder).

Now, Voyager

Warner Bros., 1942.

Directed by Irving Rapper. Produced by Hal B. Wallis. Screenplay by Casey Robinson from the novel by Olive Higgins Prouty. Camera: Sol Polito. Music: Max Steiner.

With: Bette Davis, Paul Henreid, Claude Rains, Gladys Cooper, Bonita Granville, Ilka Chase, John Loder, Lee Patrick, Franklin Pangborn, Katherine Alexander, James Rennie, Mary Wickes, Janis Wilson, Michael Ames, Charles Drake, Frank Puglia, David Clyde.

There's something about the "BIG" romantic specials of the late 30s and early 40s which robs them of any lasting emotional value. Considering how many vehicles of this type Joan Crawford and Bette Davis made, it's amazing that not one of them can truly be called a classic, and it's probably that word "vehicle" that is to blame. Joan Crawford was always a star and a personality before she was an actress, and by that I don't mean to diminish her acting ability or the qualities that brought her an Academy Award for *Mildred Pierce.* But one was always aware that one was watching Crawford, and that she was something special, tough and invulner-

able. One never had any doubts about her ultimate triumph (or, in certain roles, her ultimate defeat) and it was mainly a matter of finding out *how* and *why* the happy, tragic or at least dramatic climax would come about.

Although she was far more of an actress, Bette Davis projected this same invulnerability, and a much lesser actress might actually have done rather better with many Davis roles for the simple reason that audiences might have had less confidence in *her,* and thus have been willing to sit back and watch her being buffeted by fate without any pre-convictions as to the outcome. Even the look of Warner Bros. sets in the Bette Davis movies suggested that they were just a picturesque backdrop to *her.* They might be realistic, utterly artificial, or stylized, but they *looked* like sets, isolated in huge studio stages, and with vast expanses of mood-evoking studio sky behind them. One has the feeling in the studio sets of the 20s and early 30s that realism—or at least a romantic stylization of realism—came first, that sets were erected to look solid and real, as though the characters could just move in and live there long before the movie rolled, or their stars were selected. Certainly there's a convic-

With Janis Wilson as the repressed and neurotic daughter of Paul Henried, whom she takes under her wing.

tion to the sets of *Six Hours to Live* or *Hot Saturday* which the opulent artificiality of *Now, Voyager* lacks.

This is not to suggest that *Now, Voyager* is outdated or to be approached only with the tongue in cheek. Far from it. But its emotionalism now springs more from the responses of memory that it evokes in the audience. On a filmic level, we can marvel at the sheer craftsmanship of production, the care that went into every phase of filmmaking from editing to camerawork and music. And too there's the romanticism of the Davis–Henreid teaming, the superb (if flawlessly typecast) list of supporting players, and the absolute mastery of acting technique which makes every Davis performance a joy to watch. On a personal level—if we are old enough—it evokes the combined spirit of romanticism and nostalgia which wafts us back to the days when we were younger and more naive, and responded so well to given scenes and blockbuster lines of dialogue that we have never forgotten them. There's very much of an art in this kind of filmmaking and I don't intend to demean it. Many films that are unquestionably academic classics were never capable of evoking the emotional responses of a film like *Now, Voyager,* or of being remembered so well—or so fondly.

Now, Voyager has a story that is complex and not prone to overanalysis. Combining elements of *Brief Encounter, The Enchanted Cottage* and *Back Street,* it's not as good as any of them—yet within its own particular commercial genre, must be considered more of a *success* than they were. *Now Voyager* has been selected for inclusion here not as a kind of scapegoat, as a way for saying mildly unkind things about a much-loved film, but because it is so good in its own much larger-than-life way that it is virtually a spokesman for all those related Davis films—and especially *Dark Victory, The Great Lie, Old Acquaintance* and *Deception*—which likewise might seem to have been ignored. Based on a long and rambling novel, it's storytelling in the grand old manner—a manner that, in movies at least, has long been abandoned. Doubtless it will always bring pleasure and evoke admiration for its skill. Sometimes one really has no right to expect a film to retain what was only a transitory spell dictated by current movie fashion and, in this particular case, its supply of exuberant escapist romanticism to a world involved in a grim war. Quite unwittingly, Davis's final line to Paul Henreid in the film sums up the attitude one, in all fairness, must take towards the film today: "Don't ask for the moon when we have the stars."

177

L'Eternel Retour
(The Eternal Return)

Discina, 1943.

Directed by Jean Delannoy. Written and supervised by Jean Cocteau. Produced by Andre Paulvé. Music by George Auric.

With: Jean Marais, Madeleine Sologne, Jean Murat, Yvonne de Bray, Pieral, Jean D'Yd, Junie Astor, Roland Toutain, Alexandre Rignault, Jeanne Marken.

The modern Tristan and Isolde meet when Patrice (Jean Marais) steps in to save his father's fiancee (Madeleine Sologne) from the attentions of a brute (Alexandre Rignault).

Wounded in the fight, the unconscious Patrice is carried out. This specific juxtaposition of faces was to be a recurring image in Cocteau films.

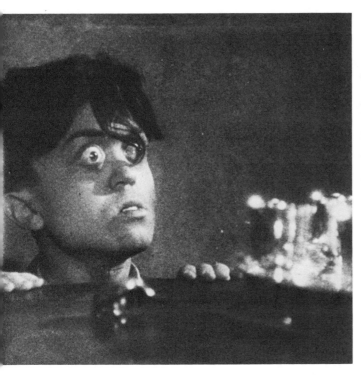

The malevolent dwarf, played by Pierral, constantly conspires against the young lovers.

Shot down while trying to see his love after a long separation, Patrice is told that she will not see him, even on his death bed. He dies moments before she arrives to join him in death.

The bodies of the two lovers are placed side by side in an old boat house which, as the camera pulls back, is transformed into a classical tomb as legend takes over totally for the fadeout.

Compositions like this constantly underscore the story's links with legend and fairy tale.

Josette Day and Jean Marais.

La Belle et la Bête
(Beauty and the Beast)

Discina, 1946.

Directed by Rene Clement. Written and supervised by Jean Cocteau. Produced by Andre Paulvé. Camera, Henri Alekan. Production design: Christian Berard. Music: George Auric.

With: Jean Marais, Josette Day, Marcel Andre, Mila Parely, Nane Germon, Michael Auclair, Raoul Marco.

These two Jean Cocteau versions of myth and fairytale need to be considered together, even though made several years apart and, in the U. S., released somewhat later and in the reverse order.

L'Eternel Retour, made under the German occupation and of course not seen by the outside world until after the war, was Cocteau's first full-scale tampering with myth: in this case, an updating of the Tristan and Isolde legend. At the time, reac-tion was mixed. On the one hand, it seemed a welcome return to the poetry and beauty in which the French cinema had been so strong in pre-war years. On the other, the decidedly ''Aryan'' look of hero and heroine persuaded many viewers that whatever it was saying was probably pro-Fascist. It was not released in the United States until *after La Belle et la Bete* and suffered by comparison with that later and much more polished film. Too, the then-powerful Catholic Legion of Decency took a very dim view of the idea of the hero falling in love with his father's new young wife—and were instrumental in causing so many cuts to be made that the tormented young lovers hardly got a moment to themselves onscreen. It's difficult to sustain a sense of passion and tragedy when its protagonists seem to be little more than pals. Reducing their commitment to each other, yet retaining all of the other legendary

Beauty and beast in the enchanted castle.

"props"—such as a love potion accidentally administered to the wrong person—threw the film decidedly off balance. Too, for reasons that have yet to be explained by psychologists, the "crazy family" of the American Depression-era comedies (*My Man Godfrey*, *Merrily We Live*) seemed to be transferred bodily to the French occupation films, particularly those (like *Lumière D'Été*) written by Jacques Prevert. But while the American families were amiably lunatic and harmless, the French equivalents were malevolent and evil. The family in *L'Eternel Retour* even included a fiendish little dwarf who poses as a lovable victim while performing the most monstrous acts!

L'Eternel Retour, has moments of remarkable beauty, with an operatic finale of the lovers eluding one another and being kept apart until Nathalie (Isolde) arrives just in time to hear Patrice (Tristan) croak out a death rattle and die.

The film, if nothing else, underscores Cocteau's reliance on Georges Auric's music by using far too little of it. When Auric's Wagnerian themes take over, the film soars to poetic and operatic heights; without it, it sometimes falls flat. It is unfair to place all the blame for the misfire elements on the limitations of music. Cocteau was feeling his way into film again after a long absence, and for the first time with the intention of *concentrating* on film as his major medium of expression. It was a dry run in many ways, and an honorable one.

La Belle et la Bête is an equally bizarre film, but a happier one. Despite the superficially horrific trappings of a grotesque castle, a mixture of Gothic tradition with Cocteau surrealism, disembodied but living arms holding candelabra, and the Beast's hands smoking after he has made his kill, the overall effect is romantic. Jean Marais' Beast, with its fascinatingly moist nose, is less werewolf than giant pussycat. The trick effects are deliberately simple: Beast (now Prince) and Beauty being wafted heavenward at the end is a visual trick far less complex than any devised by Georges Méliès a half-century earlier.

But the design of the film—the castle, its decaying grounds, the enchanted forest; or the simpler symmetry of Beauty's home, where the sisters' peaked hats and billowing sheets in the wind create their own patterns—is superb. This time Cocteau uses Auric's music far more fully, and his method of juxtaposing romantic themes with increasing undercurrents of menace creates exactly the right flavor of fairytale magic combined with the suggestion of horror.

Although Cocteau did not physically direct these two films, they are wholly his in conception and design—and totally unlike the distinguished body of work created by the two directors away from Cocteau. His own masterpiece, *Orpheus,* is a logical and climactic sequel to these two earlier works, though less of a romanticist film.

Beast transformed by Love: Jean Marais and the Prince in the film's final moments.

John Stuart (as Maddelena's husband), Patricia Roc, Angela, their daughter, Phyllis Calvert as the sedate and religious Maddelena, Reginald Tate (as the family doctor) and Alan Haines (even by British standards, a rather unprepossessing "hero") as Angela's fiancé.

Madonna of the Seven Moons

Gainsborough-Eagle Lion, 1944.

Directed by Arthur Crabtree. Produced by R. J. Minney. Screenplay by Roland Pertwee from the novel by Margery Lawrence. Music: Louis Levy; Camera: Jack Cox. (Released in the U. S. by Universal in 1946)

With: Phyllis Calvert, Stewart Granger, Patricia Roc, Peter Glenville, John Stuart, Jean Kent, Nancy Price, Peter Murray Hill, Dulcie Gray, Reginald Tate, Amy Veness, Hilda Bayley, Alan Haines, Helen Haye, Elliot Mason, Elliot Makeham, Danny Green.

After a steady diet of contemporary (and therefore war-oriented) stories in the early years of the war, Gainsborough gambled on a piece of sheer escapist romance in 1943 with *The Man in Grey.* It was such a staggering commercial success that a whole cycle followed, to continue well into the postwar period. Ironically, as the films became better and more literate, their popularity declined, and one of the best of the whole group, *Blanche Fury,* was a sad disappointment at the box office.

Next to *The Man in Grey, Madonna of the Seven Moons* was the most successful of the group. It had the added prestige of going out through Rank's new Eagle-Lion company, initially designed only for "classics" (a concept that soon fell flat) and by being so long (by the standards of the day) that on its initial release it was single-billed. Wartime programs in Britain tended to try to run short, so that theatres could close relatively early. *Madonna of the Seven Moons* ran 100 minutes in its original British version, though this was cut down (quite intelligently and without obvious continuity gaps) to 88 minutes for its U.S. release, the casualties including Stewart Granger's singing of "Rosanna" to his lady-love.

Patricia Roc, at the peak of her career as a new young romantic star, with the veteran John Stuart.

In the Florentine underworld: Peter Glenville, Phyllis Calvert, Stewart Granger, Nancy Price.

It was always one of the favorite British films of that unique American artist/author Edward Gorey, specialist in Victorian and Gothic melodrama but with a uniquely humorous touch. *Madonna of the Seven Moons* starts off like an Edward Gorey illustration, with a young girl from a convent pursued and raped (offscreen) by an unsubtly lascivious gypsy, leaving a trail of daffodils in her wake as she flees through the forest. The unnerving experience turns her into a schizophrenic.

Following her mother's disappearance, Angela tries to track her down via the clue of some of her jewelry; Elliot Makeham is the pawnbroker.

Phyllis Calvert as Rosanna, with Stewart Granger as the passionate lover, Nino, of her "other" existence.

We pick up her story years later. Now married, and very happily, to a Florence businessman, she has a teenaged daughter whose wholesome sexuality is in distinct contrast to her own matronly respectability. Periodically however, she disappears and assumes another personality, totally forgetting her other self. Maddalena, the dignified and highly religious housewife (if one can use such a term for a virtual Lady of the Manor), becomes Rosanna, fiery gypsy lover of Stewart Granger, underworld boss of a gang of Florence thieves. After a period of time, the other self reasserts itself, and she returns to her husband, unaware even that she has been away. On this occasion, the daughter takes it upon herself to track down her mother, and in a wildly improbable series of Dickensian coincidences, falls victim to the far from honorable schemes of one Sandro, lecherous brother of her mother's lover! The film comes to a colorful finish with a welter of death, redemption and *crime passionel,* the mother saving her daughter from Sandro by stabbing him (thinking it is her own lover being unfaithful to her) while Sandro manages to hurl a knife at her before he expires. The ending is romantically tragic in her case, happily optimistic for the daughter, but not unduly harrowing emotionally since no audience can have taken any of this farrago too seriously.

Madonna of the Seven Moons is designed purely and simply as an escapist costume romance, and although Patricia Roc (as the daughter) sports some very up-to-date fashions in the form of brief shorts and low-cut evening gowns, the film creates a deliberate Never-Never-Land in terms of its period, with colorful carnival costumes and venerable pseudo-Italian architecture further concealing exactly when all of this is supposed to be taking place. Only one establishing date is *ever* mentioned, and that so casually that amid the fast-moving procession of rape, religion, amnesia and *crimes passionel,* there isn't much incentive to work forward from that date and figure out that all of this is taking place in immediate pre-war Fascist Italy.

Carnival time . . . against which the film's climax unfolds.

slipping a shoulder provocatively out of a blouse doesn't really help. Moreover, she was little more than two years older than Patricia Roc, although playing her mother. And it is absurd to even call such a British stalwart as John Stuart (as the husband) by the name Giuseppe! However, Peter Glenville (later a less outstanding director than he was an actor) is marvelous as the lecherous and utterly degenerate Sandro, and Patricia Roc as always is a fresh and uncomplicated delight as his intended victim.

Obviously *Madonna of the Seven Moons* is no classic on a serious level, yet it is something of a

On the pretext of taking her to her mother, Sandro (Peter Glenville) plans to drug and seduce Angela.

Madonna of the Seven Moons is both absurd and yet wonderfully overblown in its own way, given such pictorial gloss (it was the first, and perhaps best, directorial venture by a former cameraman) and totally (and deliberately) artificial sets and art direction that there's never any need to take it seriously. The acting is earnest but inescapably British, and it is hard indeed to accept any of the cast as hot-blooded Italians, Phyllis Calvert especially is much too ladylike for the fiery gypsy temptress, and tossing her hair with intended abandon or

milestone in marking the *need* for romance and love at a time of national stress, and of the unrestrained determination with which it sets about it. Pictorially, it *does* achieve distinction too, and one of the love scenes between Phyllis Calvert and Stewart Granger is quite remarkable for a British film. They are both sitting on a bed in a darkened room, their figures merely black silhouettes outlined by the Neapolitan sun streaming through the window. Granger occasionally inhales from a cigarette and each time he does so, the glow from the cigarette

189

Rescued from Sandro, Angela watches as he and her mother die at each other's hands.

briefly illuminates his troubled face, or Calvert's ecstatically happy one. It undoubtedly draws its inspiration from the classic Garbo–Gilbert cigarette love scene in Clarence Brown's *Flesh and the Devil* (a scene that he repeated with Tyrone Power and Myrna Loy in *The Rains Came*)—but its purpose is dramatic as well as romantic.

There's perhaps a little too much religion in *Madonna of the Seven Moons* for the film's good. Although stressing Catholic ritual, it still casts a romantic enough glow not to be irksome or offensive to other religions. Yet it is an element that is sincerely motivated and obviously has to be taken seriously, and in so doing mitigates against the full zestful enjoyment of the rest of the film—which is neither as psychiatrically sound as *The Three Faces of Eve* or as unabashedly romantic as *The Man in Grey*. Still, there's never been anything *quite* like it, and it still has its own peculiar magic.

Family friend Peter Murray Hill comforts Angela as her mother lies near death.

190

Spellbound

Selznick-International–United Artists, 1945.

Directed by Alfred Hitchcock. Produced by David O. Selznick. Screenplay by Ben Hecht and Angus MacPhail from the novel *The House of Dr. Edwardes* by Francis Beeding. Camera: George Barnes. Special Effects: Jack Cosgrove. Art Direction: James Basevi and John Ewing. Music: Miklos Rozsa. Dream sequence by Salvador Dali.

With: Ingrid Bergman, Gregory Peck, Michael Chekhov, John Emery, Leo G. Carroll, Jean Acker, Steven Geray, Rhonda Fleming, Donald Curtis, Norman Lloyd, Paul Harvey, Erskine Sandford, Wallace Ford, Regis Toomey, Victor Killian, Janet Scott, Bill Goodwin, Art Baker, Teddy Infuhr, Dave Willock, Addison Richards, George Meeker, Matt Moore, Harry Brown.

 Spellbound is not too highly regarded by Hitchcock aficionados. It is sandwiched in between what many regard as his best American film, *Shadow of a*

Doubt (1943), and the film that has become something of a cult favorite, 1946's *Notorious*. Too, it was an enormously successful film commercially—which always tends to annoy critics in retrospect. At the time, it was the only real blockbuster subject that United Artists had on their roster, and nobody who walked big-city streets in 1945 could possibly avoid the huge posters that were erected to help sell it, the most oft-used illustrations being of Bergman and Peck against the famous Dali surrealist background. It was also a "fashionable" movie, another attribute that tends to irk critics. At the time it was highly touted, not least by Hitchcock himself, as being the first psychiatric movie. It was hardly that, having been preceded by items as diverse as Pabst's *Secrets of a Soul* (1926) and Charles Vidor's *Blind Alley* (1939). But it probably was the first major-scale American movie to harness psychiatry for purely romantic and commercial purposes, and as such it has much to answer for, since its success

Fleeing from the police, psychiatrist and patient (Bergman and Peck) find refuge at the home of her former teacher, Michael Chekov.

cism—at a time when this kind of Hollywood film was at its peak—has turned it into a kind of definitive classic. Had American audiences ever wanted to embrace guilt complexes and find in the immediate postwar film noir essays the same kind of nostalgic stimulation that they have found in World War II patriotic fervor and musical trivia, then *Spellbound* might easily have been turned into the same kind of cult classic that *Casablanca* has so inexplicably become. However, even if American audiences do belatedly discover the noir period (already admired by critics and students for its visual and thematic style), the chances are that it is too late for *Spellbound* to duplicate the success (or fate) of *Casablanca*. Mel Brooks's utilization of *Spellbound* as the basis for his overall Hitchcock satire, *High Anxiety* (1977) has too effectively demolished it for it ever to be taken really seriously again.

The plot of *Spellbound* is relatively straightforward. A psychiatrist, Dr. Edwardes, played by Peck, comes to take over the directorship of a mental hospital. It soon becomes plain that he is somewhat unstable himself, though the extent of his neuroses is known only by Dr. Constance Petersen (Bergman) who, in the course of trying to help him, falls in love with him. Finally forced into the realization that he is *not* Dr. Edwardes and may in fact be a murderer, but not wanting to embroil Con-

unleashed a positive welter of imitations with tortured heroes and repressed lady psychiatrists.

It's easy to be flip and to dismiss *Spellbound* as a silly film, but somehow its overwrought romanti-

Fellow psychiatrists Steven Geray and John Emery tease their colleague (Ingrid Bergman) about her apparent romantic interest in the institution's new director (Gregory Peck).

stance in his problems, he flees. Constance joins him and uses psychiatry to try to discover the truth. The police are hot on their trail, and hindering the psychiatric process is the patient's fear that the revelations may indeed prove him to be a murderer—and that he may turn on Constance. Ultimately, the secret of both his own guilt complex and the identity of the real murderer are revealed.

The story is serviceable enough, and for a long and somewhat overproduced film, maintains a remarkably brisk pace, constantly introducing plot surprises and new locations and characters. Much of its narrative byplay, as in all Hitchcock movies, is merely a means to get from point A to point B, and doesn't bear too close scrutiny. Typical of Hitchcock's occasional perverse humor at the expense of his audience is a relatively early scene in which Peck is making casually flirtatious moves toward Bergman.

He orders her to take a walk in the countryside with him, telling her that she needs to get out of the institution and into "*real* grass and *real* trees" and we cut immediately to an elaborately spacious *interior* set of rolling hills, in which the grass, trees and landscape are all patently phony!

Similarly, the secret of Peck's guilt complex is revealed as he and Bergman ski down a mountain-side, heading ever closer to the cliff edge, and destruction. Almost at the last minute, a flashback to his childhood recalls that once, sliding down a steep stone wall outside his home, he accidentally pushed his brother off the same wall to a rather grisly death by impaling him on sharp iron railings immediately below. One would have thought that such a revelation, far from removing guilt feelings, would merely confirm that they were justified, and turn the tormented hero more neurotic than ever!

However, it is the romantic trappings of the film—and most specifically, Ingrid Bergman's magnificent performance, George Barnes's glossy photography, and Miklos Rozsa's soaring romantic score—that make the film succeed so well.

Although its plot is much more that of a thriller than *Notorious* (which places all of its melodrama within the framework of a triangle love story), the overall impression of *Spellbound* is just the opposite—a love story told within the framework of a thriller. This romantic note is set within the main title design, that of leaves swirling in a violent wind (yet curiously, none of the leaves hanging from the fragile bough of a tree ever come unstuck!) while Rozsa's score—haunting, neurotic and romantic all at the same time—introduces what was to become one of the most famous musical love themes of the

The two psychiatrists continue to psychoanalyze the man who is convinced he is a murderer.

40s, and indeed won for him an Academy Award that year.

As always with Hitchock, sexual symbolism of a fairly elementary (but always picturesque) nature prevails throughout—some of it of such an explicit and clinical nature that it doubtless passed unnoticed in 1945. However, one of the great visual splendors—backed by the Rozsa strings at heights of unrestrained lushness—occurs in the first really passionate embrace between Bergman and Peck. Peck's kiss produces a state of both release and submission in Bergman, pictorialized via a striking superimposition over the giant two-head closeup of a series of doors opening, one after the other, down a corridor leading to a cloudy infinity. (The shot is a much more showy and technique-conscious equivalent of the similar scene in the Czech *Extase*, where the first kiss of passion releases Hedy Lamarr's spirit, which, in superimposition, drifts through the tight embrace.)

If Gregory Peck was miscast in the film, then Ingrid Bergman was never better (and never more predictably) cast. Her beauty, her radiance, and her musical delivery of lines comes to the rescue every time the film seems about to become too much of a "typical" Hollywood super-special. Bergman had the unique (and almost exclusive) faculty of being able to use, reuse and even exploit mannerisms without their ever once seeming to *be* mannerisms —an acting trick that even Davis, Hepburn, Maria Schell and other individual actresses were never able to master. And of course Hitchcock knew *exactly* how to use her; she may have made better films than those she made for Hitchocock, but she was *never* better directed than by him.

Spellbound may be overblown, florid, tricky— even obvious in the artifice of its romanticism. But with the exception of its shortchanging us on the Dali dream sequence (Hitchcock wasn't given the freedom to shoot it the way he wanted, and much of what *was* shot wasn't used), everything in the film works. It's the exact opposite in every way of the same year's *Brief Encounter* from England, yet each in its own way is a definitive love story for the period.

Alfred Hitchcock, at extreme left, sets up a shot early in the film. Despite the convenient Hollywood hills, most of this sequence was actually shot on a studio stage.

Brief Encounter

Cineguild-Rank, 1945.

Directed by David Lean. Screenplay by Noel Coward, David Lean and Anthony Havelock-Allan from a one-act play *Still Life* by Coward. Camera: Robert Krasker. Music: Rachmaninoff's Piano Concerto # 2, played by Eileen Joyce.

With: Celia Johnson, Trevor Howard, Cyril Raymond, Stanley Holloway, Joyce Carey, Valentine Dyall, Everley Gregg, Margaret Barton, Dennis Harkin, Marjorie Mars, Irene Handl.

Few films have succeeded as well as *Brief Encounter* because they came at *just* the right time to strike a responsive audience chord; and few films, it must be added, have dated quite as much. To be fair, the film, an exquisitely crafted piece of workmanship, really hasn't dated at all, but attitudes about love, sex, marriage and fidelity have changed so drastically that the morality of the film seems positively archaic to any audience that didn't live through and experience the 40s.

The story, it will be recalled, deals with two conventional and apparently happily married middle-class people—a doctor and a housewife—who meet accidentally, and find their casual friendship developing into a deep love that literally tears them apart, unused as they are to such violent emotion. Their love never reaches the physical stage, and their innate decency so torments them with feelings of guilt that unhappiness quite overshadows their joy. Ultimately they decide to part; the doctor has an opportunity to start a practice in Africa, and they know they will never meet again. Their last few precious moments together are ruined by a gossipy neighbor who intrudes on them at the railway station as they make their farewells. The wife almost kills herself by throwing herself under a train—but is unable to go through with it, and returns instead to her husband and small boy.

British films in 1945 had produced a number of love stories characterized by maturity, charm, and underplayed drama: *The Way to the Stars, Perfect*

Strangers (retitled *Vacation from Marriage* in the U. S., a fine little film in which a drab and smug married couple, beautifully played by Robert Donat and Deborah Kerr, find themselves transformed into more sophisticated and virtually unrecognizable individuals by their wartime service), and *The Seventh Veil.* Although the latter film was far more novelettish than its compatriots, its combination of Svengali and psychiatry was still more restrained than it might have been on other occasions, and it was well served by James Mason in one of his finest roles. It was also a major box-office hit. All of these films, and others, gained by a decidedly pro-British feeling (by no means a permanent characteristic of the British) and because British films were enjoying a new prestige at that time. Too, in comparison with the more colorful Hollywood romances of 1945 (*Song of Love, The Unfaithful, Possessed, Norah Prentiss*) the British film did seem truer, more related to life. Even its leading players were actors rather than stars, and relatively new to film. Trevor Howard in particular, a fine actor and an unconventional "type," in his first major film seemed drawn from life rather than from the casting offices.

What really sealed the film's success, however, was the unexpected support of Britain's housewives. During the war, the contribution of men, young and old, to all branches of the services—and on the home front—had been acknowledged. The women who had joined the forces or gone to work in factories had likewise been given their due in films like *The Gentle Sex* and *Millions Like Us.* But the housewife, who had had to survive bombings and food shortages, and perhaps separation from her evacuated children, had been taken for granted. And she was still being taken for granted. The men had returned to their peacetime jobs, but for the housewife, although the dangers of the war had passed, most of the problems remained. Austerity was in effect for a long time in postwar Britain, with food, clothing, and other material in short supply continuing to be rationed for several years. Here was a film extolling the nobility and capacity for self-sacrifice of the "common housewife" and doing it in a realistic, noncondescending way that admitted that the highlight of her week might be a visit to the movies, or the borrowing of a book from the lending library of a Boots' chemist store. This was a cunning little bit of flattery in itself, since using Boots' rather than the regular lending library added just a slight note of social elevation.

Though not stressed, the elements of class distinction are quite pronounced throughout the film. There is decided condescension towards the movies, and to the "serving" public—waitresses, station buffet attendants, and the like. The middle-aged couple (Stanley Holloway and Joyce Carey) indulges in harmless flirtations which smack of music-hall humor, while the brash young teenaged barmaid and her crude boyfriend clearly indulge in sexual activity in their time off. Thus sex is established as a kind of dirty joke for the lower classes, and renders more viable the shame and wretchedness that Alec and Laura feel when they are caught (innocent of any wrongdoing) in the apartment of one of Alec's friends—himself a doctor, clearly on a

The final, sad parting in the same dingy lunchroom.

higher social level than Alec. Even though he is a cloddish and unsympathetic type, it is *his* condemnation—he tells Alec that he is not shocked, "just disappointed," and asks for his key back—that finally convinces the lovers that they are wrong and forces their decision to part.

The film is played out against everyday backgrounds—shops, cafés, a cinema, the countryside, a boating lake—and against those forbidding British railway stations which seem to have been made for film noir and sad farewells. Much of it is intentionally funny, and all of it, thanks to the skill of Trevor

The comedy relief was deliberately drab and a little vulgar; station attendants Margaret Barton, Joyce Carey, Stanley Holloway and Dennis Harkin.

Howard and the somewhat mannered but still effective acting of Celia Johnson, rings true. What is not quite so true are the cinematic methods used to heighten all these emotions. Celia Johnson's voice-over narration (she is thinking her thoughts aloud, wishing she could tell them to her husband as he sits complacently opposite her, working on the *Times's* crossword puzzle) is basically unnecessary, since it tells us nothing we don't glean from the narrative itself. The almost overpowering use of Rachmaninoff piano music adds an artificial note of nobility and greatness to the recounting of a love affair which is *not* unique, but which is probably typical of thousands just like it. And the last, tidy, comfortable lines of the film, in which the husband (an unrewarding role beautifully played by Cyril Raymond) tells his wife: "Whatever your dream was, it wasn't a very happy one was it? You've been a long way away—thank you for coming back to me"—are quite out of character, since they imply a wisdom and a knowledge that he doesn't possess, although the comments work within the emotional milieu set up by the music.

Also, in the last analysis, the final outcome is *not* really a sad one. The British like security and a routine, well-ordered life, and do not welcome disruptive emotions. Only such a love for conformity and lack of stress has enabled them to endure constant deprivation and hardship, Government bureaucracy, perpetual encroachment on their rights and conveniences by nonstop strikes, and the regimentation of their leisure time by that uniquely British institution, the Holiday Camp. In due couse, Alec and Laura would doubtless have tired of one another, and trotted happily back to their respective hearths and homes. So with *Brief Encounter* the British housewife had it both ways—a tribute to her stoicism, plus the innate knowledge that her humdrum life was best in the long run.

In 1945, one British critic commented that "love has seldom been so sensitively dealt with outside the French cinema," but even at the time the French weren't impressed. They couldn't understand what all the soul-searching was about, and felt that if the doctor wanted to sleep with his lady friend, why didn't he? Today's young British audiences, when they bother to see it at all, find its restraints hilarious.

But as an emotional time capsule, and as a remarkably skilled piece of filmmaking, *Brief Encounter* doesn't really date. Max Ophuls was perhaps the first of many filmmakers to show his affection for it by copying one sequence verbatim in his own *Letter From an Unknown Woman* shortly afterwards. And nothing could stress the validity of the original more than a look at the inept British remake of the mid-70s in which superstars Richard Burton and Sophia Loren so totally mitigated against the sensitivity and believability of the decidedly nonsexual Trevor Howard and Celia Johnson.

Fate—or solution? A comfortable home, *The Times* crossword puzzle, and an ordinary but devoted husband (Cyril Raymond).

Joan arrives in the highlands, expecting to be ferried across to her fiancé's island.

I Know Where I'm Going

Rank–General Film Distributors, Britain, 1945.

Written, produced and directed by Michael Powell and Emeric Pressburger. Camera: Erwin Hillier. Production Design: Alfred Junge. Music: Allan Gray. Released in the United States in 1947 by Universal.

With: Roger Livesey, Wendy Hiller, Pamela Brown, Nancy Price, Finlay Currie, John Laurie, George Carney, Walter Hudd, Murdo Morrison, Margot Fitzsimmons, Jean Cadell, Norman Shelley, Petula Clark, Catherine Lacey, Valentine Dyall, Herbert Lomas, Graham Moffat.

I Know Where I'm Going, one of the loveliest and most lyrical films ever made, came into existence almost by accident. Writer-producer-directors Powell and Pressburger were waiting to get into production with their ambitious and expensive *A Matter of Life and Death* (retitled *Stairway to Heaven* in the U.S.) but there was a delay in the availability of Technicolor facilities. In order to keep busy, they decided on a fairly simple film for the interval. Writer Pressburger had long been kicking around a vague plotline about a girl trying desperately to get to a remote island; Powell in his turn had long wanted to get back to the Scottish highlands, an area that he loved but hadn't been able to use in a film since 1939's *The Spy in Black.* The storyline that was concocted was simple in the extreme—therein lies much of its charm—but the film itself turned out to be an elaborate, meticulously crafted film, with some time-consuming trick effects, far from the "little" film that its makers had originally envisioned. Fortunately it turned out to be a hit on both sides of the Atlantic, both critically and with the public. Nevertheless, it was conceived and produced as a labor of love, and that love—for the countryside, for the people and for their traditions—shows up in every foot of the film.

Its thesis is that love matters more than money or power, hardly a novel idea in 1945, nor, to a country at the tail end of a long and devastating war, one particularly in need of restating, in view of the problems—and priorities—of the period. Yet it managed to be both timely and time*less,* so that more than thirty years after it was made it still

199

seems quite valid, the war itself merely a background, and doubtless its universality will enable it to remain a classic during the years to come.

Even while the credits are unreeling, a narration and a deft series of images tells us that from childhood, Joan Webster has only wanted the best out of life—and has been determined to get it. As the film proper begins, she is saying goodbye to her middle-class father, prior to setting off for Scotland and the Isle of Kiloran, where she is to marry an elderly—and very rich—industrialist. Once she gets to the highlands, there are delays due to bad weather, and a disquieting meeting with Torquil McNeil. Gradually she comes to love him and the simple highland people who neither have nor want money, but refuses to allow herself to be dissuaded from her purpose. Against everyone's advice, she finally insists upon being taken to her husband-to-be, even though it means sailing into the teeth of a storm and courting death in a terrifying mid-channel whirlpool, from which she and the small crew only just escape. Shamed and humbled by the experience, she is still determined to marry her industrial-

ist—but at the last minute, accompanied by a band of Scottish pipers, strides back to embrace, and marry, the man she now really loves—Torquil. There's far more to it than that—including a Scottish curse—but the details of the plotting are unimportant. What matters is the humanity, the carefully drawn characters, the love of sea and land and a way of life, and the constantly stunning visual beauty.

Because it's a leisurely tale, there's time for small incidents to tell us a great deal about the characters. In the very first sequence, where Joan says goodbye to her father in a rather elegant (especially for wartime) London restaurant, the father's uneasiness—he is a conservative banker, and is afraid of depositors seeing him in such grand surroundings—emphasizes the rather narrow class-conscious attitudes from which his daughter understandably wants to escape. At the same time, her rather too deliberately and haughtily ordering her soup to be returned because it is now cold, shows how anxious she is to step into her new role of wealth and power. Neither father now daughter emerge as very sympa-

thetic characters from this beautifully written sequence, but they *do* emerge as very real and human ones.

,The train journey from London to Scotland provides Powell with his one justifiable chance to indulge his fondness for tricky film technique. This has sometimes been considered a flaw in his direction, but if so it's a flaw born of an enchantment with the film medium, and a desire to enjoy it to the full, and extract the very maximum from it. However, undoubtedly realizing that filmic pyrotechnics would detract from the simplicity of his film, Powell limits his trickery to this one sequence, before the plot proper gets under way. There's an imaginative dream sequence wherein Joan falls asleep while watching her wedding gown swaying to the rhythm of the train's movements, and dreams—via superimposed negative images and humorously exaggerated low-angle shots—that she is marrying not a man, but the huge industrial complex that he represents. Much of the journey is suggested by a charming miniature train chugging over tartan-like hills, accompanied by a song; this episode, not only pleasing in itself, also suggests a very gentle parody of the famous early Harry Watt documentary, *Night Mail.* When Joan has to change trains for the final leg of her journey, the transition is achieved by a direct cut from the top hat of a fawning and bowing official sent to greet her, to the funnel of the smaller train belching black smoke as it starts up. The whole train journey episode is whimsical and lighthearted, but with the arrival in Scotland the mood changes. It is almost as though Nature herself takes over, and from that point on Erwin Hillier's breathtaking photography captures every nuance of approaching storm, early morning mist, sunlight on the hills, and stark silhouettes of seamen outlined against fog or crashing waves. One can almost feel the spray and the dampness of the mist rolling in from the hills.

As the film progresses, and gets geographically further and further away from civilization and the big cities, so does the division between the "rich" people and the "others" become more apparent. Despite the temporary leveling effect of World War II, class distinction has always been a dominant factor in British society, and doubtless will be for a long time to come. The film makes no heavy-handed underlining of this fact; indeed, had it wished to do so, it could have taken the easy route of making the aristocracy decidedly unsympathetic. As it is, the film's good natured affection seems to be extended to *all*; but the rich people in the film are a somewhat dull and stuffy lot, totally unable to comprehend the

Although delayed by a storm, the bride-to-be daydreams happily of her marriage on the morrow. A fine study of Wendy Hiller as Joan.

joys and emotions of a gathering of the clans to celebrate a couple's sixtieth wedding anniversary (an entirely lovely sequence, this)—any more than the simple fisherfolk can understand why the industrialist wants to build his own swimming pool and stock his streams with trout, with the ocean and its salmon all around him. Even the millionaire himself is a jolly and decent sort, and one feels mildly sorry for him when he loses his bride.

The free spirit of the highlanders seems to reach its climax with the introduction of Catrina (beautifully played by Pamela Brown), who bursts into her home with windblown hair, rain-soaked mackintosh, and a brace of huge hunting dogs!

One of the factors most contributing to the success of *I Know Where I'm Going* is the warm and rich performance of Wendy Hiller, whose relatively sparse appearances in British films made each performance very much of an event, yet at the same time made one lament all the more for the missed opportunities and the films she might have made. This was her first film since *Major Barbara* in 1941; her next would not be until *Outcast of the Islands* in 1951, by which time her youth was behind her. In character roles from *Sons and Lovers* (1960) to *The Cat and the Canary* (1977) she was still superb, but at her peak in the 1940s, when she was in her thirties, she combined characteristics of Ka-

201

At the wedding anniversary celebrations of an aged couple, Joan gets to meet and understand the local people. At left, John Laurie.

Against his better judgment, the Laird (Roger Livesey) tries to transport Joan to her fiancé, but the storm worsens and they are almost killed when their small boat narrowly escapes destruction in a whirlpool.

tharine Hepburn and Grace Kelly with a unique inner radiance that was uniquely her own. Her zeal as the Salvation Army girl in *Major Barbara* was so intense that she was totally able to win over an audience that might otherwise have found the role rather absurd, in *I Know Where I'm Going,* even though the role is deliberately shallow and even unsympathetic, she manages to make the audience share her dilemma—grudgingly respecting her determination, yet at the same time recognizing in her hidden fires of passion and humanity that cry out for a more romantic solution. It's a magnificent performance, and since most of the other players are placid, all of the attention is focused on it.

Although far from being the most ambitious, *I Know Where I'm Going* is almost certainly the most satisfying film from the Powell-Pressburger unit, which also produced such films as *The Life and Death of Colonel Blimp, Stairway to Heaven* and *The Red Shoes.* In any writer-producer-director team, there's usually not much doubt about which half of the duo was the dominant one, and the proof usually comes when the team splits up and one has a chance to study their solo work. With Billy Wilder and Charles Brackett in the U.S., clearly Wilder's creative input was the greater. One can make the same claims for Sidney Gilliat (of Launder and Gilliat) or George Seaton (of Seaton and Perlberg). But the Powell-Pressburger union was rather different;

although Pressburger received co-director credit, Powell's directorial hand was very much in command, and Pressburger's contribution was mainly in the writing. But the writing and conception of their films was almost as important as their ultimate execution, and while—perhaps rightly—Powell tends to receive the greater credit for the finished work, at the same time their interdependency was much greater than in most such teams. Both have worked in a solo capacity, but their best films remain those that they made together.

I Know Where I'm Going is typical of their film in that it is, in a sense, a story about escape—or withdrawal from the world. *The Red Shoes* was about a withdrawal into the world of ballet; *Black Narcissus,* dealing with a group of nuns in a remote Himalayan outpost, was quite literally about a retreat from the world; *Stairway to Heaven* withdrew into *another* world, the antechamber of an afterlife. In *I Know Where I'm Going,* the heroine is retreating from her world of middle-class respectability and comparative poverty, while the hero, on leave from his naval duties, is retreating from the war. But in no sense are they defeatist films, and in most cases the withdrawals and retreats are purely temporary. Thus they have a kind of optimism and a positive approach to life which was missing from so many contemporary British films like *Odd Man Out* or *They Made Me a Fugitive,* steeped in both the

Predictably, love wins out over money, and Joan and the Laird are happily reunited.

defeatism of the immediate postwar British films, and the grimness of the then-current film noir cycle.

People who saw *I Know Where I'm Going* when it was new, and were enchanted by it, find that it is *one* film that fully lives up to its memories. Others, seeing it for the first time, are inevitably bowled over by its beauty and charm. Interestingly, the only group of people that consistently seem to *dis*like it are the filmmaking students of the 60s and 70s, brought up on the films of Bergman, Resnais and Varda, and convinced that to justify themselves, films have to make a *statement*. *I Know Where I'm Going* makes its statement immediately, and students tend to be impatient and unwilling to wait around for an ending they have anticipated They fail to realize that the totality of the film is the

"statement" and that the "love is more important than money" theme is merely the peg on which to hang an Odyssey quite as remarkable, in its own way, as Mr. Kubrick's—and a good deal less ambiguous.

I know Where I'm Going is full of pictorial beauty, technical ingenuity (the whirlpool sequence is a masterly intermingling of location with studio sequences, no less than five negatives being juxtaposed in the climactic shot of the escape from the heart of the whirlpool), delightful and unpredictable sequences, and endearing characters. My own favorite touch is the insane yet typically British logic in placing an area's *only* public telephone at the foot of a waterfall, so that all conversation is drowned out!

Flying officer comrades during the Battle of Britain: Michael Redgrave, Trevor Howard (in one of his earliest roles) and John Mills.

The Way to the Stars
(Johnny in the Clouds)

Two Cities Productions–United Artists, 1945.

Directed by Anthony Asquith. Produced by Anatole de Grunwald, Script by Terrence Rattigan and de Grunwald. from a story by Rattigan. Poems by John Pudney. Camera: Derek Williams. 2nd Unit Cameraman: Guy Green, Jack Hildyard. Music: Nicholas Brodsky. Associate Producer: Gordon Parry.

With: Michael Redgrave, John Mills, Rosamund John, Douglass Montgomery, Renee Asherson, Stanley Holloway, Basil Radford, Felix Aylmer, Bonar Colleano, Trevor Howard, Joyce Carey, Bill Owen, Jean Simmons, Anthony Dawson, Nicholas Stuart, David Tomlinson, Johnny Schofield, Charles Victor, Hartley Power, Vida Hope, Peter Cotes, Hugh Dempster.

Terence Rattigan, himself an Air Force officer during the war, became Britain's wartime chronicler, not in a historic but in a dramatic sense, recording its moods in plays and film scripts that ranged from emotional drama to lighthearted comedy. And in many ways, his *The Way to the Stars* is the definitive "Battle of Britain" film. Its three interwoven love stories—the American airman with his wife back home, the British flying officer who dies leaving a widow and child, and the younger couple who feel it is wrong to marry in wartime but finally do anyway—cover virtually all aspects of the war as it affected servicemen and the women they loved. There is no combat action at all, though it is spoken of, and virtually no physical action, other than for a brief bombing attack and a plane crash.

The film was a fantastic success at the British box office, a blockbuster that one just couldn't avoid. After a long London premiere and a saturation release on a major circuit, all the second-run theatres picked it up; then a whole circuit replayed it, and there was an official reissue within a couple of years. The critics loved it, and so did the public. Every time a film of this type comes along there is a tendency to build up a resistance to it, if only to avoid becoming one of the sheep. But the sheep can quite often be right, and they were in this case.

There are a number of reasons for the film's success. For one thing, British films were then in the midst of their highest prestige period. This was one of the biggest new British films, and it had a topheavy star roster of popular players. Too, its mood caught audiences at just the right time—as did *Brief Encounter. The Way to the Stars,* with the war at an end, preached patriotism, stiff-upper-lip and shoulder-to-shoulder camaraderie when such preachments were really no longer necessary. Although nobody would admit it, the film enabled the British to pat themselves discreetly on the back and say, "Yes, that's how we behaved, and that's why we won!"

And finally, the Anglo-American spirit of friendship was then at an all-time high. The grim postwar heritage of pizza restaurants and hotdog emporiums had only secured but a tenuous foothold in Leicester Square, and it was more fashionable to like the Americans than to like the British. Admittedly, one saw some pretty horrendous specimens stalking the London streets, but the average Britisher donned his rose-colored spectacles and forced himself to the unlikely supposition that there might even be an odd Englishman or two behaving in a like manner in the streets of New York at that very moment. No, the average Britisher's impression of the average American was not the brash loudmouth that one saw in the streets, but the open, boyish and generous young man that one took into one's home for a Sunday dinner. For the most part, romanticized or not, this impression was probably a reasonably accurate one, reinforced by movies such as this one, with Douglass Montgomery's perhaps *too* engaging and relaxed American airman, or *A Canterbury Tale,* with an American sergeant played by American nonactor John Sweet.

In any event, the film neatly confirmed the idea that there were more nice Americans than bad ones, and that even the loudmouths (like Bonar Colleano, who spent the entire war playing such roles!) were really not so bad at heart. The British wouldn't have stood for this viewpoint in an American movie of course, as they never took the Americans that seriously. Most Britishers regarded MGM's *Mrs. Miniver* as a sincerely-felt tribute, appreciated it, and flocked to see it, but it was little closer to the realities of wartime England than *Aloma of the South Seas,* and nobody believed it. On the other hand, Britain made its own equivalent—an unambitious film called *Salute John Citizen.* This could be taken seriously—but nobody bothered to see it in sufficient numbers for it to make much of an impression at the box office.

All these factors, and probably others, made *The Way to the Stars* admirably attuned to the times, and to the country. Retitled, and substantially cut, it failed in the U.S.—just as 1946's *The Best Years of Our Lives,* a huge critical and popular

Redgrave with new wife (Rosamund John) and child.

success in the U.S., created but little stir in Britain. It's rather interesting that both of these films were advertised not on timeliness or theme, but solely on the parade of stars that they offered. The posters for each film are almost identical.

Because so many years have gone by, and times and tempos have changed, *The Way to the Stars* no longer exerts *quite* the same appeal today. Some of the little bits of business seem just a shade too contrived, the characters a trifle too "typical." Such things irk not because they don't pay off, but because we know they were put in just because they *were* guaranteed to pay off. But on the whole, thanks to sensitive writing and fine performances— and not least to one of those typically pseudoclassic scores that British composers love so well (and that are all virtually interchangeable)—the film *does* retain much of its emotional and dramatic value. It's still a fine film, and its opening was good enough for director Henry King to lift in toto for the opening of his *Twelve O'Clock High.*

Anthony Asquith was a fine British director with a particular talent for handling material from the stage, yet with such a sure knowledge of film technique that a deft piece of editing here or a camera movement there could transform such material into film and not just filmed theatre. *The Way to the Stars,* undoubtedly because of Rattigan's own primarily theatrical background, could very easily have become a series of static dialogue encounters. But it never does, even though it maintains a solid sense of theatre—with well-controlled comedy used for punctuation at just the right time, and the manipulation of an obnoxious, selfish character (played well by Joyce Carey) that everybody in the film—and in the audience—has cause to dislike intensely, and who receives a rousing comeuppance between tragic climax and happy ending.

What makes the film work most, however, is its truth. Its restraint is genuine, not merely played for effect. The attitudes and moods of wartime Britain are caught with unerring accuracy, and if they seem a little idealized today, it is only because (very sadly) those attitudes have dissolved and decayed steadily in postwar England, resulting in the chaos and near-anarchy that overtook that country in early 1979. The romantic exchanges—particularly between Michael Redgrave and Rosamund John, as the slightly older couple—are superbly directed and played, and have lost not one whit of their poignancy or sense of urgency in the intervening years. And of course the impact of the film is heightened by the fact that its romanticism is interwoven with idealism.

The sacrifices of World War II were worthwhile. Younger audiences, attuned to regard later wars—such as that in Vietnam—in a purely political and certainly not in an idealistic sense, may increasingly regard the romances that use World Wars I and II as a background as artificial, wondering why the lovers aren't protesting the war rather than ac-

Just before his own death in a flying accident, Johnny, the American (Douglass Montgomery) confides to the widowed Rosamund John that he will soon be going home.

cepting it. But *The Way to the Stars* isn't that generation's kind of film anyway. It belongs to, and will continue to move, the people who lived through those years. And when they have gone the film will perhaps become a point of historic reference only—but even at that, still a remarkable and permanent emotional record of its time.

Following Redgrave's death in a bombing raid, American air force officers are stationed at the base: Bonar Colleano, Douglass Montgomery and Rosamund John.

Sylvie et le Fantôme

Andre Paulvé Productions, 1945.

Directed by Claude Autant-Lara. Screenplay by Jean Aurenche from a play by Alfred Adam. Camera: Philippe Agostina. Music: Rene Cloerec.

With: Odette Joyeux, François Perier, Jacques Tati, Louis Salou, Pierre Larquey, Julien Carette, Jean Desailly.

Sylvia is an impressionable adolescent who lives in an old castle, and who nurtures a nostalgic love for the lover of her dead grandmother; his picture (with faithful hunting dog) adorns the wall, and his ghost is said to haunt the castle. She fully believes herself in love with the ghost, which does indeed follow her about the castle, although she has never seen it. In order to please her on her sixteenth birthday, her father arranges for the ghost to make an appearance. Actually the ghost is to be enacted by three men: the castle valet, an out-of-work ham actor who intends to play the ghost in terms of traditional theatrical terror, and a handsome young amateur burglar, pressed into service at the last mo-

ment. At her party, the overjoyed Sylvia meets all three "ghosts," only to be puzzled by their difference in demeanor as they talk to her, finding that the gentle sadness of the burglar, who is falling in love with her, most fits her "image" of the ghost. Finally, the real ghost manages to get under the prop shroud and confronts her but is unable to talk to her. Accidentally, the hoax is given away, and Sylvia, saddened and disillusioned, doesn't realize that she is in the presence of the genuine ghost. She decides it is time to put aside childish fancies, and grow up—perhaps to romance. She is saddened, but matured, and doesn't witness the moment when the guests, in on the hoax, are suddenly terrified by undeniable proof that at least one of the ghosts is genuine. His haunting at an end, the ghost—accompanied by his dog—leaves the castle for a new celestial home.

As will be seen, it is a fragile little whimsy, needing delicacy of touch (which it certainly gets) and an emotional rather than a logical frame of mind while viewing it. While it may no longer be

Sylvia shows her friends the portrait of Alain and relates his romantic and tragic history.

true that *The New York Times* can singlehandedly make or break a film, it was certainly true in 1950 when this enchanting film—already delayed by five years—opened at the out-of-the-way (and now defunct) Beverly Theatre. The *Times* afforded it one of the cruelest and unkindest reviews ever given any foreign import, going out of their way to be malevolent seemingly just because it was fairytale fantasy and thus an unworthy subject for the director who had so recently made *Le Diable au Corps.*

Despite telling much of its story via dialogue (due no little to its play origin) it is a thoroughly delightful film, beautifully mixing comedy and pathos almost in the manner of James Barrie. Its trick effects are deliberately simple, often no more sophisticated than those so prevalent in the French

Alain, the ghost (Jacques Tati) and his dog are happy and benevolent in their haunting of the old French chateau.

Alain is unable to communicate with Sylvia (Odette Joyeux), who is romantically infatuated with his memory.

trick and magic films of the early 1900s (although it might be added that *they* were of an exceedingly high order). Another major asset is its truly magical score—a simple, haunting melody played on a particularly emotional tin whistle or flute, an instrument that somehow seems to have a sob built into its tone. The cast, too, is exactly right: Odette Joyeux, fresh and sensitive as the girl; an unspeaking Jacques Tati, handsome and graceful, with no trace of the ungainliness that was soon to become his Monsieur Hulot trademark, as the ghost; and Louis Salou, quite marvelous as the ham actor. The public alas never got much of a chance to discover the beauty of this film for themselves; after a very brief first run, it got a follow-up second week in 42nd Street—and vanished.

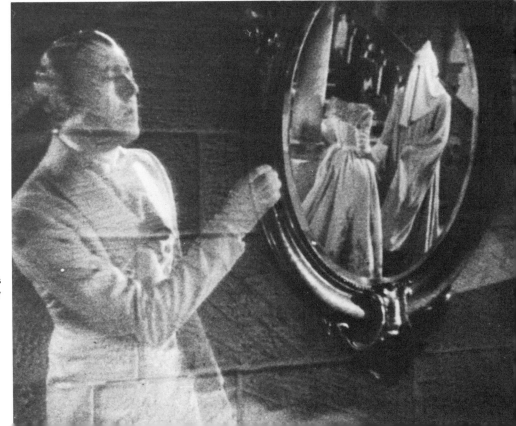

Alain watches as one of the bogus ghosts impersonates him at Sylvia's birthday party.

Dorothy McGuire, Robert Young and Herbert Marshall.

The Enchanted Cottage

RKO Radio, 1945.

Directed by John Cromwell. Produced by Harriet Parsons. Screenplay by DeWitt Bodeen and Herman J. Mankiewicz from the play by Sir Arthur Wing Pinero. Camera: Ted Tetzlaff.

With: Dorothy McGuire, Robert Young, Herbert Marshall, Mildred Natwick, Spring Byington, Hillary Brooke, Richard Gaines, Alec Englander, Mary Worth, Josephine Whittell.

It's very rarely that a love story *gains* in impact over the years. Usually the qualities that make it work when it is new are subject to constant attack from changing times, sensibilities and morality. If it is a really good film, it will withstand those attacks and remain as good as it always was. But for such a film to actually get *better* is most uncommon. (I am not talking here about films become more *entertaining* with the passage of time. That frequently happens, even with unimportant films, when their sheer technical expertise, or perhaps an outstanding cast, seem to gain in comparison with contemporary

standards.) But since *The Enchanted Cottage* deals with illusion and change, it is somehow appropriate that *it* should now seem to have changed.

Based on a play by Sir Arthur Wing Pinero that hinged on an immediate post–World War I problem, *The Enchanted Cottage* was originally staged in 1922, and a fine film version followed in 1924, starring Richard Barthelmess and May McAvoy, under the direction of John S. Robertson. It deals with a disfigured and bitter war veteran, who is even contemplating suicide rather than live with his ugliness for the rest of his life. Instead, he fortuitously meets—and marries—a plain girl who is likewise despairing of ever finding happiness. Though their marriage is based on need rather than love, they retire to a little cottage in the country, cut themselves off from the world, and find that in time they do indeed love one another. Moreover, a miracle seems to have taken place. He has reacquired his former good looks, and the girl becomes beautiful. Ultimately, thoughtless friends comment on their ugliness and they realize the truth: they are

210

unchanged, except to each other. Knowing that it is their love that has made them seem whole and beautiful to each other, they know they can easily regain that "miracle."

Though the silent film was deeply moving, there were opportunities for the updated sound remake to improve on it. John Cromwell was a better director than John S. Robertson, and moreover, as an experienced stage director and a former actor himself, he was well equipped to deal with a stage property that depended so much on the interplay between the two main characters. Furthermore, DeWitt Bodeen and Herman Mankiewicz were excellent screenwriters, among the best, most literate and most imaginative in Hollywood. They could use dialogue subtly where the silent had been up against the limitations of subtitles. The scene in which the couple learn that their afflictions have not disappeared, through the thoughtless but sincere expressions of pity from a friend, is beautifully written and played.

But as a postscript to World War II, *The Enchanted Cottage* seemed both unrealistic and out of place. It was surrounded by films like Selznick's *I'll Be Seeing You*, glossy, star-laden vehicles dealing in at least superficially realistic terms with the more pressing problems of psychological maladjustments of returning veterans. Critics were almost as thoughtlessly cruel to *The Enchanted Cottage* as the

friend in the story. More than one critic pointed out that plastic surgery having reached the stage it had, there was no reason for the hero to accept his facial disfigurement; that his Frankensteinian makeup (an exaggeration of course) turned the film more into a horror film than a love story. Early forerunners of Women's Libbers emphasized how much even a "plain" girl could improve her looks with current cosmetics, and that anyway, in this day and age character mattered much more than beauty. These critics weren't necessarily wrong, merely intolerant. The film could probably have won them over by going in for some elaborate special effects (RKO after all had one of the industry's best rosters of special effects men, who'd shown their genius from *King Kong* through to *Citizen Kane*). Instead, although permitting one or two trick effects, the film opted for a simple and uncluttered visual style, the work of an excellent cinematographer (Ted Tetzlaff) who would soon be a director himself.

Now, more than three decades later, the film is no longer locked in to the post–World War II period. So much has happened since that those years seemed almost innocent and light-years away, enabling *The Enchanted Cottage* to become what Pinero always intended it to be, a fable about the power of love, not a document on postwar conditions.

Robert Young
and Dorothy McGuire.

Pierre (Marcel Pagliero) is murdered by Mouloudji, a traitor in the underground ranks.

Les Jeux Sont Faits

U.S. release title *The Chips Are Down.*
Les Films Gibes, 1947.

Directed by Jean Delannoy. Original story by Jean-Paul Sartre, with dialogue by Sartre and Jacques Laurent Bost. Camera: Christian Matras. Art Direction: Pimenoff. Music: Georges Auric.

With: Micheline Presle, Marcel Pagliero, Charles Dullin, Marguerite Moreno, Colette Ripert, Fernand Fabre, Jacques Erwin, Jim Gerald, Guy Decombe, Mouloudji.

Since *Les Jeux Sont Faits* is not a well-known film, and may never be in general distribution again, it is probably advisable to outline its plot first. (It was, incidentally, the first work written directly for the screen by French existentialist writer Jean-Paul Sartre.)

In an unnamed totalitarian state, Eve (Micheline Presle) is being systematically poisoned by her politician husband, who seeks to inherit her money and is also on the brink of consummating an affair with her sister.

Pierre (Marcel Pagliero) is a resistance worker heading an insurrection against the dictator. Eve dies, and almost simultaneously Pierre is killed in a street battle with the fascist forces. Both wander to a mysterious little street leading to heaven's ante-room. There, the busy and efficient secretary (Marguerite Moreno) explains that under certain conditions those who might well have met and become lovers in life may return to life on an experimental basis. If they can prove their love, they can live out their normal lives; if they fail, they must return, with no further appeal. Eve and Pierre, appalled by the soulless existence after death, in which the dead can witness the living but can communicate only with the dead, and without emotion, welcome the chance to return. One of the dead asks that they rescue his little girl from a loveless existence with her slatternly mother and current lover, and place her in a good home.

Back in the normal world, Eve and Pierre find their lives picking up from the instant of their apparent death. Eve is now aware of her husband's true character and intentions, and seeks unavailingly to warn her sister. Pierre, who in his hours of death had visited the dictator's palace, now knows that the dictator actually wanted the insurrection, and is merely using the resistance movement to further his own ends. Pierre's attempts to persuade his fellow resistance workers of this merely arouses their suspicions, suspicions that are increased when he re-establishes contact with Eve who, as wife of a

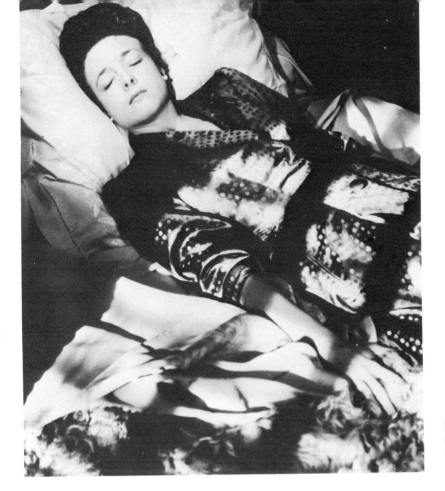

Eve (Micheline Presle) lies dying; the hand clutching at a rough-textured fur or rug is a recurring motif throughout the film.

governmental official, is regarded as being in the enemy's camp. Both Eve and Pierre are too concerned with their own problems to concentrate on their future; moreover, Pierre is embarrassed by encounters with Eve's society friends. They do however remember their promise, and rescue the child from her wretched home life.

Convinced that Pierre is a traitor, the resistance plans to assassinate him; however, he is warned by a friend, and the killers, believing him to be out, leave him and Eve alone in the apartment. They consummate their love, both out of necessity and desire, and feel sure that they will be allowed to remain with the living. Next day, however, Pierre has pangs of conscience, and feels it his duty to warn his comrades of the folly of an operation they

After her death, Eve places a consoling hand on the shoulder of her grieving sister Lucette (Colette Ripert), and does not yet know that her husband (Fernand Fabre) actually poisoned her, for her money and to possess Lucette.

Returned to life, Eve tries in vain to convince Lucette that her husband plans her seduction.

plan for that day. Eve, failing to dissuade him, goes to her husband's home to make one final attempt to reason with her sister. A traitor in the pay of the police shoots and kills Pierre just before his allotted 24-hour trial period is up, while simultaneously Eve dies again, aware now that her husband has already seduced her sister. Hopelessly, they return to the afterworld. As they are about to part for the last time, they are approached by a young couple who have committed suicide, and who ask about the possibilities of returning to life. "You can always try," they tell them, without conviction, as they separate.

Although Sartre's defeatist existentialist phi-

Pierre (center), accompanied by the shade of an executed French Revolution aristocrat (Charles Dullin, right) visits the palace of the dictator.

Eve reaches the mysterious little street that links life and death.

215

losophy influenced most of the purely dramatic and very downbeat French films of the post–World War II period (*Les Portes de la Nuit* in particular), actual filming of his works was delayed until the later 40s. *Les Jeux Sont Faits* (a gambling term, meaning in effect that the die is cast, that the wheel is already spinning and there is no way of changing the outcome) was his first foray into writing directly for the screen. It was not well liked in Europe, where critics resented the fact that Sartre's ideas were mystical yet at the same time atheistic and/or antireligious. It was not released in the U.S. until 1949, where a basic unfamiliarity with Sartre was a handicap. The film got tepid reviews and soon disappeared. It is, however, a most interesting and worthwhile film in many ways, with wry humor, a beautifully controlled performance from Micheline Presle, a surprisingly good one from the Gabin-like Marcel Pagliero (whose dialogue had to be dubbed, since he spoke no French) and a hauntingly melancholic score from Georges Auric at his Wagnerian best.

Despite the philosophic content of Sartre's dialogue, it is a film that is very easy to understand since it is so full of visual symbols: the repeated motif of a hand clutching at hair or fabric, signifying a desperate attempt to cling to life; the little dead-end street between life and death, dead trees on one side, living ones on the other, emphasizing the dividing line between the two worlds and the absence of half-measures; the gestures of the dictator as he practices a speech before a mirror, trying to decide whether expressions of dominance or supplication will most win over the populace. Thanks to the playing, and to Auric's score, the film is far more persuasive emotionally than it is intellectually, which is probably not what Mr. Sartre had in mind. It's a pessimistic film, but, like a Keaton movie, not a depressing one since the pessimism is so taken for granted. And there are moments of particularly joyful comedy, particularly from the magnificent Marguerite Moreno as the efficiently fussy secretary of the anteroom to Sartre's particular heaven or hell.

But in the long run, thanks almost entirely to Micheline Presle's playing, it winds up as a love story—something that cannot usually be said of life-and-death and other-world fantasies. Whether they be whimsical comedies like *Here Comes Mr. Jordan* or serious essays on social or political

Eve and Pierre, unseen, watch a street musician and, for all his poverty and wretchedness, envy him, for he is *alive*.

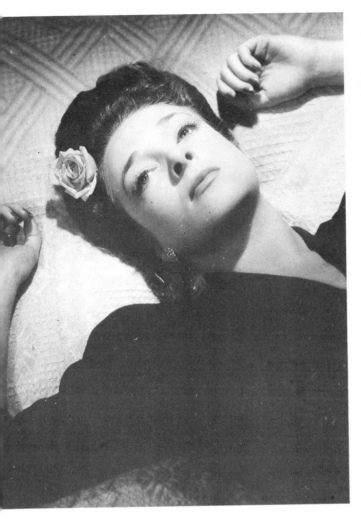

Eve reminds Pierre that they *must* love each other if they are to make their return to life permanent.

Having tried in vain to save Lucette, Eve is talking on the phone to Pierre and, hearing him shot down, dies again herself.

themes, as in the British *They Came to a City*, plot, and the novelty of the framework, command most of our attention. Michael Powell's *A Matter of Life and Death* (*Stairway to Heaven* in the U.S.) and *Les Jeux Sont Faits* (coincidentally very similar films made at almost the same time; indeed Sartre may well have been influenced by the Powell film, while reversing its optimism) are two exceptions in that we don't really care too much about the philosophies involved, but we *do* care about a happy ending for the romantic protagonists.

The major love scene in *Les Jeux Sont Faits* has rather strange undertones in that it comes somewhat too early in the association of Pierre and Eve for it to be entirely natural. Thus, while their emotion is genuine, there is a feeling of pressure: they not only have to prove themselves to each other,

but to the higher court which will determine if they are to remain alive. They are in a sense on display, and this gives a vaguely voyeuristic quality to the scene. However, even the standard cinematic tactics of those less explicit days—the camera panning around walls and ceiling, or catching a quick reaction shot of eyes or a hand—doesn't lessen its emotional impact. Micheline Presle, one of the finest of the newer French actresses at that time, was as expert then at suggesting women much older than she was in reality, as she was—in her years of maturity—at playing women much younger. Although such films as *Boule de Suif* and *Le Diable au Corps* probably tested—and proved—her versatility rather more, her performance in *Les Jeux Sont Faits* remains one of her best and most moving.

Stefan (Louis Jourdan) takes Lisa (Joan Fontaine) to his apartment.

Letter From an Unknown Woman

Universal, 1948.

Directed by Max Ophuls. Produced by John Houseman. Screenplay by Howard Koch from the novel by Stefan Zweig. Camera: Franz Planer. Music: Daniele Amphitheatrof. Art Direction: Alexander Golitzen. a Rampart production.

With: Joan Fontaine, Louis Jourdan, Mady Christians, Marcel Journet, Art Smith, Howard Freeman, Carol Yorke, John Good, Leo B. Pessin, Erskine Sanford, Otto Waldis, Sonja Bryden.

Incredible as it may seem, this exquisitely crafted film was greeted with apathy, if not hostility, on its original release. It ran into considerable censorship trouble in the U.S., entailing some minor cuts. Universal seemed embarrassed by it, and made little attempt to sell it. In Britain, where the Rank Organ-

ization contractually took all Universal films, it happened to coincide with a time when Rank was temporarily overstocked with both domestic and U.S. product, and thus was one of a group of Universal films that was shunted instead to a small independent company—resulting in second-rate and limited playing time (though a certain amount of favorable critical attention). In the U.S., *The New York Times* dismissed it as "tommyrot" and "schmaltz," and didn't even see fit to mention the name of the director! Such kudos as it was willing to bestow all went to star Joan Fontaine—who certainly deserved recognition not only for her fine performance, but also for her faith in the property, which she acquired for herself, and arranged for her husband to produce. Not at all incidentally, she also had the wit to recognize that the one man who should direct it was Max

Ophuls, European emigré with thus far only one Hollywood film to his credit, the highly stylized Douglas Fairbanks, Jr. swashbuckler *The Exile.*

It's hard to understand the press's castigation of the film as a kind of genre cliche, as though a *Letter from an Unknown Woman* rolled off the assembly line every other week. It may have represented a genre unto itself in Europe—where indeed Max Ophuls had specialized in such films (*Liebelei* in particular). But those films made little inroads on the U.S. market outside of the art theatres, and in Hollywood the tradition was split between such films as *Only Yesterday* and *Back Street*, firmly planted on U.S. soil, and the Lubitsch pastries,

ranging from *The Smiling Lieutenant* to *The Shop Around the Corner.* There really hadn't been a full-fledged film of its type since von Stroheim's silent (and quite different) *The Wedding March.* And even if the critics were more aware of the genre than their readers, one would have thought they would have applauded the idea of a European director, a master in his genre, coming to Hollywood to be given a free hand and all the money and technical expertise denied his earlier work.

Letter from an Unknown Woman didn't make the *New York Times*'s "Ten Best" list for 1948, while *Apartment for Peggy* and several other minor films did. No matter; they have been forgotten or

Lisa leaves the railway station after having said goodbye to her young son, unaware that a brief period spent in a quarantined carriage has exposed them both to plague.

relegated to their appropriate position based on box-office receipts, while Max Ophuls's film lives on.

Its plot, admittedly (like those of many filmic and literary classics) is fairly negligible. It details a hopeless, through-the-years love of a young girl for a famous and traditionally romantic pianist. At first as a child she loves him from afar; later they meet, and, convinced that he is truly falling in love with her, she savors every moment as they dine and walk through the snowy park, and that evening in his apartment she gives herself to him. Almost immediately he forgets her, and she resigns herself to being just one of his many affairs. She bears his child without complaint, and without notifying him, and enters into a loveless but ultimately satisfying marriage with an older man to provide security for the child. Years later, she meets the pianist again. His inspiration is gone now, and he is approaching dissolution, but his lifestyle is unchanged. Once more he woos her, never realizing who this woman is. She leaves him, this time for good—not knowing that her husband, aware of the previous liaison which she had promised not to renew, has followed her. Both mother and child die as a result of an outbreak of plague; in her last hours, she has written a long, detailed letter to the pianist, telling him

of her love and the child that he never knew. The husband, meanwhile, has challenged him to a duel —and as was his custom, he had planned to leave town without regard for his honor. But the letter changes things and reawakens his honor and his conscience: he leaves to keep his rendezvous in the morning, and almost certain death.

As can be seen, such a story could well be maudlin or melodramatic. It is neither, and its only illogical note is that the pianist could forget the woman so quickly, so sensitive and loving does she become in Joan Fontaine's hands, and thus so totally different from the women he must have been used to. In any case, story is of far less importance here than style—and by any standards, *Letter from an Unknown Woman* is one of the most elegant films that Hollywood ever produced. The art direction is superb, creating a completely convincing Viennese milieu out of Universal's standing sets (including the Frankenstein village) and of course many elaborate new ones. Counterpoint and irony are used throughout: the couple enjoying the romantic voyage of their dreams (or of the woman's dreams anyway) as they sit in a fake fairground carriage while views of the world are trundled past the window on painted canvas, or dancing rapturously to the strains of a romantic waltz—while the

220

plump women in the orchestra munch on sausage and complain about the overtime.

Ophuls and cameraman Planer had worked together in Europe, and their collaboration here shows a refinement of their teamwork. The camera glides and dollies as it always does in Ophuls films with incredible smoothness, but while the technique is dazzling in itself, it doesn't hide the thought behind individual compositions or camera movements. When, breathless with excitement, the woman is finally taken up to the pianist's rooms, the camera duplicates exactly the angle and movement of an earlier shot, when the then young girl had watched the pianist take one of his casual affairs up the same stairs. When, towards the end of the film, Fontaine returns to him for the second time, bringing a small bouquet of flowers, the camera follows her into the room and doesn't even stop to emphasize the symbolic point as she lays the flowers down casually on a chessboard. It is a thoughtless, natural gesture on the part of the woman, and Ophuls isn't going to make more of it than that by moving into a closeup, or halting the camera's movement to punctuate the point. A few minutes later the camera stays on Joan Fontaine's face—first happy, then quickly disillusioned—as in the background we hear Jourdan sending his manservant down to the delicatessen for a midnight snack—". . . the *usual* things."

In many ways, *Letter from an Unknown Woman* is far more Ophuls than Stefan Zweig. Several of Zweig's novels have been adapted to the screen, many of them with more fidelity to the original than this one. While they sometimes work well dramatically, they are not particularly successful or satisfying in a romantic sense, due in part to Zweig's inherent harshness. The original novel *Letter from an Unknown Woman* is far less romantic than the movie adaptation; at one point the woman of the title is frankly a prostitute, a turn of events that would certainly have dismayed both Miss Fontaine *and* the Production Code. In fact most changes in the film seem to have been made because of censorship restrictions, and yet they do not emerge as compromises, merely as changes totally in keeping with the Ophuls method of mellowing and romanticizing. (Later, as in the work of John Ford, bitterness and even harshness would creep into his final films.)

Although the movies have much to answer for in their many desecrations or distortions of literary classics, there are occasions when the shoe is on the other foot. Stanley Kubrick's *Barrie Lyndon* is far more successful on *its* filmic level than Thackeray's original novel is on *its* literary levels, and one day the movie may well come to be regarded as the "definitive" version of that work. So, very probably, will *Letter from an Unknown Woman*.

Lisa with her husband Johann (Marcel Journet), who is aware of Lisa's love for Stefan, and after her death, challenges him to a duel.

Micheline Presle, one of France's finest actresses, gives a superb performance as Martha.

Le Diable au Corps

France, 1949.

Directed by Claude Autant-Lara. Screenplay by Jean Aurenche and Pierre Bost from the novel by Raymond Radiguet. Camera: Music: Rene Cloerec. Produced by Paul Graetz.

With: Micheline Presle, Gerard Phillipe, Jean Debucourt, Denise Grey, Palau, Jean Varas, Jeanne Perez, Charles Vissieres, Germaine Ledoyen, Maurice Lagrenee, Andre Bervil, Richard Francoeur, Jacques Tati.

In its day, *Le Diable au Corps (Devil in the Flesh)* was almost as much of a cause celebre as *Extase* had been, and release in the United States seemed extremely unlikely. In view of the rigidity of censorship at the time, and the power wielded by the Catholic Legion of Decency, it is quite a remarkable tribute to the common sense that in this case was lurking behind all the bureaucracy, and that finally prevailed.

The problem this time was not so much explicit

detail—there's no nudity and none of the erotic symbolism of the earlier film—but *theme*, and even more important, *attitudes*. The story deals with the love affair between a teenaged schoolboy and a married woman, and it deals with it in a relatively sympathetic way. What probably saved it in the eyes of the American censorial moralists was that the affair could hardly be termed a happy one, and all those involved suffered far more moral retribution than their "sins" really justified.

The film begins at the point where *A Farewell to Arms* leaves off. It is Armistice Day in Paris, but a rainy, depressing day in which all the noises of celebration seem hollow. François (Gerard Phillipe) witnesses, casually, the preparations for a funeral —which gives the film a doom-laden opening, even though the audience knows nothing as yet about the person who has died. The film then goes into flashback, to chronicle François's first meeting with Marthe (Micheline Presle), a novice nurse at a military hospital (the groans and the blood are too much

Martha meets François (Gerard Phillipe), a schoolboy, during the first day of her new duties as a nurse.

for her, and she faints while working on her first case). Francois is still a high school student, she older, and being urged by her parents to marry. François is smitten by her and pursues her; she is flattered, and permits a romantic relationship to develop. However, Francois is still too young and immature to understand or to be able to handle real love; he is given to temper tantrums and moody fits

of suspicion and jealousy. He deliberately fails to keep one all-important date, though he watches secretly to make sure that Marthe is there. Despairing of his attitude, Marthe allows herself to be pushed into marriage with an older man she does not love, who is about to leave for the front.

Shortly afterwards, François contacts her again and wants to resume their relationship. Reluc-

Though the relationship is discouraged by Martha's mother, François continues to pursue her.

as the railway station background to the lovers' partings in *Brief Encounter*.

Superbly photographed, and with a sparse but rich score by Rene Cloerec, which manages to convey a sense of mounting passion mixed with melancholy, *Le Diable au Corps* is directed with incredible sensitivity by Claude Autant-Lara and beautifully acted by its two stars who, in addition, are cast to perfection.

Phillipe plays the seventeen-year-old youth with remarkable conviction; his almost gauntly slim body suggests the adolescence which his sensitive face might otherwise deny. He appears haunted throughout, gripped by passions he gives in to without understanding. And lovely, tender Micheline Presle—who seems both lover and mother to the boy—gives what is unquestionably her finest and most delicately shaped performance. Physically too, she is also *exactly* right, full (but not provocatively) figured, her face suggesting both the physical

Reunited after a long separation, Martha, though now married, realizes that she still loves Francois and invites him to return to her apartment that night.

tantly, but not really able to help herself, Marthe agrees, and they make love one night when François tells his parents that he has gone on a camping trip. They continue their relationship openly; Marthe's mother is very bitter, and the couple plan to tell the husband but can never bring themselves to do it. Meanwhile, his letters go unread and he cannot understand why he never hears from his wife. At one point, his unit is traveling through Paris and he will be between trains at the station for a short period; he begs Marthe to join him there, but out of loyalty to François, she refuses to do so. Marthe becomes pregnant by Francois, and gets to the hospital too late. She dies. For the first time, Francois is aware of what his selfishness has caused. The husband is grief-stricken, but believes the baby to be his.

The whole film has a sad, gray tone to it. Everything seems to be happening at twilight, or in the rain, yet the use of Paris locations offsets this apparent artifice. One particularly effective location is the ferryboat station on the Seine for the scene where François fails to keep his appointment, serving much the same dramatic and symbolic purpose

Martha awaits François's arrival. He has told his family that he is going on a camping trip.

With her husband away at the front, Martha continues her affair with François quite openly.

and spiritual love which would so inflame a sensitive and idealistic older schoolboy.

Autant-Lara directs the film—and the two stars play it—so that while we experience a sense of outrage and shock, and great pity for the husband, at the same time we cannot help but feel intense compassion for the entrapped lovers too. *Le Diable au Corps* is a surprisingly long film for its basically uneventful (in terms of incident) story, but there's not a wasted moment in it, and it is virtually a perfect movie. Certainly nothing that could be done with the story on today's anything-goes screen could in any way enhance it, and the only jarring note in the entire film is the obligatory panning away from the lovers in the bedroom scene to a dormant fire which suddenly blazes into life. Even this cliché is to a large degree covered by Cloerec's music, but still it's the one moment when we are aware that this is a *movie* and not life itself. (Despite the intimacy of the whole film, its overriding taste and tact prevent the audience from ever being put into a voyeuristic frame of mind.)

Perhaps the clincher to the film's claim on our emotions is the knowledge that the short novel was admitted to be largely autobiographical—and that the tormented author, Raymond Radiguet, committed suicide at age twenty.

Francois joins the now pregnant Martha for an evening of celebration (the armistice is expected momentarily) before she checks in to the hospital. There are complications, however, and Martha dies. In an unusually moving climax, she dies with François's name on her lips; but her husband believes it to be the name she has selected for "their" child.

Elizabeth Taylor was at the peak of her youth and beauty in 1950, and those qualities brought distinction to many a movie that might otherwise have been routine. One of them was THE CONSPIRATOR, which managed to be quite a solid little love story, until it was revealed that co-star Robert Taylor was playing a Communist traitor, at which point the film sidetracked into melodrama.

From the Fifties On

Typifying the studios' attempts to appeal to younger audiences by creating younger and, eventually, even teen-age stars, were Piper Laurie and Tony Curtis, Universal's popular duo of the fifties. They appeared, not always with total conviction on Curtis' part, in everything from historical swashbucklers (*The Prince Who Was a Thief*) to modern motor-racing sagas (*Johnny Dark*).

The last three decades are perhaps still too close to us for enough true perspectives to develop, and the purely contemporary scene is discussed in the final pages. However, the love story—if it didn't dominate the movie screens in the early fifties—certainly occupied a substantial portion of it. Hollywood had met, and overcome, the initial competition from television, and was expending its best energies to sustain the great new audience it had attracted during the war years. It was also fortunate in being blessed by the presence of a number of newly developed female stars of unusual and even spectacular beauty—and in some cases exceptional acting ability too. Ava Gardner, Grace Kelly, Claire Bloom, Kim Novak (a much maligned actress whose work can now be seen to have an instinctive, naturalistic quality that is most appealing), Elizabeth Taylor, Patricia Neal, Eleanor Parker and Deborah Kerr represented quite a pool of talent—and beauty—from which the Hollywood love story could draw, just as such talented directors as George Stevens, Joseph Mankiewicz, Alfred Hitchcock, Fred Zinnemann, John Ford, Elia Kazan and Carol Reed were working at, or near to, their creative peaks.

In RIO GRANDE (1950), Maureen O'Hara and John Wayne played an estranged married couple, a state often emphasized by the composition of the frame—as here, where the tent pole divides them and sets up a stiff, formal relationship. (Later, again under John Ford's direction, they celebrated a far more joyful wooing and wedding in *The Quiet Man*, one of the decade's loveliest romantic films, and one of its biggest hits.)

Lovely French star Micheline Presle brought grace and maturity to a brace of 1950 movies; above, with John Garfield in UNDER MY SKIN; left, with Tyrone Power in AN AMERICAN GUERRILLA IN THE PHILIPPINES.

SO LITTLE TIME (1952) was a moving British-made tragedy of a doomed wartime romance between Maria Schell and Marius Goring.

LIMELIGHT (1952) was one of Charles Chaplin's best films, and one of the few to deal honestly with genuine love between an old man and a young girl. With Chaplin and Claire Bloom.

MOGAMBO (1953): Gable pretends to be carousing with Ava Gardner in order to disillusion Grace Kelly; a more serious and less rambunctiously comic remake of *Red Dust*.

Stevens's *A Place in the Sun,* Zinnemann's *Teresa,* Reed's *The Man Between,* Mankiewicz's *Five Fingers,* Lewin's *Pandora and the Flying Dutchman,* Chaplin's tender *Limelight* and Hitchcock's *Vertigo* were all outstanding romantic films from this period. At the time, we looked back to the 40s and 30s and felt that the movies were going downhill fast—but the fifties represented the last great stand of the studio system, and the films from its first five years have a relaxed confidence in their own quality—and appeal—that was soon to disappear in a renewed and more desparate onslaught against the competition of television.

Many of the films of those years have improved tremendously with age. The unrestrained romanticism of *Pandora and the Flying Duchman*

Hitchcock's TO CATCH A THIEF (1954) was also comedic with thriller overtones, but the director managed to create both eroticism and passion in its romantic interludes. Cary Grant and Grace Kelly were ideally cast.

Although a comedy, the British GENE-VIEVE (1954) was notable for both the charm and sophistication of its handling of married life, with John Gregson and Dinah Sheridan giving beautiful performances as the married couple very much in love but driven to frequent frustration and temper flareups by the everyday friction of the marriage institution.

ROOM AT THE TOP was somewhat of a breakthrough film in 1958 for its straightforward treatment of sex. Its acceptance without censorship battles paved the way for rapid relaxing of long-held censorship restrictions. Laurence Harvey and Heather Sears drive off to a loveless marriage at the film's climax.

Married off-screen, Joanne Woodward and Paul Newman made interesting on-screen lovers (this scene is from 1960's ON THE TERRACE) but their movie vehicles were chosen for their own merits rather than as star showcases, and thus they never quite developed the boxoffice value of Elizabeth Taylor and Richard Burton.

was welcome, but seemed rather quirky in the 50s. Now it seems to have joined the ranks of Cocteau's modern legends. Too, its bold use of color, before color became a commonplace commodity, reminds us today how little color has really been tapped for dramatic and exotic expression. Hitchcock's *Vertigo*, considered at the time purely on its values as a thriller, was criticized for its occasional obtuseness. But today, *Vertigo* can be seen to have been considerably ahead of its time—a trite and overused phrase, but one very applicable to this particular film. It may well be Hitchcock's masterpiece; quite certainly it deserves to be studied as a love story rather more than as a thriller, and it contains Kim Novak's finest screen acting—even admitting that Hitchcock capitalized on her well-known lack of self-confidence, and manipulated that trait in his di-

rection of her. Her work in *Middle of the Night*, a transposed (and slightly romanticized) transference of Paddy Chayevsky's play about the love affair of an elderly man with a young girl, and the marital problems that ultimately develop, likewise is a sensitively acted interpretation of a difficult role.

Alas, the real competition from TV brought forth a full-scale war rather than a carefully planned battle from Hollywood. Its compeititon was to be unsubtle: wide screens, 3-D, color, size, spectacle, shock, sensation, horror films, an increased catering to the young via teenage rock-and-roll and beach-party movies, attempts to push back the barriers of censorship via films which increasingly dealt with sex. The love story was affected as much as any other genre, perhaps more so, since it lost its simplicity. All of the old romantic chestnuts were

HOLIDAY FOR HENRIETTA (1955) was a film within a film, a satire of movie-making. It was difficult to keep track of what was real at any given time, but Michel Auclair and Dany Robin, whether taken straight, or as lampoons of familiar French romantic types, were a delightful team.

The misfire THE MISFITS (1961), dogged by disaster during and after production, was nevertheless an extremely interesting film that took on added poignancy after the deaths of stars Clark Gable (whose last film it was) and Marilyn Monroe.

Stanley Kubrick's SPARTACUS (1961) offered an interesting, off-beat, and quite effective romantic teaming in Jean Simmons and Kirk Douglas. It too benefitted from the as yet not overly exploited new sexual freedom on the screen.

dragged out and reroasted. With the right director and star combination, as happened with *An Affair to Remember,* the results could still be agreeable. But far too many of these remakes were blown up and distorted to a point where they lost all their real values. The new *A Farewell to Arms* became such an epic that its love story was lost in the shuffle; and the detailed agony of a childbirth scene left one only with the need to escape the theatre, not to settle down for a quiet and touching finale, as in the original version.

Universal's spectacular remakes of their biggest 30s successes—*Imitation of Life, Magnificent Obsession, Back Street*—became top-heavy star vehicles, overloaded with decor, fashions and glamour. In the third version of *Back Street,* the almost

Much underrated and one of the best films of the sixties, THE AMERICANIZATION OF EMILY was somewhat overshadowed in 1963 by the similar (in mood) DR. STRANGELOVE. The cynicism, desperation and passion of a wartime romance were beautifully depicted by James Garner and (especially) Julie Andrews, neither of whom have topped those performances since.

Frequently imitated since, but never quite equalled, TOM JONES (1961) was a remarkable mixture of bawdiness and romanticism. With Albert Finney, Susannah York.

The science fiction spoof BARBARELLA was one of the major delights of 1968, with Jane Fonda's comic timing and casual sensuality its biggest asset. Above, she joins David Hemmings in space-age sex; below, in angel John Phillip Law's "nest" for a more traditional expression of the romantic urge.

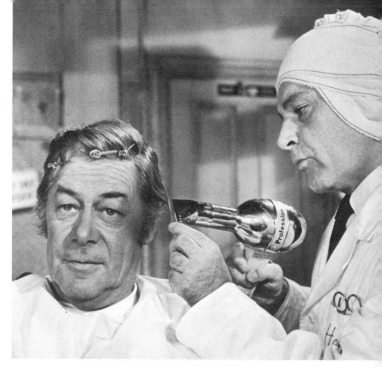

waiflike heroine (Irene Dunne in the 30s, Margaret Sullavan in the 40s) had become a dynamic, aggressive ruller of a fashion empire, and Susan Hayward, in such a role, not only towered over her male vis-a-vis (John Gavin), but was hardly in need of our sympathy or compassion.

From the 60s on, and of course more so in the Hollywood film than in the European, sex has generally replaced love—and yet the new filmic freedom has not produced an erotic masterpiece to match an *Extase.* Many films—like Kubrick's *Bar-*

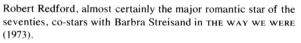

Robert Redford, almost certainly the major romantic star of the seventies, co-stars with Barbra Streisand in THE WAY WE WERE (1973).

rie Lyndon—have resisted the temptations to use the new erotic freedoms, and instead have been romanticist rather than romantic. There has been a tendency too to laugh at sex, love and marriage—not necessarily a bad thing, but again a tendency that takes one away from genuine emotion. And emotion is what is most needed in the love story, and is most *lacking* in the average contemporary film, even so sincere (if somewhat loaded) a film as *Coming Home.*

However, the sixties and seventies have been unusually turbulent and complex periods. It may well be that the best and most perceptive films about these years have yet to come—just as the

1979's PLAYERS was in many ways an appalling film—rather like a 1930's Republic "B" movie stretched to ponderous Tolstoyan proportions. But the seriousness with which it took its parade of cliches, and the care and production polish—spread over locations on two continents—certainly indicated a recognition of the *need* to get back to the older style of romantic movie. With Ali MacGraw and Dean-Paul Martin.

best films about World War II appeared well after the fact. And already, 60s films that seemed shallow at the time are beginning to take on a more interesting patina as being reflective, if not always in a complimentary way, of the era. Now is much too early to pass generalized judgments on the romantic films of these years—other than to salute the passing of the traditional Hollywood love story in those first years of the 50s.

234

A Place in the Sun

Paramount, 1951.

Produced and directed by George Stevens. Screenplay by Michael Wilson and Harry Brown from the Theodore Dreiser novel *An American Tragedy*. Camera: William C. Mellor: Music: Franz Waxman.

With: Montgomery Clift, Elizabeth Taylor, Shelley Winters, Keefe Brasselle, Fred Clark, Raymond Burr, Frieda Inescort, Shepperd Strudwick, Kathryn Gorney, Ann Revere, Walter Sande, Ted De Corsia, John Ridgely, Lois Chartrand, Ian Wolfe, Douglas Spencer, Paul Press.

A Place in the Sun is one of the best of a number of lushly romantic films (in varying ways, *Pandora and the Flying Ducthman* and *Limelight* were others) that seemed to usher in the 50s, only to disappear when new technology—wide-screen and 3-D processes—and a desperate attempt to combat the competition of television took over, pushing the romantic film aside in favor of spectacle and shock.

A Place in the Sun was somewhat criticized for having soft-pedaled and distorted the crusading social criticism of Theodore Dreiser's important but unwieldy novel. Even its title is a romantic displacement of the original intent, and to have seen it as a film parallel to Dreiser's conception would probably have meant the quickly aborted Eisenstein conception of the early 30s, which soon gave way to the much criticized (and one might say maligned) version by Josef von Sternberg, an interesting film, however, and not without pictorial influences on Stevens's remake.

More than with most films, *A Place in the Sun*

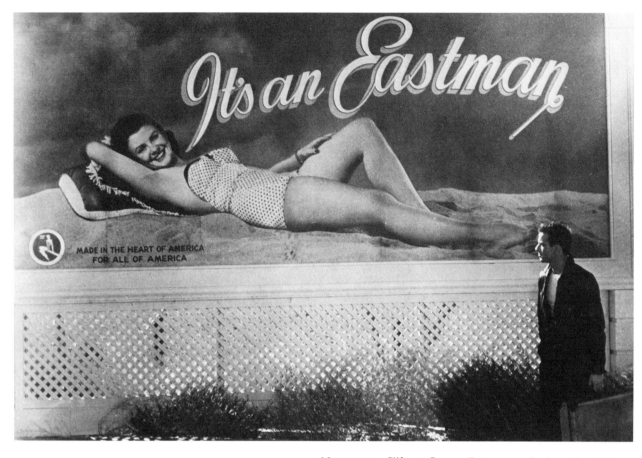

Montgomery Clift as George Eastman, arrived on the West Coast and about to take a menial job with the conglomerate industry owned by rich but distant relatives.

depends not so much on writing or on great acting as it does on directorial technique. Stevens's later films all had this in common; they were the work of a perfectionist, who would shoot endless takes of the same scene, plus alternate and protection shots, and then fuss further in the editing stages until every scene was honed to its peak. Since most films are (or at least, were) intended to be seen just once, the method is understandable, since the initial impact of a "perfect" film can be overwhelming. But on repeat showings, the perfection gradually becomes a flaw, lacking the minor mistakes that often give a film life, or the relaxing of control that sometimes gives it spontaneity—as in the films of John Ford. A Stevens comedy like *The More the Merrier* or even a classic Western like *Shane,* begins to lose something on repeat viewings. On the other hand, a love story like *A Place in the Sun,* unlike a comedy or a Western, exerts an appeal that is wholly emotional, and the director is justified in manipulating that emotion by all the means at his disposal. It is *because* the technique in *A Place in the Sun* is so perfect—ranging from the casting to the haunting

score and the languidly romantic photography, with its huge closeups and slow, dreamlike fades and dissolves—that it does work so well on repeat viewings. True, as in Leo McCarey's *Make Way for Tomorrow,* one is occasionally *aware* of being used. One tended to resent it in that film because in many ways the story was basically dishonest; one knew it, yet had to admit at the same time that the emotional impact was there because of McCarey's skill.

In one way, the casting disarms one in *A Place in the Sun* since it immediately places the film on an almost symbolic, rather than realistic plateau. Elizabeth Taylor is the embodiment of so many unattainable American dreams—perfect beauty, wealth, unselfish love—that we sense from the very beginning that any love story with this virtual goddess is doomed. Montgomery Clift is so likable, sensitive, and so deserving of happiness, that we likewise cannot believe that, as Dreiser intended, he is merely being swept along by forces he can't control. Lastly, the dull, whimpering girl who serves a momentary need for Clift's loneliness—as he does for hers—is, as played by Shelley Winters, so abra-

236

An early meeting with Angela (Elizabeth Taylor).

Parties and weekends with Angela introduce George to a dream-like existence that he never thought possible for him.

Examples of the huge, intimate closeups with which Stevens shot many of the love scenes.

George Stevens directs Shelley Winters.

Contrasting scenes from the 1931 version: Phillips Holmes with Frances Dee as the society girl, and with Sylvia Sidney as the factory girl.

sive and dispiriting that there is almost no need for a moral choice, and anything that is planned for her seems justifiable! Von Sternberg's version at least played fairer with the audience in terms of its casting of these key roles. Frances Dee, as the rich girl, was beautiful and elegant—but not an unattainable dream. Phillips Holmes as the boy was far more of a schemer and certainly lacked the basic integrity of the Clift characterization. And finally Sylvia Sidney as the factory girl, while a distinct contrast to the worldly-wise sophistication of Dee, still had a waif-like appeal and vulnerability. One felt that if convention and class distinction had forced a marriage between the two, it wouldn't have been that bad a match—whereas the Shelley Winters role, as written and played, makes one feel that the George Eastman character as played by Clift must have been absolutely desperate, rather than merely lonely, to enter into a relationship with her.

However, these are feelings that enter the mind only when one draws back from the film to study it coldly. While it is on the screen, the emotions are too fully engaged, the eye too dazzled by Taylor's beauty and sensitive playing, to consider these limitations logically.

Despite knowing how Stevens is doing it all, the cumulative effect is tremendous, even if it more resembles Greek than American tragedy. It is one of the supreme achievements of the American romantic cinema.

Vernon Gray and Janette Scott.

Now and Forever

Associated British Picture Corporation–Pathé,
1956.

Produced and Directed by Mario Zampi. Photographed in Technicolor by Erwin Hillier. Story and screenplay, R.F. Delderfield and Michael Pertwee. Music by Stanley Black.

With: Janette Scott, Vernon Gray, Kay Walsh, Jack Warner, Pamela Brown, Sonia Dresdell, Moultrie Kelsall, David Kossoff, Wilfrid Lawson, Marjorie Rhodes, Ronald Squire, Charles Victor, Guy Middleton, Thora Hird, Bryan Forbes, Michael Pertwee.

Even in 1956, *Now and Forever* was a complete anachronism, something like a Deanna Durbin musical romance with*out* the music. (And fifteen years earlier, the Durbins would have been archaic too, without their music). Since it is virtually unknown in the U.S., some brief indication of plot is necessary before one proceeds to its charm—and its sad fate.

Janette (Janette Scott) and Mike (Vernon Gray) are two teenagers who meet when Mike, a garage mechanic, is kind to her and sees her through a school concert when her mother, a society snob, prefers to play golf. Janette idolizes her father, who has been separated from her mother for some years. When he dies, she has only Mike to turn to. The love that develops between the two is entirely innocent, and approved of by both Mike's father and Janette's school headmistress. However, they keep their love a secret from Janette's mother, knowing that she, with her possessive and snobbish attitudes, would forbid it. A malevolent schoolteacher informs the mother however, and the latter surprises the two youngsters in an apparently compromising situation. To her announced decision of sending Janette to live with an aunt in Canada, a distraught Janette attempts suicide. While the parents thrash out the problem, the young lovers take matters into their own hands by eloping, heading for Scotland and Gretna Green, where, as per tradition, runaway lovers can marry without delay or bureaucracy. In their dash to the North, the couple encounter both kindness and hostility, always with the police at their heels, for the mother has trumped up a robbery charge. Eventually, their money gone and their car wrecked, they are cornered by parents and police just as they are about to cross the border into Scotland. However, their case has attracted nationwide sympathy. On the mother's promise to relent, they agree to go back and wait until they are old enough to make their marriage work.

When it was first screened for Allied Artists executives (Allied held the United States franchise for the Associated British movies), almost none of them stayed through the whole film, one even remarking as he stalked out that it was high time that Jan Grippo (producer of the Bowery Boys series) was sent over to England to show them how to make movies! It got a resolute thumbs down, and was never heard of again in this country in terms of a theatrical release. (Allied didn't really *want* the British films anyway, and only took them because they were contractually obligated to do so, since Pathé released *their* films in England.)

Pathé was always a very conservative and even Victorian company, and few of its films had ever made really notable dents in the U.S. market. Their 1939 *Dark Eyes of London* had been a surprisingly grisly Bela Lugosi horror film that had done well, *The Queen of Spades* had been a prestige success on the U.S. art-house circuit, and a very few comedies or dramas (*Last Holiday, Laughter in Paradise*) had achieved some popularity because of the omnipresence of Alec Guinness or Alastair Sim. But the majority of the Associated British films got but sparse exhibition in the U.S., and then mainly in areas and theatres with strong pro-British leanings. *Now and Forever* was obviously a very old-fashioned movie,

too evenly (and unconvincingly) divided into blacks and whites. Even in England, the long sustained market for this kind of film was rapidly dying out. Nevertheless, with a little thought and imagination behind the advertising, it *could* have been sold in a limited way, and despite its (unfortunately) outdated morals and attitudes, might well have charmed and pleased the right audiences. Seen today, a quarter of a century after its production, it's a visitor from another world, a shattering and rather sad reminder of how values, moral and otherwise, have changed in the intervening decades. In some ways, it could be considered a companion picture to introduce the 1966 Hayley Mills film, *The Family Way*. Both could have complemented one another rather well, not only for their story content, but in showing the changes that had come over the movies' treatment of love and sex. *The Family Way*, considered a somewhat daring movie in its day, likewise seems rather archaic at the end of the seventies, and one would really have to add an *Emmanuelle* epic to complete a triple-bill that would fully illustrate the new "sophistication" that has come to movies about love and marriage.

Now and Forever lay dormant for ten years or more, when it was sold to (but almost never shown in) a package for American television. As a film, *Now and Forever* is a little slow getting under way, due mainly to the stereotyped nature of the adult roles. But once the elopement is under way, it takes off with warmth and real humor, and spends most of its time in the heart of the English countryside. Occasionally, the lily is gilded just a little, with fa-

Kay Walsh (as the understanding headmistress) and Janette Scott.

mous beauty spots juxtaposed into (apparently) a single location. For example, Bourton-on-the-Water, one of the loveliest villages in the Cotswolds, lends itself to being just a *part* of the town in which the heroine lives. England *is* beautiful—but its charm lies in its naturalness and lack of perfection, and the country is not quite as breathtaking in every direction as this film seems to imply!

The whole film has a pleasingly naive fairytale quality, and its kinship to the Durbin films, mentioned earlier, is probably no accident. It is particularly close in spirit (and even individual incident) to Durbin's *First Love*—even to the school concert, the elements of class distinction, and the sympathetic treatment of "underlings." (A waiter and a housemaid are two of the most likable and helpful lesser characters.) Many of the pictorial compositions are designed purely to stress beauty, color and youth—as for example, when Janette Scott throws open windows that are surrounded by flowers, an image so identical to one in the old hand-colored Méliès film *The Flower Fairy* that it can hardly be coincidental.

Just as the Durbin films depended so much on the gaiety and vivacity of their star, so does *Now and Forever* rely a great deal on the beauty and sensitivity of its star. Janette Scott, making a graceful transition from child roles to adult ones, gives a most appealing and moving performance. And even though one can occasionally sense that she is being directed, it is still the best thing that she has ever done. The shift from schoolgirl to near maturity is achieved very effectively, over and above such obvious devices as getting rid of pigtails and switching to lower-key lighting. It's pity that so many of her

subsequent films, primarily comedies (*Double Bunk, School for Scoundrels*) and later, sci-fi thrillers (*The Day of the Triffids, Crack in the World*) were content to use her youth and beauty, instead of carefully developing her as a dramatic star as well, as Rank had done with Patricia Roc in the 40s. Scott seemed on the threshold of major stardom in Britain at one point, and was certainly one of the most publicized of the newer players. Following *Now and Forever*, she was absolutely ripe for roles calling for youth and perhaps whimsy—she'd have made a marvelous Barrie heroine in remakes of *Peter Pan* or *A Kiss for Cinderella*. But unfortunately she was tied to Associated British at the critical stage in her career, and their unimaginative formula (both in the films that they made and in the stars they developed) aborted what might have been a unique career.

Throughout, *Now and Forever* is a thoroughly pleasant film. One can't really believe in the near-satanic evil of the vindictive teacher (Sonia Dresdell) or the casual bitchiness of Pamela Brown as the mother—or, for that matter, in the good-natured virtue of the hero, a somewhat more idealized version of the Robert Stack of the Durbins. But there's much more conviction in the cameo roles, especially Ronald Squire's kindly but worldly-wise waiter, and best of all, Wilfrid Lawson's hilarious yet frighteningly accurate study of an innkeeper, greedy, lazy, lecherous and harmlessly crazy!

The fate of the film in America is particularly sad, since its theatrical exposure was nil and its television exhibition minimal. Moreover, the television prints were all printed not in Technicolor, but in the very unstable Eastmancolor, which tends to

242

become faded or distorted very quickly. Apart from being a paean of praise to the English countryside, its background of springtime was essential to the story of exuberant young love. When the film finally *did* get a single showing away from television late in 1978 (nontheatrical, but at least on a large screen at one of New York's universities), the inevitable had happened, and color fading was seriously impairing the film's visual beauty. Now, thanks to the miracle of modern technology, spring had been turned into autumn. The trees had been changed from greens to browns; green fields looked like rain-parched deserts; even the heroine's gaily colored dance costume had reverted, like Cinderella's gown at the stroke of midnight, to a drab gray. Future historians (or even some of the more pretentious contemporary ones) might well look at prints like this in years to come and decide that director Zampi was using color stylistically, to symbolize the antagonistic destiny and autumnal gloom that threatens and defeats youth in contemporary England! Even if one considers *Now and Forever* a relatively unimportant film (and nobody *should* make a judgment like that, for film has a disquieting way of changing its values, or revealing new ones, as time passes), then one must realize that there are other films which are indisputably important, and where true color rendition is critical (Nicholas Ray's *Rebel Without a Cause* for example) and the same thing is happening to them.

Despite the fading color and the by now spectacularly changed attitudes, 1978's belated unveiling of *Now and Forever* in the U.S. showed that its innate charm and taste still worked, and that the sincerity of Janette Scott's performance was still equally valid. Only one moment raised an unintended (though affectionate) laugh, and this was towards the end of the film, when a closeup of a newspaper carried a seemingly exaggerated headline to the effect that the elopers were still at large. Surprising as it may seem, this was *not* an instance of dramatic license or exaggeration. At one time, the race by elopers from England to Scotland's Gretna Green was a centuries-old romantic tradition; so much so that the film took it for granted, and didn't bother to actually state it. The only reference to Gretna Green was on a sign-post in the film's closing reel. Moreover, in England at the time—apart from news items of above-average interest in the war years—nothing *ever* happened. This was well before the race riots, the punk-rockers and the political scandals a la Jeremy Thorpe, and newspapers did indeed pounce on such elopement stories, giving them both extensive coverage and even the headlines shown in the film. Today of course, eloping is almost as outdated as marriage, but *Now and Forever,* a delightful breath of fresh air, is a lovely reminder of the days when it wasn't. Even if life was never *quite* that innocent, it's good to think that we once believed that it could be.

P.S.: Events came full circle in England in the summer of 1979. Two teen-agers *did* run away from home to get married. With the exception of some typical 70's permissiveness—they were on the run for a longer period and managed to set up house for themselves —their adventure paralleled *Now and Forever* exactly, even to a sympathetic parent on one side opposed to an unsympathetic one on the other, and an eventual surrender to the police. Their escapade occupied the front page headlines of *every* English newspaper virtually *every* day for weeks, every near-miss by the police being reported with special glee and public support for the youngsters growing day by day. Incredibly, nobody had the acumen to revive the film on television during all the hullaballoo. One of the few people to recognize the remarkable parallel was star Janette Scott, now a Hollywood resident but then on vacation in England, and much amused by the confirmation that those aspects of *Now and Forever* if anything *under*stated the case.

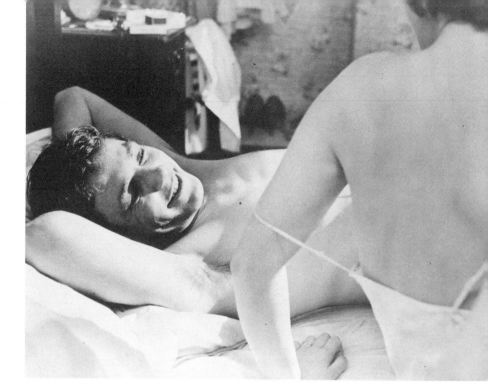

Saturday Night and Sunday Morning

A Woodfall Production, 1960.

Directed by Karel Reisz. Produced by Harry Saltzman and Tony Richardson. Screenplay by Alan Sillitoe, from his novel. Camera: Freddie Francis. Editor: Seth Holt. Music: Johnny Dankworth.

With: Albert Finney, Shirley Anne Field, Rachel Roberts, Hylda Baker, Norman Rossington, Bryan Pringle, Robert Cawdron, Edna Morris, Elsie Wagstaff, Frank Pettitt, Avis Bunnage, Colin Blakeley, Irene Richmond, Cameron Hall, Alister Williamson, Louise Dunn, Anne Blake, Peter Madden.

Although *Saturday Night and Sunday Morning* is quite certainly about love—and sex—it is actually the very antithesis of the romantic film. As a love story, if one can call it that, it is perhaps less interesting than as a dramatic story—but circumstances have caused it to be a film that is unusually reflective of its times, both artistically and socially, and therein lies its importance.

In an artistic sense, the very late fifties and early sixties represented a rare peaking for British film (and for certain other arts too). Generally speaking, for a multitude of reasons ranging from economy to national characteristics, British films were rarely innovative. There might be (and often was) superb craftsmanship, fine writing, brilliant acting—but in terms of content, or style, it had always been done somewhere else, earlier—and usually by Hollywood. Not necessarily *better*, but earlier. David Lean's Dickens films were the best of their kind, for example, but MGM had beaten them to the punch by a full ten years. Somehow, the spirit of optimism that (temporarily) pervaded Britain in the late 50s resulted in a kind of artistic leadership in certain areas. The Beatles' music was new —and influenced the world. For good or ill, the miniskirt was new—and influenced fashions around the world. And the tough, cynical, honest writing, loosely termed the "angry young man" school, was innovational too—in literature, in plays, in film. *Saturday Night and Sunday Morning* is, almost inarguably, the best film to come out of this school—

despite some very notable runners-up. Moreover, in a purely social sense, the film is an honest and invaluable record of conditions—and attitudes—prevalent in Britain at that time. After the dismal austerity of the immediate postwar years, things seemed to have taken a definite turn for the better. Rationing disappeared (although housing was still a major problem) and employment soared. Wages soared too, and, protected by powerful unions, workers were earning handsome salaries—at least by prevailing British standards.

The mediocrities found themselves comfortably off, with money flowing in, and good security. Those with ambitions, on the other hand, found themselves frustrated. England has never had much of a free-enterprise system, or provided real incentive for an individual to strike out on his own. Too, many of the young men of that time had either had their careers interrupted by the war, or, as youngsters, had had their education affected by the war. The only really practical ambition was to do *more* work, and, via overtime, earn more money. That done, there was nothing else to do or to look forward to. So a kind of complacency set in: ambition vanished, and the only aim was to have a good time—usually by waiting until the weekend, and then going on a spree of dancing, drinking, and womanizing. This was particularly true of the factory workers of the midlands and the North, the milieu represented by *Saturday Night and Sunday Morning.* The young men of the early sixties grew into the middle-aged men of the late 70s—the time that Britain was plagued by strikes and economic slowdowns from a work force totally without ambition or pride, and concerned only with making more money to enjoy more comforts in a land now beset by drastic unemployment and incredible inflation.

Not only is *Saturday Night and Sunday Morning* a fascinating signpost to the troubles that lay ahead, but it is perhaps even a warning for the United States. America's *Saturday Night Fever* is virtually a remake of the British film, transposed to metropolitan America of the 70s, and its title is an acknowledgment of that.

The hero—or antihero—of *Saturday Night and Sunday Morning* is presented with rare candor. It was not unusual for the protagonist of a British film at that time to be casual about love and sex, and to use it as a means of getting ahead. Laurence Harvey's Joe Lampton in the earlier *Room at the Top* was such a type. But the film clearly condemned his behavior, and in an ironic way, he was punished for it. However, Albert Finney (an excellent performance, especially for a newcomer to film) does not use sex as a means to an end, but as the end itself. His sole purpose in life is pleasure, even though this means the continuance of a love affair with his work-mate's wife, and an attempt to procure an abortion for her when she becomes pregnant by him. Not only amoral, he is also a liar and has other far-from-admirable characteristics—yet the film presents this as a kind of norm (despite occasional chiding from his pals) and contrives to have us find him rather charming, in a way.

As in *Saturday Night Fever,* the character does achieve, finally, some sense of responsibility, but there's little that he can do with it. The film's final outlook is far from optimistic, either on the national level (rightly, as later events showed) or on a personal level. He seems about to escape from a dull

Albert Finney as the young malcontent who wants only "a good time."

Rachel Roberts as the married woman with whom he has an affair . . .

family life, with a father oblivious to everything except television, to an equally dull married life with the "nice" girl, well played by Shirley Ann Field. Field, who could be an extremely animated actress, does a far better acting job than may have been realized (especially in the carefully controlled monotony of her dialogue delivery) in making her character "nice," temporarily exciting (she is withholding sex until after marriage) yet ultimately drab, merely underlining the boredom that is the hero's problem since he has, at best, traded his freedom for a kind of routine stability. Britain certainly has its share of the "English Rose" beauty—the Patricia Rocs, the Janette Scotts and the Rosamund Johns—but unfortunately it also has more than its share of the plain housewives and dull girlfriends, so flawlessly delineated by Rachel Roberts and Shirley Ann Field in this film.

Academically, *Saturday Night and Sunday Morning* is an almost perfect film, beautifully directed by Karel Reisz, and a textbook illustration of his definitive book on the art of film editing. It is full of acute and honest observation, some of it funny, much of it painful. There are occasional echoes of

classic French cinema; somehow the scene in which Finney and his mate, philosophizing about the inevitability and entrapment of marriage as they fish from the banks of a canal, seem to parallel the closing sequences of Duvivier's prewar *Poil de Carotte* in which the estranged father and son come to terms with life without really expecting a great deal from it.

Although there were few specific follow-ups, *Saturday Night and Sunday Morning* probably influenced more British films than it has been given credit for—and quite certainly it influenced the more showy but quite outstanding *The Comedy Man* (1963).

Saturday Night and Sunday Morning may well be unique in its pessimism about love. In his 1924 silent *Isn't Life Wonderful?,* about the miseries of life in starvation- and inflation-ridden post–World War I Germany, Griffith insists that, despite everything, love can make life beautiful. In the less desperate period of World War II's aftermath in Britain, Reisz and Sillitoe seem to be saying that love, at best, can make life tolerable—that it isn't much, but it's all there is.

. . . and Shirley Anne Field as the "nice" girl with whom he will finally settle down.

Annie Hall

Charles H. Joffe Productions–United Artists,
1977).

Directed by Woody Allen. Written by Allen and
Marshall Brickman. Camera: Gordon Willis.

With: Woody Allen, Diane Keaton, Tony Roberts,
Carol Kane, Janet Margolin, Paul Simon, Colleen
Dewhurst, Shelley Duval, Christopher Walken,
Donald Symington, Helen Ludlam, Marshall Mc-
Luhan, Jonathan Munk, Mordecai Lawner, Joan
Newman.

Annie Hall, in a sense, is Woody Allen's *Sullivan's
Travels.* But whereas that classic early 40s film was
Preston Sturges's way of taking stock and ponder-
ing which way his career should go (and in the
course of the film successfully letting it go in *both*
of the directions that his onscreen equivalent was
so undecided about), Woody Allen seems not one
whit concerned about his career. He uses the film
instead to take personal stock, to consider, through
a thinly disguised fictional equivalent, the success
and failure of his private life. Since it is well known

that the film is largely autobiographical, it has something of a voyeuristic look to it all, especially in
those sequences dealing with the "fictional" comedian's romantic liaison with the "fictional" Annie
Hall of the title, played by Diane Keaton. Depending on the subsequent turns that their private and
public lives take, *Annie Hall* may well increase in
interest. Reports that Keaton and Allen were to
wed were soon quashed by replacement news of a
liaison between Keaton and Warren Beatty, which
itself soon seemed to be recycling some of the Keaton–Allen problems.

Purely as a film, quite divorced from its personal elements—a divorce proceeding that is
frankly rather difficult to accomplish—*Annie Hall* is
almost certainly Allen's best picture. For one thing,
by its very nature—flashbacks presented via a
voice-over narration—it depends more on talk and
on flip, throwaway wisecracks, the basis of all of
Allen's humor, and far less than usual on elaborate
sight gags that in the past have all too often adver-

Despite the rhapsodic and virtually un-precedented raves that their subsequent *Manhattan* (1979) received, ANNIE HALL is a superior work and likely to remain the definitive Woody Allen–Diane Keaton collaboration.

tised their reliance on the work of Lloyd, Keaton and Chaplin. Even the sight gags that it does have are visual equivalents of one-liners, and, like the sunlight gags in the Hollywood automobile sequences, closest in spirit to the underplayed visual gags of Jacques Tati.

As always, Allen is the butt of most of the jokes, and is cunning in the way he invites audience sympathy for his character even as he contrives to have the audience laugh at that character. The candor of the romantic scenes is well under control, always stopping—though sometimes only just—on the credit side of potential bad taste and/or masochism. The film also benefits immeasureably by Diane Keaton's (deservedly) Academy Award–winning performance as Annie, though in some ways it was a borderline performance. Chauvinistic remark though it may be, Diane Keaton—a lovely woman and a very graceful one—was always best when she was willing to be just that. In her immediately prior films, there were signs of a determination to be an *actress,* and a disturbing piling up of mannerisms. *Annie Hall* survives these because of the character's basic relationship to the *private* Keaton, but in

subsequent films, without that safety valve, the aggressive actress characteristics have taken over, and much of the relaxed grace has fled.

In view of the rather special personal and career relationships of Allen and Keaton, and the interweaving of those relationships with career demands of New York and Hollywood, it is rather surprising—and very much to Allen's credit—how well the film works even with audiences that have no intimate knowledge of the two cities and their relative cultures. European audiences, for example, seem to catch on right away and laugh at "inside" innuendoes about the two lifestyles as readily as New Yorkers or Hollywoodians.

Saturday Night Fever may well, in time, prove to be the "definitive" and most representative movie about 70s lifestyles. But of all the other romantic and often sexually obsessed love stories of the 70s—ranging from *Last Tango in Paris* to *An Unmarried Woman* and *Coming Home, Annie Hall* may equally well turn out to be the warmest and most likable love story of that decade. In its own very special way, and dealing with a totally different kind of survival, it's 1977's *The Crowd.*

LOOKING AHEAD

At this book goes to press, midway through 1979, one can only conjecture as to what lies ahead in the 1980s.

In the past, most decades have telegraphed their filmic intentions—and trends—in the last year of the prior decade. 1909, 1919, 1929 and 1939 in particular were years which provided quite a remarkable "coming attractions" survey of the artistic, innovational and entertainment patterns of the following ten-year spans.

No really clearly defined signals have thus far presented themselves for the 80s—except for the fact that, capitalizing on the new freedom of the screen, the 70s has been, in a sense, an era of high-cost exploitation films. The kind of films that were once made by small independent companies, to do the things (still within certain limits) that were denied to the Production-Code controlled major companies, have now become the *norm*. In the 40s, assuming it could have been made at all, *Hard Core* would have been a cheap little picture promising far more than it could deliver, and the same might be said for earlier equivalents of *An Unmarried Woman* or *First Love*. Except of course that the 30s "exploitation" film knew its market, made no pretense at class or integrity, and offered its wares quite honestly (if with unfulfilled expectations) under such titles as *Child Bride, Marijuana the Weed from Hell* and *The Love Life of a Gorilla*.

It is unfair to such well-made (and well-intentioned) films as *Hard Core* and *Coming Home* to label them as exploitation films. They are not. But they *do* have the content, and the explicit sexual material, to enable them to be *sold* that way. Most of the big 70s hits have been highly exploitable films —from the sex and nudity of the new breed of love story (*First Love, The Sailor Who Fell From Grace With the Sea*) to the sense of shock in both biographies (*Valentino*) and comedies (*Blazing Saddles*) and of course to the sheer sensation of increasingly bloody horror films and increasingly cataclysmic disaster movies.

There is, at the close of the seventies, a sense of this "super-hype" film having passed its apex to be replaced by something simpler. Whether the replacement is being caused by audiences seeking out and, by box-office receipts, *justifying* the simpler movie, or whether by Hollywood, realizing that the novelty is gone from the purely sensational film, trying to *develop* an audience for the quieter film, it is, as yet, too early to say. However, one can have cause for guarded optimism. With vampirism having been taken both to bloody extremes *and* kidded and satirized to a point from which one would have thought there could be no return, it *is* encouraging to note that for *his* vampire film, *Nosferatu*, Werner Herzog has returned to the chilling yet unsensational style of the original (1922) Murnau film of the same title, that is clearly his inspiration.

It would be nice to think that the same thing was happening to the romantic film: a return to old values is not necessarily a step backwards. A number of the films of the late 70s have striven, rather consciously, to recreate the flair of an earlier day. Luis Buñuel's *That Obscure Object of Desire* (1977), the fifth filming of Pierre Louy's *The Woman and the Puppet,* managed to be both a thoroughly "now" film (to use a clumsy but expressive phrase) and one of the most elegant films since the heyday of Lubitsch—although its story of a woman's destructive impact on a man who loves her hopelessly was hardly Lubitschian material! Another 1977 film, *The Turning Point*, while lacking the style of Michael Powell's *The Red Shoes* (in a loose sense its inspiration film), nevertheless in trying for the style, acknowledged the need for it—and the box-office results were rewarding.

Among a rather grim and fatalistic collection of films in 1979—*Hard Core, When You Comin' Back, Red Ryder?* and sundry others, most of which seemed to be made by the ubiquitous Robert Altman, one film—*Ice Castles*—stood out for its directness and simplicity. Like *The Turning Point*, it is a tale of achievement, and the struggle that goes with it. Unavoidably, the virtues can't be as clean-cut as they would have been in films of the 40s. Some of the language is pretty rough, characters sometimes less than admirable, and morality—in a sexual sense—a little dubious at times. Nevertheless, these elements are present enough to lend an air of contemporary realism, restrained enough to remind one of the older romantic films. The performance of Lynn-Holly Johnson as the ice-skating Olympic hopeful is both relaxed and charming, and as a professional skater herself she is obviously perfectly cast. However, the film falls short in two all-important areas which are symptomatic of problems facing *all* films today, but particularly the romantic films.

First, there's the question of sheer craftsmanship, the skill with which a film is put together. At one time we could take all that for granted: a routine commercial film in the 40s might be totally devoid of imagination, and in a narrative sense might have nothing to say, but it would always be magnificently professional in its assembly: perfectly matched cuts, no microphone booms hanging down from the top of the screen, flawless lighting control. Obviously mechanical expertise is no substitute for creativity: far better to have a stimulating film with something to say, than a "perfect" film mechanically which is an empty void artistically. But too many films today, aimed at nothing more than sheer entertainment, are still woefully lacking in the elementary requirements of good filmmaking. 1979's *Grease* was *so* inept even in its editing and camerawork that it literally looked as though it had been made by first-year film students still doing practical experimenting on 8mm. *Ice Castles* is well above the level of *Grease*, but it still has some shortcomings, especially in the skating scenes—which, after all, are rather important in a story about the training of a young novice skater. Far too often the skater's figure is clumsily framed so that one doesn't see the feet; and at no time do the skating scenes duplicate the grace—and with it, the sheer exuberant joy of achieving that grace—which, for example, marked the old Sonja Henie musicals, in which the camera glides and tracks and almost pirouettes on the ice in rhythm with the star.

A far more major weakness of *Ice Castles* is its male star, Robbie Benson, who inexplicably gets star billing ahead of Miss Johnson. At best, Benson is a fourth-rate John Travolta; at worst, he has none of the sympathetic or inspirational qualities that could motivate a girl to win over all obstacles including, in this case, blindness.

The Benson syndrome is, alas, by no means confined to *Ice Castles*. The screen at the moment is unusually rich in women who are beautiful, graceful, sensitive *and* good actresses, as well as covering a range from youth to relative maturity: Candice Bergen, Jane Fonda, Vanessa Redgrave, Lee Remick, Diane Keaton, Jenny Agutter, Mikki Olsen, Judy Morris, Carol Lynley, Olivia Hussey, Lesley Anne-Down, Carole Bouquet, Sally Field, Meryl Streep. The list is a random, not a definitive or comprehensive one, and perhaps, compared with a like number of star names from any one year in the 30s, may not seem, at first glance, too impressive. But every one of those names has proven her talent and versatility, and all of them—in one way or another, be it via beauty or acting ability or personality—has that special quality that used to mark the star (and not just the Hollywood star). Yet, attempting to compile a similar *male* list would not only be problematical, it would be impossible. We certainly have good contemporary actors, and even one or two good-looking leading men in the rugged tradition of Cooper, Gable or McCrea. But the overall image of the male star has changed, while that of the female star has remained fairly constant. The chemistry that used to ignite sparks from the Gable/Harlow, Powell/Loy, Mason/Lockwood, Dietrich/Cooper and Gaynor/Farrell teamings has long since gone. Dustin Hoffman and Vanessa Redgrave are certainly both fine performers, but as an acting team in *Agatha* they just did not work, and because the role was much stronger, it was the Redgrave contribution that stood out.

Hollywood's male stars today seem to fall into one of three categories: those who *look* like stars and, fortunately, are also good actors, a small group headed by Robert Redford, Paul Newman and Robert de Niro; those (like Al Pacino, Jon Voigt and Dustin Hoffman) who may well be fine actors, but lack star magnetism; and a distressingly large group (from James Caan, Elliot Gould and Robbie Benson up—or down) who have neither quality to recommend them, but have secured a kind of permanence on the screen for sheer lack of competition. With the male population so fragmented, and the aggressive women's lib movement being pushed by female stars with clout, it's not too surprising that the majority of the new romantic films have been dominated by women—both in plot and performance. This way well be why so many recent attempts to re-establish the classic romantic novel as a source for new screen fare—witness the remakes of *Wuthering Heights* and *Jane Eyre*—have fallen so flat. Stories such as those *need* the interplay of two equally strong and dynamic male and female characters, not one dominating at the expense of the other.

The ladies certainly deserve their chance for prominence, after having yielded center-stage to the men through the sixties and seventies. Hopefully, the eighties will restore a more even balance. Why not a *Taming of the Shrew* with Jane Fonda and Alan Bates? Or a musical *Blood and Sand* with matador John Travolta married to Jenny Agutter and tempted by Carole Bouquet?